MURDER IN CALIFORNIA

The Topography of Evil: Notorious California Murder Sites

marques vickers

1

MURDER IN CALIFORNIA
The Topography of Evil: Notorious California Murder Sites

MARQUIS PUBLISHING
LARKSPUR, CALIFORNIA

Version 1.2

Published by Marquis Publishing
Part of Marquis Enterprises
Larkspur, California

Vickers, Marques, 1957

    MURDER IN CALIFORNIA
    The Topography of Evil: Notorious California Murder Sites

For my daughters Charline and Caroline, who have chosen the light.

MURDER IN CALIFORNIA
THE TOPOGRAPHY OF EVIL: Notorious California Murder Sites

PREFACE: The Spirits of Stolen Lives

ASSASSINATION KILLINGS
Dr. Marcus Foster: A Marginalized Death Meriting Remembrance
The Mob Permanently Severs Relations With Bugsy Siegel
Chauncey Bailey: The Price of Constitutional Protection
The Mickey and Trudy Thompson Morning Driveway Execution
The Political Killings of San Francisco Mayor George Moscone and Supervisor Harvey Milk
The East/West Coast Vendetta and Killing of Christopher Wallace
The Marin County Courthouse Shootout: Thirty Minutes That Forever Altered Courtroom Security Procedures
Robert F. Kennedy: The Assassination of Hope
Joseph "The Animal" Barboza: The Inevitability of a Lifestyle Path
The Contract Killing of Vic Weiss: The Rewards For Stealing Fire
The Severe Reality of the Wonderland Gang Killings Transcended the Fantasy Sex Industry

ABDUCTIONS
The Patty Hearst Kidnapping: The Final Nail into the Coffin of Idealism
Nicholas Markowitz: The Stolen Boy and Unforeseen Execution
The Kidnapping of Brooke Hart and Resulting Mob Justice
An Execution Amidst Rural Darkness: The Onion Field Killings
Polly Klaas: The Abrupt Death of Innocence
Ramona Irene Price Strolls Innocently Into A Vanished Past
Kristin Smart: The Tangled Web Involving Fifth Amendment Silence
Kevin Collins: A Solitary Bus Bench Memorial to Every Parent's Nightmare
Rex Allen Krebs: Predestined Towards Violence
Karen Mitchell: Vanishing Into Speculation

HISTORICAL LEGACIES AND SPECULATIONS
Fung *Little Pete* Jing Toy: 19th Century Chinatown Gangland Slaying

Fatality Victims:
Raphanar Or, Ram Chun, Thuy Tran, Sokhim An, Oeun Lim. Sebastian Holzer, Vincent Holzer, William Holzer, Sheila Holzer, Bryan Zuckor, Randy Gordon, Chen Liang, Preston Lowrey III, Constantinos Lyrintzis, David Caouette, Randy Lee Fannin, Michelle Fournier, Lucia Kondas, Victoria Buzzo, Christy Wilson, Michelle Fast, Laura Webb, Seth Fessenden, Stephen Becker, Paul Herzberg, Bruce Jacobson, Donald Aarges, Frank Teplansky, Deborah Paulsen, Burton Wragg, Mike Suchar, Sylvia Ortega-Pardo, Alicia Sotomayor Ortega, Joseph Ortega, Charles Ortega, James Ortega, Cheri Lynn Ortega, Teresa Ortega, Alicia Ortega Ortiz, Michael Andre Ortiz, Cheng Yuan Hong, George Chen, Katherine Cooper, Veronika Weiss, Christopher Michael-Martinez, Weihan Wang, Joanie Harper-Brothers, Marques Brothers, Marshall Brothers, Lyndsey Brothers, Earnestine Harper, Bonnie Lee Bakley, Emil Matasareanu, Larry Phillips, Jr., Nicole Brown-Simpson, Ronald Goldman, Jose Menendez, Kitty Menendez, Sue Morency, Dorothy Stratten, Matthew Pavelka, Demetrius DuBose, Thomas Guerry, James Pence, George Alleyn, Walt Frago, Roger Gore, Captain Walter Auble, Sam Cooke, Sal Mineo, Ronni Chasen, Ramon Novarro, Lana Clarkson, Phil Hartman, Marvin Gaye, Mabel Monohan, John Stompanato, Haing Nogor, Ennis Cosby, Kevin Dean Reida, Charles Hogan, Joel Kocab, Ned Doheny, Hugh Plunkett, Ted Healy, William Desmond Taylor, Kym Morgan, Geneva Ellroy, Raymond Washington, Elizabeth Short, Yolanda Washington, Judith Miller, Lissa Kastin, Dolores Cepeda, Sonja Johnson, Kristina Weckler, Jane King, Lauren Wagner, Kimberly Martin, Cindy Hudspeth, Cyndi Vanderheiden, Henry Howell, Robin Armtrout, Howard King, Paul Cavanaugh, Chevelle Wheeler, Kimberly Ann Billy, Joann Hobson ,Cornelia Crilley, Ellen Hover, Jill Barcomb, Georgia Wixted, Charlotte Lamb, Jill Parenteau, Robin Samsoe. Lucinda Schaefer, Andrea Hall, Jackie Gilliam, Jacqueline Lamp, Shirley Ledford, 41 Members of the Heaven's Gate Cult, Mei Leung, Jennie Vincow, Maria Hernandez, Christina Caldwell, Mary Caldwell, Dayle Okazaki, Tsai-Lian Yu, Vincent, Maxine Zazzra, Harold Wu, Edward Wildgans, Peter Pan, Elyas Abowath, Bill Doi, Mary Louis

Cannon, Joyce Nelson, Lela Kneiding, Maxon Kneiding, Chainarong Khovananth. Dr. Robert Offerman, Debra Manning, Charlene Smith, Lyman Smith, Keith Harrington, Patrice Harrington, Manuela Witthuhn, Cheri Domingo, Gregory Sanchez, Janelle Cruz, 50+ Medically Assisted Homicide Victims by Efren Saldivar, Donald *Shorty* Shea, Leno LaBianca, Rosemary LaBianca, Sharon Tate, Jay Sebring, Abigail Folger, Wojciech Frykowski, Steven Parent, Gary Hinman, Billy DeVerell, Ron Launius, Joy Miller, Barbara Richardson, Vic Weiss, Robert Kennedy, Christopher Wallace, Mickey Thompson, Trudy Thompson, Benjamin Bugsy Siegel, Ramona Irene Price (Presumed Dead), James Campbell, Nicholas Markowitz, Dr. Marcus Foster. George Moscone, Harvey Milk, Chauncey Bailey Jr., Judge Harold Haley, Joseph *The Animal* Barboza, Kevin Collins (Presumed Dead), Kristin Smart (Presumed Dead), Brooke Hart, Polly Klaas, Rachel Newhouse, Aundria Crawford, Fung Little Pete Jing Toy, Virginia Rappe, Diane Whipple, Huey P. Newton, Laci Peterson, Conner Peterson, Oakland Policemen Mark Dunakin, John Hege, Ervin Romans and Daniel Sakai, David Nadel, Kim Allen, Lori Lee Kursa, Yvonne Weber, Maureen Sterling, Carolyn Davis, Therese Walsh, Lindsay Cutshall, Jason Allen, 918 Victims of the Jonestown Settlement Massacre in Guyana, Ivan Stineman, Annette Stineman, Selina Bishop, Jennifer Villarin, James Gamble, Deborah Fogel, John C. Scully, Allen J. Berk, David Sutcliffe, Shirley Mooser, Donald Michael Merrill, Victor Ohta, Virginia Ohta, Dorothy Cadwallader, Derrick Ohta, Taggart Ohta, Oscar Grant III, Denise Louie, Calvin Fong, Paul Wada, Donald Quan, Fong Wang, Mel Grimes, Elizabeth Grimes, Tshering Rinzing Bhutia, Doris Chibuko, Sonam Chodon, Grace Eunhae Kim, Katleen Ping, Judith Seymour, Lydia Sim, Hugh Scrutton, Thomas J. Mosser, Gilbert Murray, Cesar Gonzalez, Jose Vasquez, Jose Delores Salazar, Edmund Emil Kemper I, Maude Matilda Hughey Kemper, Mary Ann Pesce, Anita Luchessa, Aiko Koo, Cindy Schall, Rosalind Thorpe, Alice Liu, Clarnell Strandberg Kemper, Sally Hallett, Ambrose Griffin, Theresa Wallin, Evelyon Miroth, Daniel Meredith, Jason Miroth, David Michael Ferreira, Kenneth Whitacre, Andrew Zatko,

Norman Metcalfe, Danny Cizek, David Law, Joe Garcia, Kris
Staub, Ruth Munroe, Dorothy Miller, Benjamin Fink, Leona
Carpenter, Lawrence "Whitey" White, Mary Guilfoyle, Father
Henri Tomei, Jim Gianera, Joan Gianera, Kathy Francis,
Daemon Francis, David Francis, David Oliker, Robert Spector,
Brian Card, Mark Dreibelbis, Fred Perez, Edda Kane, Barbara
Schwartz, Anna Mejivas, Anne Anderson. Shawna May, Diane
O'Connell, Cynthia Moreland, Richard Towers, Ellen Hansen,
Heather Scaggs, Anna K. Menjivar, Mary Frances Bennett, Quita
Hague, Frances Rose, Saleem Erakat, Paul Dancik, Marietta
DiGirolamo, Ilario Bertuccio, Neal Moynihan, Mildred Hosler,
Tana Smith, Vincent Wollin, John Bambic, Jane Holly, Thomas
Rainwater, Nelson Shields IV, Betty Lou Jensen, David Faraday,
Darlene Ferrin, Cecelia Shepard, Paul Stine, Charles Crawford,
Herbert Spencer, Father Eric Freed, James Olive, Naomi Olive,
Claude Snelling, Karen Mitchell (Presumed Dead), Sebhrenah
Wesson, Elizabeth Wesson, Illabelle Wesson, Aviv Wesson,
Jonathon Wesson, Sedonia Wesson, Marshey Wesson, Ethen
Wesson, Jeva Wesson, Dale Ewell, Glee Ewell and Tiffany
Ewell.

Convicted and/or Deceased Killers:
Patrick Purdy (Deceased), Nicolas Holzer, Charles Andy
Williams, Frederick Davidson, Scott Dekraai, Edward Charles
Allaway, Brenda Spencer, Bruce Pardo (Deceased), Elliot
Rodger (Deceased), Vincent Brothers, Erick Menendez, Lyle
Menendez, John Morency, Paul Snider (Deceased), Ramon
Arranda (Deceased), David Garcia, Bruce Bowersox (Deceased),
Frank Bowersox (Deceased), Bobby Davis (Deceased), Jack
Twinning (Deceased), Carl Sutherland (Deceased), Lionel Ray
Williams, Harold Martin Smith (Deceased), Paul Ferguson, Tom
Ferguson (Deceased), Phil Spector, Brynn Hartman (Deceased),
Marvin Gay, Sr. (Deceased), Emmett Perkins (Deceased), Jack
Santo (Deceased), Barbara Graham (Deceased), Indra Lim ,
Jason Chan, Tak Sun Tan, Mikhail Markhasev, Michael Clark
(Deceased), Angelo Buono (Deceased), Kenneth Bianchi,
Wesley Shermantine, Loren Herzog (Deceased), Rodney Alcala,
Lawrence Bittaker, Roy Norris Marshall Applewhite

(Deceased), Richard Ramirez (Deceased), Efren Saldivar, Bruce
Davis, Leslie Van Houten, Steve Grogan, Patricia Krenwinkel,
Charles *Tex* Watson, Mary Brunner, Susan Atkins (Deceased),
Bobby Beausoleil, Charles Manson, Sirhan Sirhan, Michael
Goodwin, Gregory Powell (Deceased), Jimmy Lee Smith
(Deceased), Ryan Hoyt, Jesse Rugge, William Skidmore, Jesse
James Hollywood, Graham Presley, Donald DeFreeze
(Deceased), Joseph Remiro, Russell Little, Dan White
(Deceased), Yusuf Bey IV, Devaughndre Broussard, Antoine
Mackey, Ruchell Magee, Jonathan Jackson (Deceased), William
Christmas (Deceased), James McClain (Deceased), Harold
Thurmond (Lynched Without Conviction), Maurice Holmes
(Lynched Without Conviction), Richard Allen Davis, Lem Jung
(Deceased), Chew Tin Gop (Deceased), Marjorie Knoller, Robert
Noel, Tyrone Robinson, Scott Peterson, Lovelle Mixon
(Deceased), Jim Jones (Deceased), Glenn Taylor Helzer, Justin
Helzer (Deceased), Gian Luigi Ferri (Deceased), John Linley
Frazier (Deceased), Johannes Mehserle, Tom Yu, John Franklin
Kenney, One L. Goh, Ted Kaczynski, Edmund Kemper III,
Richard Trenton Chase (Deceased), Juan Corona, Lynwood C.
Drake III (Deceased), Dorothea Puente (Deceased), Herbert
Mullin, David Carpenter, Larry Green, J. C. X. Simon
(Deceased), Manuel Moore and Jessie Lee Cooks, Gary Lee
Bullock, Marlene Olive, Charles *Chuck* Riley, Wayne Adam
Ford, Marcus Wesson, Dana Ewell and Joel Radovcich.

Currently Incarcerated:

Napa State Hospital
Edward Charles Allaway
One L. Goh

**United States Penitentiary, Administrative Maximum
Facility (ADX), Florence, Colorado**
Ted Kaczynski

Pleasant Valley State Prison, Coalinga
Gary Lee Bullock

California State Prison in Lancaster
Joseph Remiro
Antoine Mackey
Jason Chan
David Garcia
John Morency
Frederick Davidson

Crossroads Correction Center in Cameron, Missouri
Paul Ferguson

Santa Barbara County Sheriff's Facility
Nicolas Holzer

California Health Care Facility in Stockton
Phil Spector
Manuel Moore

Mule Creek State Prison, Ione
Herbert Mullin
Charles *Tex* Watson
Lyle Menendez
Joel Radovcich

California Institution for Women in Corona
Patricia Krenwinkel
Leslie Van Houten
Brenda Spencer

Calipatria State Prison
Jesse James Hollywood

Ironwood State Prison, Blythe
Charles Andy Williams

Correctional Training Facility
Indra Lim

Salinas Valley State Prison, Soledad
Yusuf Bey IV
Tak Sun Tan

Valley State Prison For Women in Chowchilla
Marjorie Knoller
Dawn Godman

California State Prison, Corcoran
Juan Corona
Charles Manson
Rodney Alcala
Mikhail Markhasev
Efren Saldivar
Dale Ewell

California State Prison, Sacramento
Tyrone Robinson

California State Prison Solano, Vacaville
Tom Yu
Peter Ng
Edmund Kemper III
Larry Green

R.J. Donovan Correctional Facility, San Diego
Michael Goodwin
Sirhan Sirhan
John Franklin Kenney
Jesse Lee Cooks
Roy Norris
Erick Menendez

California Men's Colony in San Luis Obispo
Ruchell Magee
Bruce Davis

Orange County Central Men's Jail
Scott Dekraai

San Quentin
Ryan Hoyt
Richard Allen Davis
Rex Allen Krebs
Scott Peterson
Glenn Taylor Helzer
David Carpenter
Lawrence Bittaker
Wesley Shermantine
Vincent Brothers
Wayne Adam Ford
Marcus Wesson

Oregon State Penitentiary, Salem
Bobby Beausoleil

Washington State Penitentiary, Walla Walla
Kenneth Bianchi

LaPalma Correctional Center, Eloy Arizona
Devaughndre Broussard

Presumed Living But Whereabouts Unknown:
Lionel Ray Williams (Presumed Completed Prison Term), Mary
Brunner (Released From Prison), Russell Little (Released From
Prison), Robert Noel (Completed Prison Term), Juan Rivera
Perez (Wanted For Murder), Johannes Mehserle (Completed
Prison Term), Sai Ying Lee (Wanted for Murder), Melvin Yu
(Presumed Completed Prison Term), Curtis Tam or Stuart Lin
(Presumed Completed Prison Term), Jesse Rugge (Presumed
Completed Prison Term), William Skidmore (Presumed
Completed Prison Term), Graham Pressley (Presumed
Completed Prison Term), Marlene Olive (Completed Prison
Term) and Charles *Chuck* Riley (Completed Prison Term).

Preface: The Spirits of Stolen Lives

The spirits of stolen lives have evaporated into time until periodically summoned into random recollection. Time ultimately creates amnesia towards public catastrophes that society once considered *unforgettable*.

The private trauma remains fresh to the immediate victim's families, friends and diverse relationships. The ghosts of recollection are prevalent, searing and painful. They never recede.

For the innocent victims of homicides, their stilled voices are silenced, but their identities and legacies should never be forgotten.

My introduction into the consequences of murder began with the December 20, 1968 killings of David Faraday and Betty Lou Jensen by the Zodiac serial killer. The shocking executions were committed on an isolated stretch of Lake Herman Road near the city limits of my hometown, Vallejo, California. I was acquainted with Faraday through my involvement with Boy Scouts. My older sister knew both of the victims.

One cannot forget the trauma a random double homicide inflicts upon an intimate suburban community. Seven months later, the same killer attacked a couple in the parking lot of a local park all of us had frequented since childhood. One victim survived but the Zodiac's death toll was mounting. He would be responsible for at least two additional deaths and another surviving victim. His evil became personal.

The cowardly murderer publicly taunted law enforcement authorities and the citizenry via the news media. He was never apprehended. Abruptly we realized that Vallejo had changed. Our illusions of invulnerability were permanently destroyed. The reputation of the city of Vallejo would continue its decline over time and acts of senseless violence would become more commonplace.

It is often difficult to feel empathy for perpetrators. Detachment remains difficult when so many have suffered. They are responsible for substantial loss and yet many offer no expression of remorse. The acknowledgement of the victims often pales in comparison with the exposure of the murderers. The California justice system rarely judges the guilty expediently. The death penalty is scarcely employed, mocking its role as a deterrent.

Some killings defy explanation and understanding. Some may not properly be defined as evil. Each is uniquely tragic.

Within the context of examining each profile, many important issues are raised for discussion without necessarily culminating in resolution. These subjects include capital punishment, American racial perceptions, parental influences, child rearing, media reporting, public bias, juvenile sentencing, self-incrimination protections and the impartiality of our judicial system. Controversial options such as voluntary euthanasia for the condemned has been suggested when examining the hopeless backlog of death row and life-term convicts.

Capturing snapshots of fatality locations is never precise. Research is done via news accounts, historical images, yet much of the precise identification becomes speculative. Visual location often adds an important perspective to a profile narrative.

Crime scenes typically revert back into unremarkable landscape or unassuming buildings over the ensuing years and decades. Several have altered little since their moment of infamy. Many are passed daily by pedestrian and vehicular traffic unaware of a location's unique significance.

Makeshift on-site memorials often temporarily acknowledge the stain and the loss. Few remain permanently. Instead, layers of paint, building facade modifications and even address changes attempt to camouflage many crime scenes. The disguises are understandable. Those condemned to live amongst the lingering shadows of a tragedy sometimes become victims themselves in a sense. Society wishes to forget and move on. Murder is never tidy. Remembrance is inconvenient and uncomfortable for the living.

My hope is that these profiles and images will provide remembrance for the innocent who are no longer amongst us.

My appreciation to the following media outlets providing critical research details:

San Francisco Chronicle, Los Angeles Times, Daily News, Bakersfield Californian, Oakland Tribune, Marin Independent

Journal, Press Democrat, Monterey Herald, The Californian, Monterey County Weekly, Willits News, North Coast Journal, The Guardian, Fresno Bee, Times Standard, ChauceyBaileyProject.org, Wikipedia.org, MindControlBlackassassins.com, FBI.gov, KQED.org, CrimeLibrary.com, Hoodline.com, KlaasKids.org, SanJose.com, AliveEastBay.com, OAC.Cdlib.org, OCWeekly.com, SCSCourt.org, RamonaPrice.com, Kristinsmart.com, CharleyProject.com, SanLuisObispo.com. Murderpedia.com, Independent.com, KCET.org, BloodInTheFields.com, AtlasObscura.com, MurderByGaslight.com. SFCityGuides.org, KTVU.org, YouTube.com, DiscoverTheNetworks.org, YesMagazine.org, About.com, Fdsauk.freeforums.org, California Department of Corrections and Rehabilitation Inmatelocator.cdcr.ca.gov, WoodTV.com, Bermuda-Triangle.org, Santarosahitchhikermurders.com, Pinterest.com, MostWantedHoes.com, CityRating.com, KSBW.com, InsideSoCal.com, CountryHomesOfAmerica.com, Websleuths.com, CodysInvestigations.com, Edhat.com, AJC.com, CNN.com, CBSNews.com, DailyMail.co.uk, New York Daily News, Agaarchitects.com, Law.Justia.com, Brockmorris.com, SFWeekly.com, Ssristories.org, TheTribune, ExiledOnline.com, CBSNews.com, KTLA.com, Keyt.com, The Huffington Post, CNN.com, TurnTo23.com, ODMP.org, Web.Archive.org, Camemorial.org, Seattle Times, PoliceChiefMagazine.com, SourceOfTitle.com, Pineconearchive.com, Cielodrive.com, Biography.com, Berkeley.edu, The Atlantic Magazine, Britannica.com, SbSheriff,org, VCStar.com, Heretical.com, TheZebraProject.blogspot.com, Zebra by Clark Howard, FrontPageMag.com, HeavensGate.com, SacramentoPress.com, MisterSF.com, SparselySageandTimely.com, FresnoAlliance.com, Social.Stanford.edu, CountryHomesOfAmerica.com, OfficialColdCaseInvestigations.com, EvilBeings.com, LAWeekly.com and Murderfacts.com.

Dr. Marcus Foster: The Marginalized Assassination

Perhaps the most tragic and least remembered link from the notorious Patty Hearst abduction was the November 6, 1973 assassination of Dr. Marcus Foster, the Oakland School District Superintendent. His needless death launched the public ascension of the Symbionese Liberation Army (SLA) into a revolutionary terrorist organization. Three gunmen, Joseph Remiro, Russell Little and probably SLA leader Donald DeFreeze ambushed Foster and his deputy superintendent Robert Blackburn near their parked cars at dusk following a school board meeting.

The parking lot today remains paved and lined as it did during the 1973 slaying. The Oakland Unified School district building has fallen into decay and disrepair. The building and parking lot are fenced in and the only evidence of activity is the sole security guard employed daily to prevent vandalism and break-ins.

Foster was killed instantly sustaining between seven to nine cyanide tipped bullets. Blackburn was critically wounded but miraculously survived. A team of surgeons labored throughout the night to stop the bleeding and prevent further internal organ damage from twenty-three entry and exit shotgun wounds and multiple heart stoppages.

Ironically upon Blackburn's recovery, he assumed Foster's Superintendent position for the next two years. Professionally he continued a distinguished academic career.

What Foster may have accomplished as Oakland's Superintendent and beyond is impossible to gauge. He was universally respected after arriving from Philadelphia in 1970 to assume the head position.

His death was both senseless and erroneously motivated. The SLA assassins targeted Foster because they believed he supported student ID cards and a police presence in schools. In

20

reality, Foster had opposed the identification cards and publicly announced that he would not allow police officers in the schools.

The deterioration of the Oakland Unified School District, encompassing over 120 schools, has been well documented. The carcass symbolized by the former administration building is testament to decades of administrative incompetence, urban decay and financial mismanagement. The district declared bankruptcy in 2011.

Two of the assassins, Joseph Remiro and Russell Little, were arrested after a shootout with police in Concord in January 1974 and charged with Foster's murder. The kidnapping of Patty Hearst on February 4th was an idiotic attempt by the SLA to bargain their release and divert attention away from the Foster fiasco.

The SLA was uninformed and naïve about their potential negotiating adversary. Then California governor Ronald Reagan would have never sanctioned a prisoner exchange in any form.

On May 17, 1974, the third suspect Donald DeFreeze was involved in a shoot-out with the Los Angeles Police force. Outgunned and trapped with five other SLA members, DeFreeze committed suicide by shooting himself in the right side of his head while apparently burning alive.

Convicted in 1974 for Foster's murder, Joseph Remiro began serving a life sentence at the Pelican Bay State Prison. He remains incarcerated today at the California State Prison facility in Lancaster. Russell Little was also convicted of first-degree murder but due to a technical error in the jury instructions, was later retried and acquitted. He was released in 1983 and reportedly changed both his name and his residence to Hawaii.

The SLA never regrouped or captured the same level of media attention following the fatal Los Angeles shoot-out. Other members disbanded or were imprisoned over the subsequent years. Their impact on society ultimately proved as empty as their political agenda and rhetoric.

Pathway Leading to Execution

Parking Lot Murder Site

District Building Exit to the Parking Lot

The Mob Permanently Severs Relations With Bugsy Siegel

Post-World War II American gangster lore found its iconic hero in the guise of Benjamin *Bugsy* Siegel, The charismatic and outrageously perceived Siegel was the celebrated public face of organized crime making him a prominent target.

His reputation for violence and ruthlessness made him both feared and respected amongst friends, associates and rivals. Siegel's organization began with bootlegging during Prohibition and expanded later into more lucrative drug, protection, murder and prostitution operations. His greatest skill may have been his ability to forge alliances with diverse crime families effectively creating *organized* crime.

Beneath his cultivated public veneer as a flashy dresser, womanizer and pseudo celebrity, Siegel was marginally more than a common hoodlum. He had compiled a criminal record that included armed robbery, rape and murder dating back to his teenage years. He detested the moniker *Bugsy* branded to him due to his sometimes ferocious intensity bordering on psychotic. He wished to be regarded as a sophisticate, but such reverence was personally unattainable.

His most insightful enterprise proved to be his promotion of gambling operations in the then near barren desert of Las Vegas. Seizing an opportunity to be perceived as a legitimate businessman in 1945, Siegel coerced William Wilkerson, by threat of death, to sell his entire stake of the under construction Flamingo Hotel to the mob. Siegel hired himself in the role of operations director.

His aim was to control the totality of Las Vegas' gambling potential. The Flamingo would become his showpiece and headquarters. Siegel understood that a gambling destination would likewise require tourist amenities to tap into a secondary market of vacationers. In 1945 Las Vegas seemed as far removed from most tourism itineraries as the Sahara Desert.

History concurred with Siegel's vision, but he would not be allowed to witness its fulfillment. In 1946, the construction cost overruns for his signature palace had far exceeded initial estimates. Siegel's quest for extravagance and personal enrichment significantly surpassed his budget. His financial accountability proved vague. A habitual criminal rarely perceives financial discipline with the same stewardship as a traditional corporate CEO. Squandering other people's money is never a practice ensuring professional longevity.

Money was vanishing and the official opening date festivities of December 26, 1946 were a disaster. For the ceremony, the property and amenities remained unfinished and the normally stable weather rained a deluge. The catastrophe worsened as after two weeks, the gaming tables were operating at an inconceivable loss. By the conclusion of the first month, operations were shuttered.

Three months later, the casino was reopened and began cultivating positive press and profitability. Siegel was offered an opportunity for redemption, but the agreement proved a charade. Associates and superiors were simultaneously formulating plans to eliminate him from meetings in Havana.

Siegel's arrogance and boasting façade were affronts to an organization that insisted upon discretion and secrecy, especially since their activities were illegal.

On the evening of June 20, 1947, Siegel and an associate were lounging at his girlfriend Virginia Hill's Beverly Hills home. The residential property is easily accessible from the street and the landscaping makes concealment simple. The mobster, whose own national syndicate was nicknamed *Murder Incorporated*, became a victim by an assailant who fired at him through a viewing window with a .30 caliber military M1 carbine. Siegel was struck multiple times including two fatal head wounds.

The surprise and fury of the attack eliminated any opportunity for return response. The shadow of Bugsy Siegel was gone and his violent assassination proved instrumental in thrusting Las Vegas into national media exposure. He was only 41. Within days of his death, another crime family took over the operations of the Flamingo Hotel and Casino. Siegel's promotional legacy proved more valuable with the man himself absent.

Today he would likely revel with paternal pride at contemporary Las Vegas. The gambling and entertainment colossus ultimately matched and far exceeded his dream. Organized crime has presumably disappeared from a dominant influential and operational role. At least, that is the narrative promoted by the local Chamber of Commerce and a Gangster Museum honoring the dubious mob era.

Have they really left and why should they?

Criminality has the capacity to adorn the clothing of respectability as effortlessly as Siegel could be replaced. Perception is eternally subject to modification.

Virginia Hill's Beverly Hills Mansion

Chauncey Bailey: The Price of Constitutional Protection

Our Freedom of the Press is a constitutional protection that Chauncey Bailey paid dearly for to defend. It is ironic that amidst today's spin journalism and advertising sponsored content, reporting the truth remains as potent and relevant as ever.

Chauncey Bailey, Jr. was an American journalist, noted for his writings primarily on African-American issues. His most prominent position was as editor of *The Oakland Post* from June 2007 until his death less than two months later.

At 7:30 a.m. on August 2, 2007, Bailey was shot dead execution-style on a downtown Oakland street as he followed his customary route from his apartment to work. His lone assassin fled on foot to a parked van and drove off. Bailey was killed while working on an exposé about the finances, contract killings and fraud involved with *Your Black Muslim Bakery* and the organization's impending bankruptcy. The story had been temporarily withheld from publication due to its potentially incendiary nature.

The sidewalk stretch of 14th Street where Bailey was slain is less than 50 feet from intersecting Alice Street, where the getaway vehicle was parked. A mature tree to the right and a fenced-in postal distribution facility to the left with scattered landscaped shrubbery shade the concrete. Numerous pedestrians pass the location daily en route to their workplaces or simply to loiter in the neighborhood.

The killing site was unremarkable and could be transplanted to any major urban center. The brazenness and early hour of the killing were the most shocking elements. Shootings in downtown Oakland streets ceased to become novelty years ago. The confrontation between killer and victim was brief. Bailey very likely knew his fate, his killer and the motive.

The notoriety of Bailey's killing immediately collapsed the fortunes of *Your Black Muslim Bakery*.

Early the following morning, Oakland Police officers and SWAT team members closed off a number of blocks of San Pablo Avenue. Their search warrants and area of focus included homes and business properties of the bakery facility, which operated two business sites within the area.

The bakery and its operators were a Black Muslim splinter organization originally founded by Yusuf Bey, and consequently led by his son Yusuf Bey IV. The pre-dawn raids followed a two-month investigation into a variety of violent crimes, including kidnapping and murder. Bailey's death prompted immediate response and caught the residents unprepared.

During the raid, police arrested Devaughndre Broussard, who confessed to both stalking and then killing Bailey on orders from Yusuf Bey IV. Bailey's murder weapon was recovered during the raid. Bey IV denied ordering the killings. It wasn't until April 2009 once Broussard agreed to cooperate with prosecutors that he and one of his bakery associate's Antoine Mackey were charged in Bailey's killing.

On the same day after Bailey's death, U.S. Bankruptcy Judge Edward Jellen ordered the immediate financial liquidation of the bakery. The organization's fragile facade collapsed swiftly and definitively.

Bey IV and Mackey were found guilty in June 2011 of three counts of murder in ordering the deaths of Bailey and two other former bakery associates. Bey IV is presently interned at Salinas Valley State Prison. Mackey was convicted of murdering one bakery associate and helping Broussard kill Bailey. He is serving his sentence at the California State Prison facility in Lancaster. Both first-degree murder charges carry a mandatory sentence of life in prison without the possibility of parole.

Devaughndre Broussard, the triggerman, accepted a plea deal in exchange for his testimony and was sentenced to 25 years in prison. He was originally served his term at the Salinas Valley State Prison before being transferred to the LaPalma Correctional Center in Eloy, Arizona.

Chauncey Bailey was the first journalist killed over a domestic story in the United States since 1976. That year, Don Bolles of *The Arizona Republic* died in a car bombing. Bailey's death is a reminder despite the flaws of modern journalism, its role remains critical to preserving a free society.

Bailey's Killing Site

The Mickey and Trudy Thompson Morning Driveway Execution

Marion Lee *Mickey* Thompson was an undisputed icon of American off-road racing fame. Maximum acceleration was his forte. Establishing land speed records during his 20s and early 30s, he channeled his obsession into winning numerous track, hot rod and dragster championships. He later formed sanctioning bodies for the sport.

At the height of his renowned on March 16, 1988, he and his wife Trudy were gunned down at their hillside home in Bradbury. A pair of unknown assailants, waiting outside of the Thompson's gated house, committed the precisely timed killings. While preparing to depart for work in the morning, Mickey opened the garage door for his wife to pull out. As he approached his own car, he was wounded and dragged out to his driveway.

Unknown to Trudy, she began to back her vehicle out into the driveway. She was shot dead in her car. The shooter then returned to Thompson and finished him with a bullet to the head. Both assailants pedaled bicycles away to their escape.

The execution involved neither robbery nor any other apparent motive. For thirteen years, the mysterious case remained open without resolution.

In 2001, a former business partner, Michael Goodwin was charged with orchestrating the murder. He was convicted in 2004 on two counts of first-degree murder and sentenced to life imprisonment without parole.

The evidence was entirely circumstantial. Goodwin's reported role was to have hired the killers and assisted them with logistical details in the planning stages. He became the prime suspect based on the nature of previously reported threats against the Thompson's. In reported comments he had made to associates, he expressed an absolute certainty that he would never be caught.

A curious aspect of his arrest was that the charges were filed in Orange County instead of Los Angeles County where the murders were committed. The Orange County prosecutor initiated the proceedings within their jurisdiction citing that Goodwin planned the murders there. The Los Angeles County district attorney's office had refused to file charges against Goodwin claiming there was an absence of incriminating evidence.

Physical evidence tracing Goodwin to the shootings such as payments, telephone records or any eyewitnesses to direct meetings with the shooters was unavailable. Goodwin was identified as being present in the neighborhood with binoculars and another person a few days before the murders. The defense team claimed that the prosecution witnesses including an ex-girlfriend of Goodwin were unreliable.

Motive ultimately became a determining factor. A district attorney's office and jury concluded that Michael Goodwin was the sole individual with sufficient self-interest to order a killing for hire. Goodwin is currently imprisoned at the R.J. Donovan Correctional Facility. The shooters have never been identified.

Despite a life dominated by speed, the expediency of capture and justice for the Thompson's killers has proven excruciatingly protracted.

The Fatal Driveway

The Political Killings of San Francisco Mayor George Moscone and Supervisor Harvey Milk

It is not a stretch to suggest that former San Francisco Supervisor Dan White may qualify as the city's most historically reviled political figure.

Nine days following the People's Temple massacre at Jonestown in Guyana, on November 27, 1978, White executed Mayor George Moscone and Supervisor Harvey Milk. The killings were calculated and cowardly with absolutely no remorse for the victims, their families or any subsequent consequences. In itself, the murders were reprehensible, but what followed at White's trial was considered one of the worst travesties of American justice.

White shot Moscone in his office because he had refused to re-appoint him to his seat on the Board of Supervisors. White had officially resigned over two weeks previously but changed his mind regarding the decision. Milk had lobbied heavily against his re-appointment and was a habitual adversary with White on city legislative issues.

San Francisco politics during the 1970s was turbulent and volatile with the nature of local representation undergoing a radical transformation. White and Milk were both elected during the 1977 election when district based representation was first introduced.

Before politics, White had been a San Francisco police officer and firefighter. He and his district aligned themselves with a slim majority that characterized the Board of Supervisor's pro-growth philosophy. White, however, often found himself isolated on issues that required a broader consensus and participation base. He was the lone contrary vote against the historic San Francisco gay rights ordinance passed in 1978.

White faced tremendous financial difficulties due to a failing restaurant he owned and his marginal salary as a supervisor. He was fed up with the workings of city politics and his exclusion from insider status. The accumulated stress from his circumstances, prompted him to resigned on November 10.

His resignation suited the designs of Moscone who leaned towards a more controlled, decentralized growth agenda. Moscone was empowered to appoint a successor and since White often constituted the swing vote on local issues, he would be able to exert his influential preferences towards the future direction of the city.

White's supporters urged him to rescind his resignation by requesting reappointment from Moscone and promised him some financial support. White appealed to the Mayor to re-appoint him. Moscone had little interest in such a decision and was lobbied heavily by more liberal city political interests.

Moscone ultimately decided to appoint Don Horanzy, a federal housing official. On the day he was planning to formally announce Horanzy as his replacement, White initiated his premeditated rampage.

Concealing his loaded police service revolver and ten rounds of ammunition in his coat pocket, White entered City Hall through a first floor window evading the building's metal detectors.

White began by entering Moscone's reception office and requested an appointment. It may be conceivable that he still thought his re-appointment prospects possible. Moscone immediately informed him of his decision clarifying any uncertainty. White began arguing heatedly with the Mayor who discreetly moved the conversation to his interior private lounge to avoid further public unpleasantness. Once inside, White removed his revolver and fired four rounds, including two into Moscone's temple killing him instantly.

White proceeded to his former office and intercepted Harvey

Milk on the way. Milk agreed to join him in his office unaware of the preceding events. He was peppered with four shots before a conclusive fifth bullet was fired into his skull. Neither victim was armed nor had a premonition of White's motives.

Dan White left City Hall unchallenged and later that day turned himself in to a former police colleague. He maintained then and throughout his trial that the killings were not premeditated. The callousness of the acts confirmed otherwise.

White was tried for first-degree murder with special circumstances, which could have qualified him for the death penalty. At trial, his defense team miraculously recruited an intellectually challenged and gullible jury.

White's defense team claimed that he had been *depressed*, evidenced by, among other things, his eating of unhealthy junk foods. The defense argued that White's depression led to a state of mental diminished capacity, leaving him incapable of the necessary premeditation skills to commit first-degree murder. The jury accepted these arguments during their deliberations. White was found guilty of the lesser crime of voluntary manslaughter.

The verdict sparked outrage and riots in San Francisco, and eventually led to the California legislature abolishing the diminished capacity criminal defense.

White served a mere five years in prison for his double homicide before being paroled in 1984. As a supreme irony, he committed suicide less than two years later closing one the most tumultuous eras of San Francisco politics.

Today, the mere mention of Dan White still provokes disgust over the injustice of his sentence. Harvey Milk has become lionized as an iconic symbol of the gay rights movement. George Moscone is best known as the namesake for the city's convention center complex.

The San Francisco of today does not resemble Moscone's vision for the city. The post-Millennium vertical development of downtown San Francisco has trivialized the politically lethal discussions over growth policy from thirty-five years ago. History has shown that urban development ultimately prevails and eclipses any elected political body that attempts to control or moderate it.

San Francisco eulogized their murdered leaders but in the end followed the political agenda of their assassin.

San Francisco City Hall Entrance

The East/West Coast Vendetta and Killing of Christopher Wallace

The murder of Brooklyn's Christopher Wallace, more renowned as rapper Biggie Smalls or The Notorious B.I.G. on March 9, 1997, punctuated a purported bi-coastal feud between factions of the warring rap music industry.

The signs for imminent disaster were ominous. Wallace represented the East Coast faction and performer Tupac Shakur the West Coast. Shakur was assassinated on September 13, 1996 in a drive-by shooting on the Las Vegas strip. The killing enflamed a rivalry that escalated shooting violence and threats of retaliation. The warring resembled the savage gang behavior the music frequently sensationalized. Despite the adverse stigma, the rap music industry generates substantial international revenue, youth followings and performing icons.

The orchestrated killing prompted more speculation than resolution. The convenient East/West Coast feud theory offered a convenient explanation. Despite eyewitnesses and a composite drawing of the killer, no definitive answers or arrests were ever made.

Two days before his death, Wallace presented an award to singer Toni Braxton at the Soul Train Music Awards to a mixed audience reception. A post-event party, hosted by several music industry organizations on March 9, 1997 was held at the Petersen Automotive Museum in the mid-Wilshire district of Los Angeles.

The party was charged, chaotic and closed early by the fire department due to overcrowded conditions. Wallace left at around 12:30 a.m. with his entourage in two large Suburban SUVs. He traveled with three associates in his car. Record producer Sean Combs and three armed bodyguards rode in the other. A third vehicle tailed the two with his record company's director of security.

Christopher Wallace was seated exposed on the passenger side of his vehicle. This convenience undoubtedly ranks as either the choicest piece of good fortune for his assassin or simply a deliberate set-up. A dark Chevy Impala pulled up alongside Wallace's vehicle at the intersection of Wilshire Boulevard and South Fairfax Avenue while awaiting a green light. The driver, dressed in a blue suit and bow tie, rolled down his window, smiled and raised a 9mm blue-steel pistol directly at Wallace.

Four shots were emptied, one fatal. The lethal bullet entered through his right hip and struck several vital organs. The obese Wallace was rushed to the nearest hospital but died an hour later. His bodyguards reportedly fired no retaliation shots during the Impala's escape.

Immediately following the killing, a stream of conspiracy theories and motives were formulated. Numerous subsequent researched articles and books have fingered various suspects. The investigation has been roundly criticized and reopened for examination but remains unresolved. The truth may never surface. Several of the suspicious sources have disappeared, been killed or incarcerated.

Dead musical artists often command and sustain larger paydays for their producers. The rap music world has a bloody precedent of devouring its prominent frontmen. It has fostered an environment of violence fueled by money, drugs and fashion that have provided ample incentives for this cannibalization.

Christopher Wallace during several media interviews acknowledged the inherent risks involved with his status. Why he was seated in a vulnerable passenger seat, cognizant of this threat, is a puzzling question that defies explanation.

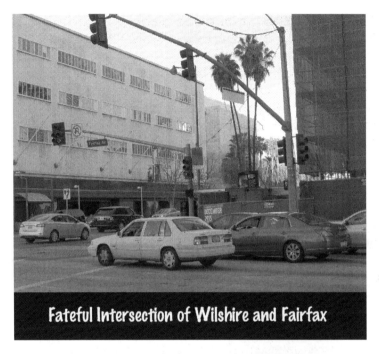

Fateful Intersection of Wilshire and Fairfax

Setting Up For The Kill

The Marin County Courthouse Shootout: Thirty Minutes That Forever Altered Courtroom Security Procedures

The final commission of architect Frank Lloyd Wright was the design of the majestic Marin Civic Center and Administration Building in San Rafael. Groundbreaking for the complex was initiated in 1960 after Wright's death and completed in 1962. The Hall of Justice section was begun in 1966 and completed in 1969.

On August 7, 1970, only one year after completion of the Hall of Justice, the Marin County Superior Court was the scene of an attempted jailbreak and hostage trade led by 17-year-old Jonathan Jackson, the brother of Black Panther militant George Jackson.

Jackson's motivation was an attempt to negotiate the freedom of the Soledad Brothers by kidnapping Superior Court Judge Harold Haley and other courtroom hostages. The Soledad Brothers consisted of George Jackson. Fleeta Drumgo, and John Clutchette, who were being held in San Quentin Prison awaiting trial for the murder of prison guard John Mills. Mills had been beaten and thrown from the third floor of Soledad's Y wing. George Jackson was a co-founder of the Black Guerrilla Family gang while incarcerated whose member, Tyrone Robinson would later murder Huey P. Newton.

The thirty-minute long ordeal began by a routine trial of defendant James D. McClain, a prisoner at San Quentin, who Haley allowed to represent himself. He had been charged with possession of a knife and stabbing a prison guard. As part of his defense four fellow prisoners from San Quentin were called to testify on his behalf. Ruchell Magee was on the witness stand when Jonathan Jackson rose from the audience and disrupted the proceedings by raising a pistol towards the judicial stand.

In the chaos that followed, Jackson removed two additional guns from a satchel, which he had carried in. He distributed his pistol and the two guns to Magee, McClain and William Christmas, who had been in a holding cell waiting to be called to testify. He then produced a sawed-off shotgun hidden from within his raincoat. The kidnappers, after some debate, secured five hostages whom they bound with piano wire: Judge Haley, Deputy District Attorney Gary Thomas and jurors Maria Elena Graham, Doris Whitmer, and Joyce Rodoni.

Judge Haley was forced at gunpoint to call the courthouse bailiff with the intention of convincing the police to refrain from intervening. The sawed-off shotgun was held against Haley's neck as the four kidnappers and four other hostages then moved into the corridor of the courthouse inching their way towards the elevator.

The corridor was crowded with responding police but no action was taken against the kidnappers at that point.

The group entered the elevator demanding the freedom of the Soledad Brothers by 12:30 p.m. that day. The kidnappers then sheparded the hostages from the building into a rented Ford panel truck Jackson had left in the parking lot behind the courthouse.

Jackson's plan was ill-conceived and doomed. Then California Governor Ronald Reagan would have never accommodated a hostage trade. Law enforcement personnel onsite had no intention of allowing the vehicle to leave the main driveway, the only exit, towards their destination of nearby Highway 101.

Police and San Quentin guards had set up a roadblock on both sides of the Hall of Justice driveway in anticipation of the group. According to eyewitnesses,, law enforcement officers began to open fire on the van almost immediately after it had left the lobby pick-up point. A shootout resulted in which Jackson, McClain and Christmas were killed and Magee was seriously injured. Reports indicated that Thomas grabbed one of the kidnapper's guns and began firing at them from inside the van.

Blood splattered everywhere from the resulting carnage.

Haley was slain by a discharge of the shotgun by Magee. Thomas was seriously wounded in his back, leaving him wheelchair-bound and Graham suffered a wound to her arm. Magee was shot in the chest and was taken to the hospital for emergency surgery.

The drama did not conclude with the August 7th butchery. A warrant was issued for the arrest of Angela Davis, a renowned communist activist and former professor in the University of California system. She had lived with and had a relationship with George Jackson prior to his incarceration. Davis was the registered owner of each of the employed guns including the sawed-off shotgun. Circumstantial evidence and eyewitnesses placed her in Jonathan Jackson's company just prior to the attempted kidnapping.

Davis became a glamorized *cause celebre* amongst anti-establishment causes during this era. Was she singled out for persecution by authorities or an active participant? She evaded capture for two months, hiding amongst her political connections before finally being arrested in New York City. She was charged as an accomplice to conspiracy, kidnapping, and homicide. She was tried in 1972 and found *not guilty* on each of the counts.

Ruchell Magee pled guilty to the charge of aggravated kidnapping for his part in the assault. He was sentenced in 1975 to life in prison and is currently imprisoned at the California Men's Colony in San Luis Obispo.

George Jackson, who's *hoped for* release prompted the tragedy, was killed three days before he was to go on trial for prison guard Mill's murder. He was fatally shot in 1971 during a San Quentin riot attempting to escape. Ironically Drumgo and Clutchette, the remaining Soledad Brothers were acquitted of the murder.

Two unidentified men shot Fleeta Drumgo to death on November 27, 1979 on the streets of Oakland. He had been released from prison in 1976 after serving nine years for a Los Angeles burglary and was living with John Clutchette at the time. His killers were never caught. John Clutchette is currently serving a life sentence at the California State Prison Solano in Vacaville for a 1980 first-degree murder conviction. He was convicted of shooting Robert Bowles in the back of the head without warning or provocation over a drug-deal dispute.

In retrospect, many factors were conveniently ignored in assigning sole blame for Jonathan Jackson's actions. It is inconceivable that a seventeen-year-old man would have had the capacity or capability of orchestrating a suicidal hostage kidnapping. At seventeen, Jackson could not have legally rented a van or secured the necessary firearms without assistance.

Any potential associate conspirator(s) have never been condemned to their due justice. Their hands remain stained by the shed blood of two honorable judicial figures and a teenager who simply wanted his older brother reunited with him. Jackson's motive was clear, misguided, but understandable. For those who evaded punishment by manipulating Jonathan Jackson to die in their place, their role is unconscionable.

The system of tight security prevalent in courtrooms today began with this incident in Marin County. Local courts were immediately wired with direct communication to the sheriff's department, and metal detectors were installed in all the courtrooms.

We take these precautions today for granted. One cannot fathom the vulnerability of a facility that could enable firearms to be effortless smuggled into a courtroom. This expectation of preventative security illuminates the level of eroded and vanished respect for our institutions of authority. Far worse, no one is even astonished.

Shoot Out Site

Frank Lloyd Wright Designed
Marin County Courthouse

Police Sniper's Perspective of Escape Van

Robert F. Kennedy: The Assassination of Hope

Robert F. Kennedy represented many diverse inspiring images to Americans. Long before the term *Hope* was employed by Barrack Obama's presidential campaign, Kennedy epitomized hope and change for societies disenfranchised.

America in June 1968 had arrived at a crossroads. Amidst the contagious rebellion against an increasingly unpopular war in Vietnam and a general malaise within American culture, Kennedy represented a sense of coherent dignity and clarity.

Some of his appeal may have been rooted by the high public regard for the Kennedy family name. Robert Kennedy was unmistakably unique. He was often reviled as much as admired for his blunt candor.

He was firmly against the Vietnam War, a military conflict his presidential brother John had escalated while in office. Serving in the Kennedy administration as the United States Attorney General, he dealt with controversial Civil Rights issues and exposed corruption within organized labor.

He completed the majority of his term under a hostile presidential successor Lyndon Johnson before resigning to run for the U.S. Senate. He was successfully elected by the State of New York and assumed office in 1965.

During his tenure in the Senate, Kennedy became an outspoken advocate of Israel. His unwavering support had been formulated during a residence in the country in his early twenties and a genuine admiration of the Jewish inhabitants.

The Presidential election of 1968 became an alternating shift of preferences within Kennedy's Democratic Party. President Lyndon Johnson's popularity suffered severely due his Vietnam War policies and the magnitude of social unrest. To Johnson's credit, he introduced more anti-poverty and anti-discrimination legislation than any predecessor or successor. Johnson obstinacy imagined he could salvage victory in an unwinnable and demoralizing war.

His narrow victory in the New Hampshire primary against anti-war candidate, Minnesota Senator Eugene McCarthy convinced him of his electable vulnerability

Following the primary, he made a national speech indicating he would no longer seek re-election. This announcement left the Democratic field wide open.

One month following his announcement, Vice-President Hubert Humphrey, also from Minnesota, declared his candidacy. He did not enter any primaries. His status as front-runner was based on previously declared delegates whose commitments were not permanently binding.

McCarthy's initial campaign success was based on his open opposition to the Vietnam War and efforts to empower younger voters. Kennedy delayed his entry into the race until after the New Hampshire primary on March 16. He immediately seized popular momentum. McCarthy's appeal began to subside. With Humphrey absent from the primary ballots, Kennedy ran exclusively against McCarthy and captured the majority of the primaries.

On April 4th, Civil Rights leader Martin Luther King was assassinated in Memphis and a stewing cauldron of racial turmoil and violence erupted nationally. The United States was in tumult and experiencing a collective disillusionment towards central leadership. A sense of change appeared necessary. Opposing perspectives became polarized and debate antagonistic. In the eyes of many, the election of Robert Kennedy represented the potential for fulfillment of the idealistic and interrupted dreams of his assassinated brother.

Views of history can effortlessly lapse into a speculation sport.

Probable outcomes are not tested by actual events. Was Robert Kennedy the calming influence America required? Would the subsequent trajectory of American history been altered? We will never know.

On June 4, 1968, Robert Kennedy narrowly won the California primary over Eugene McCarthy. At that moment, he ranked second to Humphrey in delegates for the Democratic nomination.

His delegate momentum surge had clearly ascended him on an accelerated course to overtake the front-runner. That evening signified the final influence either McCarthy or Kennedy would exert on the Democratic Party. McCarthy's popularity never regained popular traction. Kennedy was shot to death.

Shortly after midnight, four hours after the California polls had closed, Kennedy addressed his campaign supporters in the Ambassador Hotel's Embassy Ballroom located in the mid-Wilshire district of Los Angeles. His mood was optimistic and jubilant. Kennedy was on target to gain the nomination and very likely the presidency.

During that era, the government provided secret service protection for incumbent presidents but not declared candidates. Kennedy's security force consisted of a former FBI agent and several professional athletes serving as unofficial bodyguards.

The chaos following his victory speech created media deadline complications due to the late hour. Kennedy was originally scheduled to meet with an additional group of supporters in another section of the hotel, Instead, he was escorted through a hotel kitchen pantry to an awaiting press conference.

The crowd hemmed in Kennedy as he threaded through the kitchen while shaking hands en route. From the crevices of a narrow passageway, Sirhan Sirhan, a 24-year-old Palestinian national emerged and began firing a .22 caliber revolver into a distracted Kennedy and his entourage.

He shot Kennedy three times. He wounded five others and was finally wrestled to the ground and struck repeatedly by Kennedy's protective guards.

Kennedy did not die immediately. He reportedly asked about the welfare of the other victims before slipping into unconsciousness. He lingered for 26 hours before finally expiring. One of the bullets had entered behind his right ear and dispersed fragments through his brain. He was only 42-years-old.

Speculation began immediately towards the killing being a calculated conspiracy. It remains unclear how Sirhan anticipated the divergent routing through the kitchen passage.

Initially, Sirhan's strong anti-Zionist beliefs were identified as the obsession behind the killing. A purportedly discovered diary of Sirhan's confirmed his resolution to kill Kennedy. In subsequent rambling interviews, Sirhan has since blamed brainwashing tactics and memory loss for his inability to pinpoint why he was present at the Ambassador Hotel that fateful evening. He remains incarcerated at the RJ Donovan Correctional Facility in San Diego awaiting a much-welcomed demise by many.

His elimination of a potential history transformer resulted in profound domestic and international consequences. The August Democratic Convention in Chicago resulted in combative protests. Hubert Humphrey emerged from the chaos nominated by the party, but tainted. Former Vice-President Richard Nixon secured the uncontested Republican nomination and handily defeated Humphrey in the national election. He ran on a campaign platform promising to restore law and order.

Both candidates sidestepped the Vietnam War issue during campaigning. Nixon ultimately signed a peace treaty four years later ingloriously ending the conflict. Despite several notable foreign policy achievements, he would self-destruct his own legacy through the Watergate cover-up scandal.

The morale of Americans would stagnate through an extended period of economic woe and international military conflicts. Idealists suggest that Kennedy's leadership may have avoided the accompanying dissatisfaction.

The Ambassador Hotel ceased hospitality operations in 1989, but remained open for filming and private events. During 2005, the majority of the building was demolished leaving only the annex that housed the hotel entrance, shipping arcade, coffee shop and a portion of the Cocoanut Grove Nightclub. The kitchen pantry area, the site of the shooting was included in the demolition.

The Central Los Angeles New Learning Center, along with the Robert F. Kennedy Inspiration Park was built on the Ambassador grounds. An extensive peace memorial adorns the Wilshire Boulevard frontage. The metal memorials are testimonies to peace but cannot adequately capture the loss and significance of the promise Kennedy once offered.

Robert Kennedy briefly represented the same progressive change and options his brother John symbolized for so many. It is impossible to conclude whether a divided nation had the capacity to heal immediately amidst such era of rupture. It is equally debatable that our nation, with its entrenched two-party system influenced by special interest monies, may ever fully recover onto a single united course.

The Reconverted Ambassador Hotel Site

Joseph *The Animal* Barboza: The Inevitability of a Lifestyle Path

The longevity prospects of an East Coast Mafia hitman and informer would not appear substantial. When such an individual, under the U.S. government witness protection program returns to his previous profession and risky lifestyle, his prospects diminish into an inevitable death sentence.

The killing of Joseph *The Animal* Barboza surprised no one. The San Francisco location of the contract slaying was unusual and the source of his betrayal, an evident surprise to the victim.

Barboza was a confirmed New England mobster and feared hitman whose life did nothing to further the advancement of humanity. Acknowledged appropriately by his long-term legal council, F. Lee Bailey, the news of his assassination brought the quip *no great loss to society.*

An individual such a Barboza cultivates many associates of unsavory nature and few friends amongst the cesspool they inhabit during their lifetime. His background and criminal exploits make intriguing but repulsive viewing even to those sharing a fascination with the mobster lifestyle. The ultimate betrayal by an associate, inflated self-promotion and later return to criminal activity in Northern California contributed towards his predictable outcome.

Barboza's most noteworthy distinction was assuming the role of FBI informant and becoming one of the initial participants in the Federal Witness Protection Program. His testimony proved influential in securing convictions against several organized crime figures. A fresh identity and vocational occupation however could not alter his sociopathic tendencies. When one has spent an entire lifetime cultivating influential enemies, violent death becomes simply a question of where, when and in what manner.

51

The litany of death attributed to Barboza may have exceeded double digits on both coasts. Exact numbers are difficult to quantify from imaginative boasting and speculation. A proficient hitman rarely acknowledges his handiwork as someday he may face accountability.

An individual such as Joseph Barboza who acquired a nickname *The Animal* is clearly respected but doubtlessly psychotic. His second-degree conviction for the killing of a man in 1971 in Santa Rosa exposed his actual identity while he was on trial. He served a marginal five years in Folsom prison for the murder, but his fate was sealed. Out on parole in October 1975, Barboza was targeted for revenge.

His February 11, 1976 death was a classic set-up and pristine assassination arranged in conjunction with one of Barboza's *friends*. Following lunch at his friend's residence in his Sunset District neighborhood, Barboza returned to his parked car adjacent to the house. He was armed with a Colt .38 but ambushed at close range by four shotgun blasts before he could respond.

Reportedly defiant to the end, Barboza shouted obscenities at his killers as they sped away. He died immediately afterwards.

There were no eyewitnesses. The killing site and neighborhood today is serene and nearly deserted during daylight. No one has ever been charged with his death. The responsible party(s) has been rumored to be another mob hitman. The investigation remains open but with minimal enthusiasm towards resolution.

Joe *The Animal* Barboza's death became simply another combat casualty in the warfare between society and organized crime. Morals may be drawn from his sordid life and demise. They tend to be dismissed with the public's continuing fascination with cult criminal personalities. Barboza's contribution to the campaign is largely forgotten.

There remained then and now numerous candidates to supplant him. Compliance and acceptance of society's regulations make uneventful television and motion picture viewing.

The Location of the Shooting

Barboza's "Friend's" House

The Contract Killing of Vic Weiss: The Rewards For Stealing

The double existence of Vic Weiss culminated in the closely confined trunk of his luxurious red and white Rolls Royce.

Weiss impersonated business prowess and the epitome of skilled achievement. His acquaintance base included high-level athletic personalities. He postured in designer suits, a gold Rolex watch and prominent diamond ring. Most of his friends and acquaintances assumed he had acquired his fortune through real estate, insurance ventures and ownership stakes in a Ford and Rolls Royce dealerships in Van Nuys. Weiss had a reputation for always paying any entertainment tab involving his friends and business associates.

In 1979, his highest profile friend was University of Nevada Las Vegas (UNLV) Basketball Coach Jerry Tarkanian, a Pasadena high school classmate. Their formative bond and mutual respect were sustained over the ensuing years as Weiss began to dabble professionally in sport management. Tarkanian become one of his early clients and Weiss was in the midst of negotiating a prestigious contract on his behalf.

Real Estate developer Jerry Buss was in the final stages of purchasing the Los Angeles Lakers from Jack Kent Cooke and wanted a renowned winning coach to lead the Lakers. He desired the services of Tarkanian whose reputation for winning and feuding with the NCAA were legendary. The NCAA (National College Athletic Association) is the organizing authority, which legislates and governs amateur athletics within the American university sports system.

On the afternoon of June 14, 1979, Cooke, Buss and Weiss met at the Beverly Comstock Hotel to negotiate and finalize verbal agreements for Tarkanian's services. The session ended positively. The concurring terms were handwritten on a piece of paper and dropped into Weiss' briefcase upon the session's conclusion.

Official notification and consent by Tarkanian and a signed printed contract were the sole obstacles to a finalized agreement.

Weiss was supposed to telephone Tarkanian with the encouraging news. Afterwards he was scheduled to dine at a San Fernando Valley restaurant with his wife. Neither the anticipated call nor the dinner materialized.

Weiss disappeared. Four days later a security guard at the Universal Sheraton Hotel parking garage spotted his Rolls Royce with the stunning gold interior and putrid odor. Investigators found Weiss' decomposed remains shoved into the trunk. Robbery did not appear to be the motive. He was still wearing his diamond ring and Rolex. His briefcase was conspicuously absent. He had been efficiently executed by two gunshots into the back of his head.

His illusionary posed lifestyle and a motive eventually became exposed.

He was not wealthy. His business ventures and car dealerships proved fictitious. His Rolls Royce was leased. Emerging details clarified his actual occupation as an organized crime money launderer. He was in significant debt due to gambling losses. To substantiate his image, rumors circulated that he may have siphoned funds from his employers.

The code of conduct demanded by the criminal class is *absolute* fidelity and ethics. Non-compliance or violation is punished by immediate disposability. Weiss pilfered from the wrong source and his compensation became academic.

To reinforce discipline, silence becomes paramount, particularly with law enforcement authorities. The investigation into Weiss' death led only to additional suspicious deaths of related parties with no conclusive answers or cooperation. Investigators concluded that Weiss' killing was a professional contract hit. No one has ever been arrested for the crime.

The Los Angeles Lakers did not hire Jerry Tarkanian. The exemplary playing talents of Ervin Magic Johnson and the coaching by three relative unknowns, elevated the team into one of elite sports franchises of the 1980s. Tarkanian remained at UNLV until 1992, peaking his stint with a title at the NCAA Championship in 1990. Two years later, he accepted a head-coaching job with the San Antonio Spurs professional basketball club. He was unceremoniously fired after a single season. He returned to college basketball and authority defiance at Fresno State University between 1995-2002. He retired with an enviable head coaching record of 706 wins and 198 losses. He died in February 2015.

His success, strategy tactics and accompanying controversy altered a perception of amateurism within college basketball. His vehement supporters argued that he accomplished incredible results with inferior talent. His critics claimed his flagrant recruitment violations often involved unscrupulous financial offers.

The divisions between professionalism and amateur athletics continue to blur. Winning college athletic programs with their accompanying financial benefits remain the justifiable motives for stretching ethical boundaries. Within professional athletics, gambling interests have always tested the legitimacy of outcomes. The scale and infusions of betting that taint performances are revealed periodically. Only inside manipulators know the extent of how rampant the disease affects sporting competitions globally.

The example of Vic Weiss' killing had absolutely no adverse impact on the expansion of sports wagering. Global betting has since proliferated multifold. Internet sports sites, fantasy fan programs and television programming relentlessly fuel spectator's insatiable demand.

Individual performance, team examinations and highlight filming are marketed ceaselessly as viewing spectacles. Professional athletics has elevated itself into an international and cultural obsession diverting attention from more immediate, substantive and profound social and political issues.

Vic Weiss became a casualty of his gambling compulsion. His excesses are hardly unique. At some juncture, contemporary society will be obliged to reconcile the damage, blindness and sickness imposed by our *healthy* obsession with organized sporting competitions.

Universal Sheraton Parking Garage

The Wonderland Gang Killings and Fantasy Sex Industry

Pornography legend John Holmes lived a multiple existence. While considered an industry icon due to the size of his penis and acting appearances in over 2,500 films, Holmes was a notorious drug addict.

His addiction ingratiated him into distribution rings including organized crime figure and nightclub owner Eddie Nash and the Wonderland Gang, based in a wooded Laurel Canyon neighborhood in the San Fernando Valley.

These ruthless acquaintances culminated in disaster when Holmes skimmed currency and drugs from the Wonderland gang to support his own habit. Holmes tipped his debtors off about an extensive stash of drugs, money and jewelry Nash had stored in his residence. On June 29, 1981, the gang broke into Eddie Nash's opulent home and staged a large-scale armed robbery.

Robbing a competitor is always a poor idea. Retribution was swift and within two days. Holmes, whose acting range withered in proportion to his most marketable asset, was unable to mask his participation. Nash forcibly coerced his confession and obliged Holmes to accompany a revenging group under his hire.

Nash ruthlessly avenged the theft. During the early hours of July 1, the Laurel Canyon drug headquarters were invaded. Five of the members were attacked and four died from extensive blunt force trauma injuries from hammers and pipes.

The dead included leader Billy DeVerell, Ron Launius, Joy Miller and Barbara Richardson. Launius's wife, Susan Launius, miraculously survived the attack but had to have part of her skull surgically removed. These casualties were not innocent victims. The crime scene and the carnage was brutal and excessive. John Holmes was a spectator to insure his silence.

Nash, his bodyguard Gregory Diles and Holmes were arrested,

tried and acquitted for the murders. Holmes refused to testify or cooperate for obvious reasons. His participation would have insured his death upon release. He remained in jail for several months adamant in his refusal and noncompliance. Diles died in 1995.

In 1998, Holmes died of complications as a result of AIDS. An accumulated lifestyle of promiscuous sex with both genders and intravenous drugs ultimately caught up with him. Even on his deathbed, he refused to cooperate with law enforcement authorities.

The Wonderland Gang murders remain officially unsolved. They were loosely depicted in the successful film *Boogie Nights*. Despite Holmes' ability to earn premium wages for film appearances, he died destitute in a VA Medical Center in Los Angeles. The majority of his earnings lined his nasal passages via an unconquerable cocaine habit.

Holmes is still regarded as the most renowned male pornography actor of all time. The price and value for this fame was devalued by his pathetic addictions, betrayals and their accompanying consequences.

Wonderland Gang Murder Site

The Patty Hearst Kidnapping: The Final Nail into the Coffin of Idealism

The kidnapping and subsequent odyssey of Patricia Hearst began on the evening of February 4, 1974. A band of armed men and women knocked on her Berkeley apartment door and within minutes had abducted her, beaten up her fiancé and tossed her into their car truck. They then returned to their headquarters in a Western Addition apartment in San Francisco.

Their 19-year old victim was no average UC Berkeley college student. She was the granddaughter and heiress of publisher William Randolph Hearst.

The kidnapping elevated the status of a group of armed idealists, named the Symbionese Liberation Army (SLA), led by an ex-con named Donald DeFreeze. Hearst's kidnapping was motivated by the group's need to erase the memory of their only known activity up to that time. In November of 1973, the SLA had callously and stupidly murdered Dr. Marcus Foster, the Oakland Superintendent of Schools and seriously wounded his assistant with cyanide-tipped bullets. Two of their shooters were in custody for the murder.

The SLA was an extremist group loaded with guns and rhetoric and an ability to milk media exposure with empty clichéd ideology. Their ranks included both genders, blacks and whites, anarchists and idealists from diverse walks of life.

The SLA had significant propaganda plans for Patty Hearst. After all, what could be more potent to their revolutionary cause than the successful recruitment of an heiress from the elite establishment? Their stated goals included an overthrow of contemporary society.

But first, they had to brainwash and destroy any potential resistance by her.

By her account, she was clandestinely housed in a Golden Gate Avenue apartment building in San Francisco. Hearst was blindfolded and isolated in a third floor closet for two months, oblivious to the enormous media frenzy stimulated by her kidnapping. She was repeatedly abused and violated mentally, physically and emotionally. Acceptance and cooperation with their agenda became her sole possibility of survival.

Their brainwashing techniques worked. Hearst was coerced into making inflammatory statements against her family and those she had been closest to before her kidnapping. She integrated seamlessly into SLA operations and ultimately participated in an armed bank robbery in the Sunset district of San Francisco. While captive, the SLA made extravagant ransom requests of her father including demands for distributing millions of dollars in free food to the poor. This audacious stipulation turned into a fiasco with much of the inventory being stolen and disappearing without any form of accountability.

Patty Hearst proved too valuable for the group to release, but their own fate was nearing a violent conclusion. While relatively secure within the Bay Area due to an abundance of safe houses, DeFreeze impulsively opted to shift his operations to Los Angeles. This decision became their undoing.

An unsuccessful petty shoplifting debacle traced the group's van to their temporary residence. The following day on May 17, the Los Angeles police surrounded the house. A massive fuselage followed. Law enforcement officers showed little interest in taking prisoners once they were fired upon. The building went up in flames. Six members of the SLA died in the blaze, including DeFreeze who shot himself fatally while simultaneously on fire.

The site of the destroyed house remained a vacant lot for decades. Today it integrates into the existing neighborhood seemingly buried amidst abundant landscaping foliage

Hearst was not involved in the South Central Los Angeles

61

firefight as she and other members were holed up in an Anaheim hotel room. The remaining SLA gang returned to northern California and disbanded around the country to avoid captures. Hearst was arrested on September 18 and charged with multiple counts including bank robbery.

The judicial circus that followed raised legal liability issues regarding illegal activities performed by forced coercion and brainwashing. Did Hearst fabricate her treatment by the SLA to avoid severe consequences for her actions? There was little doubt that she was unwillingly kidnapped but only Patty Hearst and remaining SLA survivors can attest to the truth towards her subsequent activities and motivations.

The jury at her trial discarded her brainwashing defense. She was found guilty and sentenced to seven years in prison, for which she served two. President Jimmy Carter commuted her sentence and she was later pardoned.

The Heart kidnapping was symptomatic of arguably the most turbulent era of social hostility in San Francisco's history. The abandonment of the peace and love idealism from the prior decade had been eclipsed by a cycle of violence that would haunt the city for the remainder of the decade.

Patty Hearst's Berkeley Apartment Building

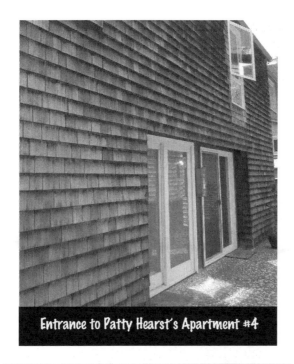

Entrance to Patty Hearst's Apartment #4

Golden Gate Avenue Safe House

Hibernia Bank Robbery Site

Former Site of the Fatal SLA Gunfight

Nicholas Markowitz: The Stolen Boy and Unforeseen Execution

Nicholas Markowitz wound up as collateral damage in a money dispute between his older half-brother Benjamin and a drug distributor Jesse James Hollywood.

The feud was based on an alleged debt of $1,200 owed by Benjamin Markowitz to Hollywood. During a visit to confront Benjamin, Hollywood and two associates, Jesse Rugge and William Skidmore observed Nicholas, 15, walking on a nearby road apparently in the course of running away from home. The trio decided to kidnapped Nicholas and hold him for ransom in lieu of the debt.

They chased him down and snatched him into their van. What followed was an odyssey that might only be believable in a movie script. In 2006, it became one. The story culminated in Markowitz's death as portrayed in the film *Alpha Dog*.

What transpired after the abduction was a bizarre road trip from their home base in West Hills, Los Angeles to the Santa Barbara region. En route, the procession stopped at numerous house parties integrating Markowitz into the festivities. He was allowed to indulge freely in their assortment of alcohol and drugs. Witnesses at these events didn't bother to notify police, as Nicholas appeared to be safe and enjoying himself.

He willingly accepted the moniker of *Stolen Boy* and by the time the entourage reached a motel in Santa Barbara, they were joined by additional acquaintances. The party atmosphere continued. It is assumed that Markowitz offered no resistance or made any attempt to escape as he felt himself in no apparent peril.

Jesse James Hollywood had other inclinations. Perhaps meaning to heighten the severity of the threat to Benjamin or aware that there were already too many eyewitnesses to the kidnapping, he opted for drastic action, He contacted another associate, Ryan

Hoyt, who owed him $200. Hoyt was given a semi-automatic firearm to dispose of Nicholas in the Santa Ynez Mountains, just north of Goleta.

On the evening of August 9, 2000, Hoyt, Jesse Rugge, William Skidmore and Graham Presley led Markowitz on a forced march to his death. At some belated point, Nicholas realized the charade was complete. He was bound with his hands behind his back and his mouth was covered by duct tape. The procession followed a narrow shrub laden trail bordering giant granite mounds. Nicholas was cruelly paraded over the uneven topography in the pitch dark before being bashed in the head with a shovel.

He was shot nine times and buried into a shallow grave with the murder weapon. The hole was covered with dirt and branches. The makeshift grave was near the popularly frequented Lizard's Mouth Trail and too shallow. Three days later, the body was discovered.

Following up on various leads, investigators arrested the four perpetrators. Jesse James Hollywood evaded immediate capture, but was arrested five years later in Brazil for having ordered the killing.

At trial, Ryan Hoyt was convicted of first-degree murder and sentenced to death. He remains on Death Row at San Quentin. Hollywood was convicted of first-degree murder and kidnapping and sentenced to life in prison without the possibility of parole. He is currently incarcerated at Calipatria State Prison.

Jesse Rugge, William Skidmore and Graham Pressley were all imprisoned for various terms for their roles in the kidnapping and murder. Each has been subsequently released and removed from public scrutiny. The film eluded Academy Award nomination.

Death March Along Lizard Mouth Trail

Lizard Mouth Trail

The Kidnapping of Brooke Hart and Resulting Mob Justice

Localized public outrage and righteous indignation appear in diminishing exhibitions today due to global and instantaneous reporting.

The transgressions committed in our own backyards appear to pale in exposure and significance with similar events occurring elsewhere. These events, though abstract and geographically distant, are magnified by the intensity of news and social media exposure. Atrocities may still shock and can provoke wrath. We may not physically participate in the outrage but often concur with appropriate revenge.

On national and even international calamities, high-profile television commentators, social activists and political leaders seize these moments to espouse their specific bias, causes or indignation. Their fury often appears more opportunistic than genuine.

Compare the intensity of this anger with local tragedies before global viewing.

San Jose in 1933 was a modest community of approximately 60,000 despite having the distinction of being California's first state capital. The entirety of its county, Santa Clara, which encompasses the majority of contemporary Silicon Valley, boasted only 150,000 residents in the 1930 census.

Today the population of San Jose hovers near one million, surpassing San Francisco as the state's third largest urban center. Aside from the change and challenges growth necessitates, citizen involvement has become more neighborhood oriented and with the commuting sector, nearly nonexistent.

In 1933, San Jose's major shopping source, Hart's Department Store was located on the southeastern corner of Market and Santa Clara Streets downtown. Giant department stores in the

1930s (until the 1960s) were the shopping and social Mecca before urban decentralization and multi-store shopping malls. The Hart family was well respected locally and wealthy but not considered pretentious. They represented examples to be emulated back when role models still mattered.

Patriarch Leopold Hart had established a dry cleaning operation in San Jose originally in 1866. The family operations expanded and thrived under his son Alex J. Hart, Sr. who founded the flagship store in 1902. His eldest 22-year-old son Brooke was being groomed to replace him. He was employed at the store as an Assistant Department Manager.

Brooke Hart had distinguished himself with his studies at Bellarmine College Preparatory and by earning a degree from Santa Clara University. He effortlessly assumed the role of *Golden Boy* and was the town's most eligible and desirable bachelor. His wavy blond hair, blue eyes and handsome appearance were coupled by an engaging personality. He personified the qualities most parents would envy in their children.

He was a trusted and responsible individual serving as the designated chauffeur for his father who had never learned to drive. His 1933 green Studebaker roadster was renowned as one of only two models navigating San Jose roads. It was difficult to imagine anything but success and prosperity for his future.

Then fate intervened. Local kidnappers abducted him.

In 1933, the United States was mired in the Great Depression. The country limped forward in economic agony, shouldering the burden of overwhelming economic stress, unemployment and disillusionment. The accumulating malaise remained pent-up and ready for expression. San Jose would manifest an eruption of this frustration.

Charles Lindbergh, Jr., the year and a half old son of the famed aviator had been abducted on the evening of March 1, 1932. Two months later, his body was discovered with a crushed skull. The nation's eyes were riveted in horror at the unfolding search, arrest, trial and execution of the convicted kidnapper, Bruno Hauptmann. Was he guilty based on the slim circumstantial evidence? Or did the actual kidnapper, a rumored acquaintance, set him up for the crime?

He maintained his innocence until his execution. Trial procedures and evidence became questionable once the verdict was announced. Some suggest that Hauptmann's German ancestry made him an ideal candidate for conviction based on the tide of popular opinion following World War I. Hauptman's widow fought vehemently but unsuccessfully for nearly sixty years to re-open the case until her death in 1994.

Brooke Hart was not a helpless infant. His popularity, kidnapping and brutal death equally stirred local passions and a response to excess. Newspaper and radio reports blatantly convicted two individuals for the crime without the benefit of a public trial. The media's utter bias towards their guilt and demands for immediate retribution incited a brazen public act that seems incredulous today...a public lynching.

Lynchings were not foreign to the California system of justice. They were employed throughout the nineteenth and early twentieth century as *frontier justice*. By the 1930s, they tended to be regarded as barbaric public expressions of revenge.

A significant number of San Jose residents ignored the shifting interpretation. The public hanging was a popularly supported display.

It is arguable that the culprits did or didn't deserve their swift justice. If found guilty, their actions would have likely merited the death penalty. But the most obvious lingering question was whether they were indeed guilty. Both perpetrators, John Maurice Holmes and Harold Thurman were judged based on conflicting evidence and potentially forced confessions.

The Constitutional sixth amendment, which in all criminal prosecutions guarantees the right of a speedy and public trial, was discarded. Vigilantes replaced the role of a jury.

Newspapers and radio from the outset explicitly documented the gruesome events behind Brooke Hart's kidnapping. Nearing 5 p.m. on November 9th, Brooke was exiting a parking garage behind his father's store with the intent of driving him to a planned civic event.

According to media reports, two men appearing armed approached him as he slowed his car. He was forced to drive to another location where the kidnappers switched vehicles. The threesome then drove to the western entrance of the San Mateo Bridge.

In 1933, the bridge was a privately owned tollway and the longest in the world. The original span was principally a two-lane causeway trestle. The bridge was neither profitable nor well traveled. Traffic did not exceed 2,000 cars per day until 1947. A modern publicly financed replacement opened in 1967 to accommodate increased traffic. A section of the original western approach remains beside the replacement bridge. It was renamed the Werder Fishing Pier in 1968.

Later during the evening of the abduction, Hart was reportedly bound with baling wire that was attached to concrete blocks. He was repeatedly bashed over the skull with these same blocks and dumped over the railing into the frigid Bay waters. Neither the violent beating nor cold initially submerged him.

Instead he flayed violently and screamed for assistance. The kidnappers had neglected to account for the low tide conditions. As Hart flailed and refused to sink beneath the surface, they began repeatedly shooting at him until he was silenced.

One may assume the combination of the bullet wounds, hyperventilation and beating trauma ultimately lapsed him into unconsciousness and drowning. The autopsy however indicated that no bullets had penetrated Hart's body.

Was the media chronological account accurate or fanciful speculation?

Upon the assumption of their victim's apparent death, one kidnapper drove to San Francisco that evening to telephone the Hart family twice with exorbitant ransom demands. Another account had the telephone calls originating from downtown San Jose pay phones located within one half mile of each other.

Ransom letters were reported to have been simultaneously mailed with postmarks from both Sacramento and Los Angeles. The deception was to confuse the police.

Police were stationed at the Hart's residence and their phones were tapped. Following the kidnapper's original calls on the evening of the abduction, renewed contact with the family followed five days later.

The abductor's capture followed an odd and almost incredulous storyline. Harold Thurmond was caught making a ransom demand from a San Jose hotel and parking garage pay phone. The phone in question was located a mere 150 feet from the San Jose Police headquarters. Could a kidnapper potentially be this incompetent and stupid? Or was the account an invented narrative?

Thurmond fingered John Holmes as his co-conspirator. In the course of separate interrogations, each provided conflicting details regarding Hart's kidnapping, the vehicle transfer and clumsy killing. Both signed written confessions implicating the other as the principle culprit. The confessions may have been valid but the operating procedures employed by investigators were suspect.

Upon the pair's capture and confession, the family was notified of their son's official death. His body still eluded police. The waters around the bridge were dragged without success for twelve days. San Jose residents waited impatiently. The confessed kidnappers were temporarily relocated from downtown San Jose to San Francisco's Potrero Hill police station. Authorities feared trouble with the mounting public anger and hysteria over the case. Their suspicions proved prophetic.

Two duck hunters discovered Brooke Hart's partially dressed and decomposed body on November 26th, just south of the bridge.

With the discovery, residents were once again stunned into revulsion over the horror and enormity of the act. Shock was transformed into rage and demands for revenge. In newspapers, there was zero column lineage reserved towards any expression of doubt or presumption of innocence. Blatant suggestions of impending mob justice made the act inevitable. The wait proved abbreviated.

Despite their probable guilt based on the discovered location of the body, the legal case against Thurmond and Holmes was far from conclusive. Their signed confessions may have conceivably been discredited by a shrewd legal defense given the questionable circumstances behind obtaining them. Prior to the establishment of Miranda Rights protection, guaranteeing legal representation upon request, forced confessions were often beaten out of suspects when evidence was marginal.

Factual discrepancies in the account of events and the dubious mental capabilities of the accused would have raised probable doubts regarding guilt or innocence.

More tellingly, there were only two confirmed eyewitnesses to any aspect of the kidnapping. A couple, who managed the San Jose Country Club, witnessed a passenger exchange between

Hart's Studebaker and another sedan, which they significantly misidentified. They further claimed to have witnessed *five* men involved in the transfer of Hart. In the FBI kidnapping file released 50 years later under the Freedom of Information Act, five *not two* unidentified males were sought as responsible parties.

San Jose residents were unwilling to settle for anything less than swift blood revenge. Their attitude then is in sharp contrast with today's extended trials and appeal process that often lengthen the guilty into an advanced age.

Judgment should have been suspended until the facts were conclusive to make a clear decision. The San Jose citizenry rushed to a frenzied judgment based on raw emotion and absent of confirmed proof. Resolution and closure, even for such a heinous action as a kidnapping demands thorough proof and due process.

We will never know for certain if the mob's instincts were accurate. Their fury eliminated the opportunity for complete disclosure. A similar killing would mirror this rashness thirty years later by an individual reacting to another national tragedy.

On November 24, 1963, Jack Ruby liquidated suspected presidential assassin Lee Harvey Oswald during his Dallas Police Station transfer. President John Kennedy had been killed the day before and the world reeled in collective shock. Upon Oswald's killing, many applauded Ruby's apparent spontaneous patriotic gesture of revenge. Over time his own motives became suspect. His act eliminated the sole individual who might have shed legitimate light on what had transpired the day before. Oswald was gone and conspiracy theories have multiplied since.

Americans lost their best opportunity for disclosure and healing.

Few today regard Jack Ruby as a patriot. Instead he has assumed the role of impediment to inquiry, truth and justice. He died

74

incarcerated in 1967 of cancer, rationalizing the impulsive nature of his action. He perished as a pathetically forgotten historical footnote.

Whether Thurmond and Holmes were ultimately innocent or guilty became irrelevant on Sunday evening November 27, 1933.

Inflammatory reporting during the preceding week suggested the assumed killers, back in San Jose custody, might avert prosecution because of their defective confessions, no eyewitnesses and *suspect* evidence.

Published accounts inferred they were consulting with a highly renowned San Francisco lawyer and were contemplating an *insanity* plea, thus evading capital punishment. Since that original article appeared, both men were subsequently declared *legally sane* by evaluating medical examiners invalidating such an option. This detail remained conveniently unreported by the press,

Absent of this confirmation, any suggestion of an alternative to a death sentence was considered unacceptable by the populous. Innocent blood had been shed and expeditious retribution was the only appropriate response.

The discovery of Hart's body galvanized action the following fateful day. The prisoners were interned at the Santa Clara County Courthouse across the street from St. James Park downtown. The park today is an idle green oasis dwarfed by an expanding base of commercial and condominium high-rises. The benches and shaded trees accommodate transients and the homeless, ignored amongst San Jose's upwardly mobile. The park's prominence has become as forgotten as giant department stores, public lynchings and the interrupted legacy of Brooke Hart.

The swelling crowd lingering across the street from the jail alarmed County Sheriff Willia Emig. He telephoned California

Governor James Rolph requesting that the National Guard be deployed to protect the prisoners. Rolph refused and further confirmed that he would pardon any participating members involved in the hanging.

The lynching, repeatedly suggested by newspapers and radio as a probable outcome, became fact. Their view was that any potential *travesty of justice* enabling the accused to escape punishment was to be prevented at all costs. Their own sensationalism instigated a farce of equal proportion.

The mob was estimated by press outlets to range anywhere between five to fifteen thousand local men, women and children. Reporters, cameramen and live radio broadcasts were poised and positioned to recount the impending spectacle. They were neither premature nor disappointed.

As the darkness descended, outnumbered sheriff's deputies fired tear gas into the crowd attempting to disperse them. Predictably, the crowd's numbers only expanded and anger intensified. A nearby construction site was raided to locate a battering ram and at approximately 9:00 p.m., an assault began. A furious group successfully broke down the doors and stormed the jail.

Sheriff Emig abandoned the bottom two floors of the jail where Thurmond and Holmes were being held. The mob leaders manhandled the partially clad prisoners whose fate was assured. Neither had yet been formally charged or indicted.

The two were expediently hung on a convenient park tree while the throng applauded. The spectacle might have easily resembled an 18th century French Revolution guillotine parties. The hanging images were explicitly broadcast throughout the United States. They still shock today. Both men swung freely with total frontal exposure and their genitals protruding.

The employed gallows tree was initially preserved to serve as a public caution against capital offenses. Souvenir hunters hacked, stripped bark and retained branches as mementos. The city council ultimately decided to cut it down due to its notoriety. Several comparably aged trees remain in St. James Park, statuesque witnesses to a historical anomaly.

It is difficult to feel sympathy for Thurmond and Holmes, particularly if they were guilty. The slaying of Brooke Hart was a profound tragedy and a loss the community legitimately mourned because of his personal and his family's decency.

Too many perpetrators continue to evade prompt justice and punishment. Their examples become an affront to our system of justice. Perhaps each of us would have identified and participated with the lynching if we were intimately affected by Hart's death.

For each survivor and victim's family that has had to experience the loss of a loved one, the impulse towards revenge is normal and difficult to repress. Over eight decades have passed since a fateful evening when righteous indignation overwhelmed the potentially arctic paced due process of our court system.

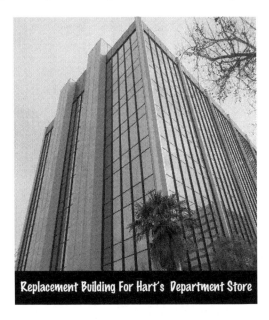

Replacement Building For Hart's Department Store

Former Site of Parking Lot Exit and Kidnapping

Site Where Brooke Hart was
Dumped Over the Bridge

County Courthouse and Jail That Was
Stormed By The Mob

Site of the Hanging: St. James Park

An Execution Amidst Rural Darkness: The Onion Field Killings

A strange homicide during the late hours in isolated Bakersfield County agricultural acreage became the subject of a sensational 1973 book entitled *The Onion Field*. Los Angeles Police Department (LAPD) Sergeant Joseph Wambach wrote the taut narrative, which detailed the kidnapping of two plainclothes officers by two criminals following a surveillance traffic stop. One of the LAPD officers, James Campbell was consequently executed.

On the evening of March 9, 1963, plain-clothes officers Campbell, 31, and Karl Hettinger, 28, pulled over a vehicle occupied by two suspicious men, Gregory Powell, 30 and Jimmy Lee Smith, 32. The pair had recently committed a series of armed robberies and wore concealed pistols tucked into their pants.

As Campbell approached their vehicle, Powell from the driver side, pulled his gun. Campbell instructed his partner Hettinger to relinquish his gun to Smith. Both officers were forced into Powell's car and driven northbound out of Los Angeles along rural Interstate 99.

A two-hour drive into the pitch night ended just shy of Bakersfield near the farming town of Mettier. There was no conversation or negotiation. The tension heightened as Powell, without explanation, steered to an obscure exit. He then drove along a roadway into a valley of freshly rowed and planted onions. Powell stopped the vehicle and unloaded his passengers.

Powell had erroneously assumed that his act of abduction would qualify as a capital kidnapping crime and automatic death penalty. Rather than spare the policemen and simply strand them in the countryside, he decided to execute them. He shot Campbell to death, but Hettinger was able to escape. The darkness adequately concealed his flight. He was able to reach a

80

farmhouse four miles away to telephone for help.

The California Highway Patrol arrested Powell that same evening for driving a stolen vehicle. Smith was apprehended the following day. Both were sentenced to death but their terms modified to life imprisonment in 1972 with the abolition of the death penalty. Powell died unrepentant while incarcerated in 2012. Smith was released in 1982 but returned to prison on multiple occasions due to drug related parole violations. He ended up living on Los Angeles' Skid Row before finally dying of a heart attack in 2007.

Karl Hettinger's life veered erratically following the kidnapping/ murder. He was ostracized and scorned by many of his fellow officers for having given up his gun and escaping. In 1966, he was forced to resign from the LAPD after being accused of shoplifting. He had the indignity of his example being used in a police training video of what *not to do* when approaching a vehicle. He would return to Bakersfield where he served as a Kern County Supervisor for multiple consecutive terms. He died in 1994 of liver disease.

Police department procedures for approaching suspects and relinquishing their weapons were modified based on the notoriety of the case. A 1979 film based on Wambach's book featured a cast of James Woods, John Savage, Franklyn Seales and the debut performance of Ted Danson.

The Agricultural Fields of Mettier

Polly Klaas: The Abrupt Death of Innocence

In the autumn of 1993, Polly Klaas was a beautiful vivacious twelve-year old living with her mother and sister tranquilly in Petaluma. Her future was limitless and prospects infinite.

Richard Allen Davis had no such optimistic projections. At 39, he was a convicted felon and had spent the majority of his adult life in prison. He was living in a Bay Area halfway house as a condition of his parole. His parole officer was based in Ukiah and en route to weekly visitations, he often detoured into Petaluma. Most of his time in the city was spent loitering around Wickersham Park, located diagonally across from Polly's residence. His extended visits to the park typically involved either getting drunk or high.

It is never been determined why Davis' and Klaas' paths fatally intersected on the evening of October 1, 1993. Klaas had invited two friends over for a slumber party. Later in the evening, Davis entered her mother's house and Polly's bedroom, carrying a knife. He tied up her two friends and abducted Polly.

The circumstantial *near misses* in apprehending Davis over the subsequent twenty-four hours mirrored the depth of frustration the case provoked both locally and later nationally. The evening of the kidnapping, Davis was actually in conversation with two Sonoma County Sheriff officers because his car had become stuck in a ditch in a remote county sector.

Due to the limited range of their broadcasting band capabilities, the officers were unaware of the kidnapping. They assisted Davis in securing a tow truck. Despite his felony status, Davis' driver's license and plate number came back with no outstanding warrants. The deputies claimed that they did conduct a search of the car before the arrival of the tow truck due to Davis' disheveled and perspiring appearance. They specified at his trial that there was apparently no evidence of anyone additionally having been in the car.

So where was Polly Klaas?

Perhaps she had already been strangled earlier that evening and left in a temporary grave or amongst the nearby thick brush. Perhaps she sat petrified in the distance awaiting Davis' promised return. Only Davis knows and throughout his interrogations and trial, his answers were vague and inconclusive.

In all likelihood, he returned to the murder site to retrieve the body for burial in a more remote and clandestine area.

Over the next two months, a massive search for Polly Klaas was conducted and broadcast nationally. On November 28, a Sonoma County property owner was inspecting her land following a timber clearing. She found suspicious and strewn clothing and immediately contacted authorities. A massive police search effort followed and turned up additional articles.

Forensic examination linked the clothing to Klaas. With an approximate idea of her burial location, resolution of the case followed swiftly. The first investigative breakthrough in identifying the perpetrator came via a review of calls in the area the day of the kidnapping. The caller log turned up the two deputies encounter with Davis. Once his name was isolated, the case against him accelerated. A poor quality palm print had been identified at the scene of the kidnapping and matched perfectly with Davis. With his convicted felon status, he was already registered in the national crime-fingerprint database.

When you are a convicted felon, there are limited concealment options. Davis had nowhere to hide. He had nowhere to flee or disappear to. He likely wallowed in the expectation that he would ultimately be caught. His profile had already been sketched by law enforcement agencies based on the descriptions given by Polly's two friends.

Under interrogation, Davis confessed to the kidnapping. He hedged on critical details about specific timeframes, knowing his revelations could secure him a death sentence at his trial. He finally led authorities to a shallow grave just off Highway 101, about a mile south of the city limits of Cloverdale.

Despite his futile efforts at cunning and evasiveness, Richard Allen Davis was convicted on June 18, 1996 of first-degree murder and four special circumstances (robbery, burglary, kidnapping and a lewd act on a child). His lengthy trial and conviction was preceded by a change in venue due to the notoriety of the case. A San Jose Superior Court jury returned a verdict of death regardless. He had ceased to become invisible from the inevitable.

In the wake of the murder, the California legislature and several states supported three strikes legislation intended to keep violent criminals in prison for life following three felony convictions. California's Three Strikes Act was signed into law on March 8, 1994, but has since been criticized as excessive and later modified by voters.

Life strangely continues for Richard Allen Davis. He remains on death row in the East Block at San Quentin. He has already reached senior citizen status. The last California execution took place in January of 2006 and the labyrinth of appeal options will certainly delay the next. Polly Klaas' bright future ceased abruptly on the autumn evening of October 1, 1993.

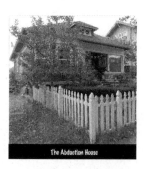

The Abduction House

Ramona Irene Price Strolls Innocently Into A Vanished Past

On the morning of September 2, 1961, headstrong seven-year-old Ramona Irene Price vowed that she would walk to her family's new house in Goleta alone.

It was her family's moving day from their former Santa Barbara residence they had just sold. Doubtlessly there were numerous tasks to complete, boxes to pack and load. Their new home was a direct five-mile walk. Ramona felt prepared to assert her independence. She informed her father of her intention and he absently and jokingly encouraged her.

Little did he imagine that very Saturday morning, she was indeed serious. Neither he nor any family member would ever see her again. Ramona was 4 feet tall, weighed 45 pounds and wore a popular pixie style haircut. She had dressed herself in a brown and white pullover sweater, brown pants with fine pinstripes and casual flip-flop sandals.

Ramona departed from Oak Avenue, continued down Modoc Road and towards the tree-lined entrance of the La Cumbre Country Club. Several eyewitnesses observed a determined little girl that day dragging a stick behind her and periodically removing her bothersome sandals.

The innocent girl evading sighting after the country club entrance and completely vanished without a subsequent trace.

Bloodhounds were inconclusively unable to trace her scent beyond the entrance. Despite exhaustive search efforts, nearby beachcombing, interviewing of known local sex offenders and numerous incoming leads...locating her proved fruitless.

History suggests that thousands of heartbreaking narratives like Ramona's exist nationally. Most accounts have remained localized. Contemporary search efforts have become more efficient with global social media outlets, milk carton ads, Amber alerts and sexual offender databases.

What touches me personally about Ramona Irene Price's story was that her kidnapping could have similarly happened to me or any of my peers during our formative years. We were naïve, open and innocent towards the intentions of potentially harmful strangers. Much more disconcerting however was that our parents rarely knew our whereabouts. We shared unlimited exposure.

Suburban childhoods during the early 1960s afforded children the luxury and landscape of indiscriminate roaming that subsequent generations no longer have the opportunity to enjoy. Parents today rightfully shepherd their children from the evident encroachment of evil and pedophilia, Most demand constant location accountability even if it requires adding an additional cellular phone account. Children seem better insulated but certainly are afforded less liberty.

In my hometown of Vallejo, the initial murders by the Zodiac serial killer in December of 1968 immediately shifted parental demands for accountability. His first two teenage victims had lied to both sets of parents as to their intended whereabouts. Parents in Vallejo realized the potential consequences from their ignorance.

In hindsight, I've often speculated why my parents chose to remain ignorant of my activities during those formative years. When queried later, both assured me that they always knew where I was. They certainly did not.

My children and future grandchildren will never share the identical unrestrained autonomy of my childhood. Ramona Irene Price never remotely suspected the peril she was openly courting with her unaccompanied stroll. She probably wanted to exhibit to her parents an independence and self-sufficiency that would make them feel proud of her.

Her body was never found. Sadly the childhood freedom I enjoyed will never be recaptured by the subsequent generations of children to come.

Setting Out Along Modoc Road, Santa Barbara

Nearing the Country Club Entance

Kristin Smart: The Tangled Web Involving Fifth Amendment Silence

California Polytechnic State University is a central California coastal school located in the pastoral community of San Luis Obispo. The institution is nationally renowned for their Agribusiness and Engineering departments. Their annual acceptance rate for applications is generally a selective 30%. Numerous college rating sources recognizes their high standard of achievement annually.

The university has graduated numerous recognized personalities in business, the military and California politics. Sports Hall of Fame alumni includes baseball's Ossie Smith and football's John Madden. Musical parodist *Weird* Al Yankovic is a graduate.

Absent of an adjacent urban presence, the city of San Luis Obispo is shortened by locals to SLO. Slow often typifies the pace of life. Pretension is absent and irreverence blatant. The most celebrated and revered public artwork is an alleyway flaring off from downtown Higuera Street layered on both sides of the lining building walls with over 100 feet of used chewing gum from top to bottom. The identical art installation exists in Seattle, but locals consider it theirs uniquely.

It would seem SLO is an ideal environment for concentrated academic study, lacking the distractions of metropolitan Los Angeles and San Francisco. Both cities are distanced approximately four hours by automobile, depending upon ones interpretation of the speed limit and traffic congestion.

In essence, SLO would seem to be the perfectly secure campus location for a perspective student and concerned parent. In general, the impression is accurate.

Appearances can periodically be deceptive and activity within a university town is no exception. Besides celebrated alumni, Cal Poly was also the Alma Mata of convicted wife killer Scott

Peterson. Illegal and inappropriate behaviors are not foreign to the community.

Student populations on university campuses nationally have reputations for reckless, immature and impulsive behavior. Cal Poly is no exception. Their fraternities and sororities have had their social activities suspended on numerous occasions in the past due to violations of alcohol regulations and related sexual improprieties.

It shocks no one that underage students drink on and off campus. The stress levels prompted by academic workloads, deadlines and the simple liberty from their home environment stimulate such behavior.

When excesses spill into public exposure, school administrations and authorities typically pay notice. Fear of an adverse reputation may harm an institution's academic prestige and more acutely, funding sources. Universities represent many ideals aimed at academic excellence, but they likewise remain a business enterprise that must sustain sufficient revenue.

In the late spring of 1996, Kristin Smart was an attractive, intelligent and promising freshman from Stockton, California leaning towards a degree in Architecture. The initial year of a college experience is a pivotal transition for out-of-area teenagers living independently for the first time. Many thrive with their newfound liberty. Others flounder and fail. They lack the necessary self-discipline and structure required to successfully navigate unlimited freedom with minimal time accountability.

By all accounts, Kristin had acclimated well to her first year of studies. She earned respectable grades and established a network of supporting friends and social acquaintances.

The three-day Memorial Day weekend symbolically concluded her first year of studies. Fraternity and Sorority parties were plentiful at this stage of the year with students winding down their academic classwork in preparation for impending final exams. For many, the Memorial Day weekend is their last opportunity for grandiose socializing. For underclassmen, it provides an excellent opportunity to boost their credential prospects for subsequent admission to one of the Greek Houses. Like many of her peers, Kristin chose to take advantage of the occasion.

On Friday evening, May 25th Kristin strolled confidently without money or identification papers to an off-campus Fraternity party. She integrated seamlessly into the festivities and was observed to have drank excessively. This behavior would not have been extraordinary at such a gathering.

At approximately 1:30 to 2:00 a.m., she departed the party alone and began staggering towards her dormitory a significant distance away. She was soon afterwards discovered by two friends sprawled out on a nearby lawn.

The two, who had also attended the party, decided to assist her home and were joined en route by another student, Paul Flores, who had likewise been there. At the juncture of Grand and Perimeter Streets, Flores offered to escort Smart alone to her dormitory since the other two students lived in a completely opposite direction. Flores' dormitory, Santa Lucia Hall was a mere hundred yards walk from the trio's separation point. Smart's dormitory, Muir Hall was an additional 200+ yards from Santa Lucia along a paved sidewalk, forking in two locations.

The sequence of events from this point forward became vague. Flores claimed to investigators that he escorted Smart only as far as his dormitory entrance instead of hers. In limiting his escort, he would have allowed Smart to navigate the remaining distance by herself in a clearly inebriated and incoherent state.

If his account were accurate, his actions would be simply calloused and irresponsible. Many have arrived at the conclusion that he did more than simply part ways at the entrance of his dormitory.

If Smart did indeed follow the paved path to her dormitory alone, a northward deviation road leads directly to an open wilderness area behind the residential living sector. During the deserted early morning hours, a vulnerable young woman could have easily been kidnapped or taken advantage of. Most investigators have dismissed such speculation.

There was no evidence or witnesses to confirm that Smart ever returned to her dorm room. Her bed and the contents on top were left undisturbed when her roommate returned from a weekend getaway on Monday, May 28th.

Once the San Luis Obispo police department became involved in the investigation, the discrepancies and later modifications by Flores' in his account of events became suspicious. He became then and remains today the prime suspect involved with Kristin Smart's disappearance.

Unfortunately the investigator's suspicions were hampered significantly due to ineptitude procedural delays from the outset.

The Cal Poly Campus police delayed notifying the San Luis Obispo police department of Smart's disappearance for four days. Their postponement was based on their unsubstantiated assumption that Kristin had taken an impulsively unannounced vacation for the weekend. Their conclusion was formulated despite her witnessed incapacity, undisturbed dorm room contents and gravely mounting concerns expressed by her parents and friends.

Smart's father drove four hours from Stockton to observe the evidence firsthand and stimulate the campus police department's lack of initiative. The Smart family sensed Kristen's silence with them was abnormal since her contact had been consistently habitual.

Her father's determination eventually prevailed. The San Luis Obispo police department was notified and immediately became directly involved. The delay and inflexibility by the campus police hindered a timely and effectively thorough initial investigation.

Shortly after Kristin Smart's disappearance was announced and before the school year concluded, Paul Flores dropped out of the university reportedly due to failing grades. He also had received a citation for driving while intoxicated costing him his license. He had not adapted well to his initial school year.

Before his official exit from the campus and a law enforcement search of his premises, he was given sufficient time to sanitize his room and remove all potentially incriminating belongings. One published report indicated that a cadaver dog utilized by investigators led them singularly to one campus location. That location was Flores' mattress in his former dormitory room. All of his other belongings were gone by the time of this discovery.

Without a body and only a circumstantial pool of evidence, formal charges would prove impossible to substantiate. An unsuccessful prosecution of Flores' would have enabled him to escape any future criminal charges based on the double jeopardy protection of the constitution. The investigation has continued to proceed cautiously since a statute of limitations concerning murder charges is nonexistent.

Kristin Smart's body has never been recovered. Concrete and confirmed witnesses of her early morning disappearance have never materialized despite substantial reward offers.

Published sources have agreed that Flores has been scathingly questioned about the disappearance since late May 1996. He has never wavered from his declaration of innocence and ignorance of events regarding Smart's disappearance or whereabouts. He was reportedly offered a plea deal based on pleading guilty to involuntary manslaughter and revealing Smart's concealed location. The deal included a reduced six-year prison term. He refused the offer.

Many diverse accounts have reported incidents of discovered and misplaced critical pieces of evidence involved with the case. An erroneous account of Smart's body being discovered on a property once owned by Flores' family has also surfaced. Unsubstantiated speculation has supplanted hard evidence.

In contrast with his professed innocent Samaritan role, Paul Flores has acted and behaved with remarkably guilty tendencies. The day following Smart's disappearance, he was observed with a black eye and evident scratches. His explanations for the injuries have varied, but none have appeased those assuming his guilt.

At a certain point in his questioning, Flores' shifted tactics. He realized that he'd become the primary suspect in the commission of a crime and was advised by legal council. Instead of responding to questions, regardless of relevancy, he began resolutely shielding himself by claiming his Fifth Amendment Right against self-incrimination.

What has distinguished Kristin Smart's disappearance from comparative cases has been the level of constancy Smart's family, friends and even volunteer private investigators have sustained towards proving Flores' guilt. Their intensive effort has not wavered despite nearly twenty years having passed.

In 1996, the family attempted to pursue a wrongful death lawsuit against Flores but the absence of a body and Flores continued refusal to answer questions made the proceedings unwinnable. Since that initial effort, the Smart family and their banded associates have been relentless in trying to obtain evidence. Numerous websites, television programs, public signage and posted online videos have retold Kristin's story with investigation updates. One website consistently tracks and posts Flores' current address, which has fluctuated over the years.

The Flores family has responded by filing a restraining order against the responsible webmaster. In 2005, they filed a lawsuit, later rescinded, against Smart's parents alleging harassment, severe emotional distress and lost income as a result of their activities.

Such obsession and passion may ultimately yield results and closure, but the still opened case remains cold. During the 2003 murder investigation of Scott Peterson, his name was suggested as a possible suspect since he was completing his senior year at Cal Poly. Further investigation provided no direct linkage between the individuals and he was eliminated from consideration.

Six years after her disappearance, Kristin Smart was declared legally dead. Her legacy remains very alive to the survivors who seek a satisfactory resolution.

Paul Flores will remain hounded by these pursuers of truth convinced of his guilt. Even if Smart's death was accidental due to her overindulgence, his silence, lack of cooperation and avoidance of disclosure is considered unpardonable by most case observers. Mercy and clemency for him would be unfathomable in their eyes.

Kristin Smart's disappearance and probable death is direct proof of the linkage between lives affected by a tragic homicide. Until future developments determine otherwise, each subsequent day's lack of resolution will expand the base of casualties sustained by one isolated tragedy.

Juncture Where the Three Escorts Separated

Road Towards Santa Lucia Hall

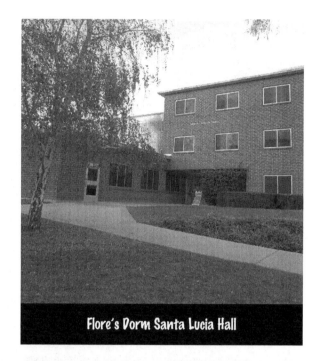

Flore's Dorm Santa Lucia Hall

Fork in the Road Towards Muir Hall

Deviation Road to Wilderness
Area Behind Campus

Road Headed Towards Muir Hall

Smart's Dorm Muir Hall

Eternal Vigilance For Closure

Kevin Collins: A Solitary Bus Bench Memorial to Every Parent's Nightmare

On February 10, 1984, Kevin Collins, aged ten, left a basketball practice early from his school's gymnasium. Shortly after 7:55 p.m. Kevin was last seen sitting on a San Francisco bus bench at the corner of Oak Street and Masonic Avenue. During February, evenings turn dark around 6 p.m. He vanished into the shadows and was never seen or located again.

Child abductions even then were not novel but typically localized. Kevin's disappearance became national news. His story inspired an unprecedented massive search including the nationwide distribution of flyers, a cover story in a national magazine, his photo image on milk cartons and pleas for his return from local politicians. His body was never found. His disappearance represented a turning point in abduction awareness as these responses later became commonplace.

For twelve years, Kevin's father David operated a search center in an effort to find his son. The strain of Kevin's disappearance and follow-up search efforts shattered his marriage. Despite his efforts and the nationwide coordinated hunt, no solid suspect has ever emerged.

The only positive consequences from the tragedy have been heightened national interest towards the plight of missing children. Law enforcement officials have also learned how to better coordinate their response to child abductions.

An isolated bus park bench remains embedded at the corner of Oak Street and Masonic Avenue. It is the sole reminder of a boy who disappeared without the slightest trace. Daily commuters, transfer riders and local transients have little idea of the grief it once symbolized to a broken family and its historical local significance.

Kevin Collins' Last Sighting

Rex Allen Krebs: Predestined Towards Violence

Rex Allen Krebs is a perpetrator responsible for at least two violent deaths. He has exhibited an extended history of sexual predatory behavior. He has identified himself as a *monster*. He requested the death penalty upon his apprehension. Many will argue that he should be granted his wish sooner rather than later. In California, the condemned, unlike their victims, die a delayed and protracted death usually by natural causes.

Rex Allen Krebs was a time bomb awaiting detonation from his earliest formation. In a February, 2010 (San Luis Obispo) *Tribune* interview following Krebs's murder conviction, his father, Allan Krebs labeled his son a *demon seed*, *cunning thief*, *innately evil* and *lacking a straight bone in his body*. Given his father's own history, his observations seemed both accurate and relevant

Are killers and habitual violent offenders born rather than raised? Krebs makes a compelling psychological case study.

In the same newspaper interview, Allan Krebs was portrayed as a chronic criminal who had been incarcerated and convicted for drug dealing and rape. The lead prosecutor in Rex Krebs's criminal conviction was quoted as vilifying the paternal influence as *one of the meanest guys on the planet... and took it out on his son*. Even Rex's defense attorney portrayed the father as *the monster who created the monster*, citing years of physical abuse coupled by the abandonment of an alcoholic mother. Yet who is ultimately responsible for violent criminal behavior?

Krebs's father acknowledged his lack of perfection and role modeling in Rex's child rearing. He attributed his poor reputation due to absence and incarceration. He refused any accountability for his son's crimes by pointedly acknowledging the blame rested solely with *the man who committed them*.

His comments appear evasive of all contributing responsibility.

The Krebs family shouldered a history of violence and death. Allan Krebs had a brother and sister murdered separately in the Pacific Northwest during Rex's childhood. Another brother killed a man during a road-rage accident. Allan Krebs was once a murder suspect of a prostitute, although never formally charged. Was Rex Krebs influenced more by nature or nurture?

The future of such a hideous upbringing would appear sadly predictable.

By the age of 21, Rex Krebs had already been arrested in three burglaries, two violent sodomy rapes and a misdemeanor sex offense. He was sentenced to 20 years in 1987 and served ten at both the Chino California Institution for Men and Soledad State Prison. Paroled for eight months and living in Atascadero, he was forced to move by a neighborhood letter writing campaign when he was discovered to be a registered sex offender. By the time he was arrested for his two fatal crimes in 1999, he had spent more than 11 of his past 15 years in law enforcement custody.

By many accounts, Rex Krebs lived a double existence. Most acquaintances found him unassuming, polite and even personable. His muscular squat physique, handlebar mustache and baldness made him appear ordinary and undistinguishable.

The sadistic rage within him created a stark contrast. During the late evening of November 12, 1998, he followed a 20-year-old Cal Poly student Rachel Newhouse who'd just left a party intoxicated from a local restaurant. She was walking nearly two miles alone to her residence. Newhouse was unaware of her stalker and mounted the Jennifer Bridge on the outskirts of San Luis Obispo that spans the Amtrak railroad tracks. Krebs anticipated her route and awaited her approach at the top of the staircase wearing a skull-faced Halloween mask.

The Jennifer Bridge amidst the darkness radiates a sinister appearance. It's twisted welded iron construction, cement

102

walkway, circuitous staircase and dim lighting make concealment easy. Upon reaching the summit of the stairway, Newhouse was overpowered, viciously beaten unconscious and dragged down by her hair. Leaving a blood and hair trail, she was hog-tied and heaved into the rear bed of Krebs' parked pick-up. Krebs' drove her to his secluded Avila Canyon house and repeatedly raped her. She was later strangled to death.

Four months later in the early morning hours of March 12, 1999, Krebs stalked and shadowed another 20-year-old college student, Aundria Crawford. He slipped and squirmed his way unnoticed into her apartment via a 12x18" elevated transom-type bathroom window facing the street front. Startling her in the early morning hours as she responded to her dog squealing, he beat her into insensibility. He repeated Newhouse's ordeal of rape, torture and ultimately murder at his property, burying both bodies separately in shallow graves onsite.

Krebs's rental residence was on an isolated hillside property accessible via Davis Canyon Road over a mile from the nearest paved roadway. The serpentine tributary perforates through layers of forest strata and uneven terrain. The surroundings accentuate a sense of foreboding doom. In the darkness, one senses they are entering the entails of Hell.

This cloak became Krebs' hellish playground. The isolation gave him an unrealistic sense of immunity from scrutiny. No one would voluntarily drive the twisting dirt pathway wide enough to only accommodate a single vehicle.

Krebs was 33-years-old and employed by a San Luis Obispo lumberyard at the time of the attacks. Fear and paranoia shadowed San Luis Obispo. No discovered bodies and minimal forensic clues had accompanied two well-publicized disappearances of young women. The abductions were spaced only a year and a half following Cal Poly student Kristin Smart's disappearance. Krebs had been briefly considered a suspect in that case but was eliminated due to his confirmed incarceration.

The criminal investigation following Crawford's disappearance focused principally on convicted sex and violent crime offenders in the region. Both women were slightly built and blond. Their forceful abductions followed a similar pattern and were consistent with the precedent violent rapes by Rex Krebs.

Two San Luis Obispo police investigators converged their attentions towards Krebs knowing of his history. Their subtle but penetrating interrogations and forensic examination of his detached Ford pickup rear jump seat eventually elicited a confession. Bloodstains on the jump seat were positively matched with Rachel Newhouse. Following the confession, Krebs identified to inspectors the precise location of the two burial sites. Crawford had been buried approximately 30 feet from the main door of his house. He had buried Newhouse deeper in the woods adjacent to Davis Canyon Road, approximately two miles away.

Were there additional women given his predatory history?

Two years later, Rex Krebs would be sentenced to death for the double homicides and a litany of accompanying charges. He was served his desired death penalty verdict but not a swift finishing stroke. His ultimate execution, as with the majority of inmates on California's death row, transition into a tedious filing of legal procedural appeals, delays and eventual judicial verdicts at the state's expense.

Still relatively young, Krebs may enjoy an extended lifespan including constant medical attention for decades while the legal system crawls forward. Critics against capital punishment prefer this pace to a culminating execution. Their objectives are clear, the total abolishment of the death penalty.

Who ultimately prospers from such tactics? Is capital punishment simply society's barbaric retribution for extreme criminal behavior or a viable deterrent? The argument remains irreconcilably polarized.

Perhaps one day, voluntarily euthanasia will become an option for the condemned and those sentenced to life imprisonment without any possibility for parole. For now, their destiny remains an excruciating wait for all affected parties.

It may be accurate to observe that a completed execution offers minimal consolation and closure for a victim's family. Too much time has usually elapsed. A killer's remorse and apologies become irrelevant. It would be difficult to presume that any of Krebs's conciliatory or apologetic remarks could be genuine.

His father's condemnation concluded that Rex Allen Krebs was not apologetic for the murders, but only sorry that he was caught. He stated plainly that his son would have continued to rape and kill until ultimately apprehended.

It is difficult to contradict such insight considering the source. A probable clone of evil, one would hope that subsequent generation's antisocial choices might be altered. The existing population of our penal institutions, which often spans multiple generations of families, poignantly confirms a contrary opinion.

Jennifer Bridge Stairway

Rachel Newhouse's Abduction Location

Aundria Crawford's Duplex

Small Bathroom Window Kreb's Crawled Through Into Crawford's Apartment

Rex Kreb's House of Horror

Vanishing Into Speculation

On November 25, 1997, Karen Mitchell left her aunt's Bayshore Mall shoe store in Eureka. She began a northerly walk along a level stretch of Broadway Street. Her destination was the Coastal Family Development Center where she worked part-time caring for children. School was out for Thanksgiving vacation and the mile and a half distance included a gradual incline. She never arrived at her workplace.

In five days she would have turned seventeen. Her life had seemingly begun to stabilize following a contentious living arrangement with her mother in Orange County. Two years before, she had moved in with her aunt and uncle, but was tiring of Eureka. She was planning to complete high school early and continue her studies at Humboldt State University the following year. She had demonstrated an interest in politics and her outspoken liberal orientation focused on environmental and child related issues.

Those who knew her best confided that she was an individual who would ultimately make a difference.

En route to her job, a witness indicated that Mitchell entered a light four-door sedan driven by a 60 to 70-year-old Caucasian male with balding light gray or sandy blonde hair. He was slightly built and wore glasses. That possible sighting was the last time anyone viewed Karen Mitchell. Her extended disappearance seemed involuntary. Money remained in a savings account and was never accessed. She still possessed a plane ticket to southern California to visit her mother for Christmas.

For months following her disappearance, regional police departments and community volunteers scoured the Eureka area including neighboring marshes and forests for clues of her whereabouts. Thousands of tips were processed without success.

One year later, the first promising suspect, trucker Wayne Adam Ford, 36, walked into the Humboldt County Sheriffs department with a woman's severed breast in his pocket. The serial killer confessed to four murders and speculation abounded that there were additional victims. He denied any involvement with the Mitchell case. Police were unable to connect him with the disappearance. In 2006, he was found guilty on four counts of first-degree murder and sentenced to death. He is currently interned at San Quentin.

The manhunt has periodically resumed with fresh interviews, cadaver-sniffing dogs and house searches. The results have yielded nothing fresh. The years passed and a more promising suspect emerged.

Robert Durst was outed as a probable serial killer following the published book *A Deadly Secret* and an HBO documentary series *The Jinx* that aired in 2015. The wealthy and eccentric Durst is heir to a New York real estate fortune. He has spent most of his adult life concealing his activities and alternative lifestyle.

Following the sudden disappearance of his wife in 1982, Durst began a nomadic existence. One of his numerous residences was located in nearby Trinidad, 20 miles north of Eureka. He was reportedly acquainted with Karen Mitchell. Their connection(s) came via her involvement with a homeless shelter. She volunteered and he frequented there in one of his varying disguises. Durst lived a clandestine way of life often cross-dressing. Reports have also surfaced that he may have known Karen from his whimsical shopping sprees at her aunt's store.

His most critical link to her disappearance was his resemblance to the composite sketch provided by the eyewitness. Was he the driver of the sedan that Karen voluntarily entered? Or was she forced into the vehicle at gunpoint?

Media scrutiny has linked Durst to murder and other unexplained disappearances. The first involved the vanishing of his wife Kathie Durst in 1982 without a trace. The second was the suspicious disappearance and presumed murder of his friend

Susan Berman, who was conjectured to have known too much about his wife's fate. The third involved the killing of Galveston, Texas neighbor Morris Black. Durst was arrested and stood trial for Black's death. He was exonerated based on self-defense. This verdict was reached despite Durst having dismembered Black's body and dumped the remains into Galveston Bay.

Slithering under the investigative radar for decades, Durst's elusiveness failed him on the final emission of *The Jinx*. Perhaps, like many precedent serial killers, Durst harbored an arrogance regarding his handiwork. Certain deluded mass murderers have considered themselves too vigilant in their disposal methods and too clever to ever be apprehended by perceived intellectually inferior investigators. These murderers consciously or subconsciously dare law enforcement authorities to prove their deeds.

A supposed Durst private musing was captured on the documentary's audiotape. His chilling admission shocked viewers and elevated ratings. He muttered to himself, *What the hell did I do? Killed them all, of course*.

This perceived confession and/or manipulative challenge prompted the Los Angeles District Attorney to charge him with the murder of Susan Berman. Her body has never been located. Before Durst could be extradited to face trial, he was arrested in New Orleans for illegally carrying a .38-caliber revolver. In April 2016, he pleaded guilty to the gun charge and was sentenced to seven years in federal prison. His request to be expediently returned to Los Angeles County to face murder charges was granted.

His highly anticipated trial began in November 2016. Durst appeared gaunt, wheel chair bound and wore a neck brace for undisclosed reasons. He succinctly declared his innocence over Berman's disappearance. Following his declaration of a *not guilty* plea, he was then was wheeled back to his county jail cell.

Was his frailty and halting voice simply another public disguise and charade?

Whatever the eventual trial outcome, his role in Karen Mitchell's discovery is likely to remain clouded. Until her body is one day discovered, a likely kidnapper or murderer may only be convicted by speculation. Throughout this lingering silence, a woman who may have made a difference during her lifetime has done so in unforeseen ways to those who've sought answers from her disappearance.

Interior of Eureka's Bayshore Mall

Broadway Street, Eureka

Former Coastal Family Development Center

Robert Durst's Trinidad Home

Fung *Little Pete* Jing Toy: 19th Century Chinatown Gangland Slaying

Within today's narrow and almost sinister alleyways of San Francisco's Chinatown, it is not difficult to imagine a 19th century concentration of opium dens, gambling houses and gangland murders. The 1906 earthquake and fire obliterated most of Chinatown. The majority of buildings and structures were destroyed. Streets, building numbers and the essential identity of the neighborhoods were altered during reconstruction.

One of the subtler but supposedly lasting changes became the declining influence and exodus of the ruling tongs. The tongs evolved out of secret societies founded by revolutionaries in 17th century imperial China. In America, they started during California's Gold Rush, helping immigrants endure the hardships of discrimination. They eventually spread to other parts of the country.

The 19th century tongs tyrannical influence extended into most sectors of Chinatown. Virile leaders emerged and were often displaced violently. No more visible leader represented the era than Fung Jing Toy, more commonly known as Little Pete. Pete was known as the *dragonhead* (the designation of leadership) of the Som Yop Tong. The title is still employed today to crown leaders of the sometimes illicit world of Chinese brotherhoods and gangs.

Little Pete rose to power via old fashion methods. He was considered the best armed, guarded and ruthless of the hatchet men (the then preferred method of execution). His empire included prostitution, gambling and opium sales. Many considered him invincible because of his steel-reinforced hat, chain mail chest protector, German shepherd companions, three bodyguards and twin pistols. He was rumored to have slain over fifty men and amassed a substantial personal fortune. Rising to the summit at 32-years-old, his fate was inevitable. He was as vulnerable as powerful.

Rival tong leaders had placed a $3,000 contract on Pete's life and on January 23, 1897, they found two takers, rumored to be the assassins Lem Jung and Chew Tin Gop. While Little Pete was finishing up a shave without his bodyguards at the Wong Lung barbershop at 819 Washington Street, the duo shoved a .45 caliber revolver under his chain mail and emptied five bullets into his spine. As trained killers, they completed the job with two more into his head.

Little Pete's fixed death stare became the only evidence for the arriving policemen. In the insulated society of Chinese tongs, no one spoke with investigators. No one ever went to public trial nor was convicted. Both assassins later returned to China wealthy men reportedly due to the contract slaying. This was never substantiated.

Today's tenant at the 819 Washington Street address may or may not be occupying the actual site of the fateful barbershop slaying. The re-designation and numbering of buildings following the earthquake created substantial identification chaos.

The tong presence has perhaps never truly vanished or disappeared from contemporary society.

Today, diversely ethnic Asian gangs still operate within Chinatown. The majority maintains discreet public profiles. The gangland past has not been fully buried within the archives. Violent acts such as the 1977 Golden Dragon Restaurant massacre or later contract killings of influential businessman Allen Leung, lawyer Dennis Natali or Vietnamese gang leader Cuong Tran remind outsiders of their clandestine presence.

The rise and swift fall of Fung Jing Toy is repeated regularly in our urban and now suburban environments. The marginalized still feel the need to collectively organize and seize their perceived due share of prosperity, whether legally or illicitly.

Approximate Location of Killing

Charles Crawford: The Fixer Loses His Influence

The Tammany Hall political machine dominated New York City politics between the mid 19th and 20th centuries. The Los Angeles equivalent of Charles Crawford and his *City Hall Gang* manipulated Los Angeles politics during the decade of the roaring 1920s.

The unelected kingmaker of Los Angeles, Crawford began his career operating dance halls and saloons in Seattle at the turn of the 20th century. He relocated and seamlessly integrated into southern California operating multiple casinos and bordellos. His activities cultivated influential political and law enforcement connections.

His influence shifted from vice to political Machiavellian. He and his associates sponsored candidate George E. Cryer victorious win for mayor of Los Angeles in 1921. For the next two terms while the city enjoyed unprecedented growth, Crawford became the primary fixer and influence peddler. His reputation and flamboyance were legendary during an era when excess was celebrated.

All roads towards city development, procurement favors and legal protection necessitated Crawford's cooperation and approval. His traditional sources of illicit revenue flowed directly into city government and dishonesty became institutionalized. His notorious greed and viciousness elevated public corruption into a new and elevated stench within Los Angeles.

Then the unforeseeable transpired.

In 1929, Cryer opted not to run for re-election and a reform candidate succeeded him. Abruptly out of power and losing his intimidating influence, a tide of media examination and judicial scrutiny began focusing attention on Crawford and his activities. His power base was evaporating, He was indicted on bribery charges involving a city councilman and later a securities scandal. The charges for both counts were ultimately dismissed when reluctant witnesses refused to testify.

With the New York Stock market collapse and the effects of the Great Depression beginning, the grazing pastures for political dinosaurs were thinning.

Crawford sought professional legitimacy and sanctuary by opening an insurance and real estate office on the 6500 block of Sunset Boulevard in Hollywood. He publicly embraced the protestant faith and made very pretentious contributions to St. Paul's Presbyterian Church.

With his influence receding, his personal vulnerability was exposed to vicious published and finally physical attack. In May of 1931, Crawford and an associate Herbert Spencer were shot at close range during a private meeting with an unknown assailant in his office. Spencer was killed instantly. Crawford regained consciousness before undergoing emergency surgery. Consistent with his criminal code of silence, he refused to identify his shooter. The fatal bullet had ruptured his liver and one of his kidneys. He died on the operating table. His funeral procession was overflowing. Some of the attendees mourned while others wanted to certify he was indeed gone.

His clandestine operations soon became publicly disclosed and the veil of secrecy that he'd constructed, disintegrated. Several weeks following the shooting, David H. Clark, a prosecutor and judicial candidate emerged from the shadows to confess his guilt for the double homicide. A jury acquitted him twice of the crime based on a presumption of self-defense. A cigar, not a gun however was lifted from Crawford's dead hand.

After Clark was acquitted at his second retrial, the untidy inconvenience of Charles Crawford was laid to eternal rest. Clark would murder again in 1953 and die shortly after his imprisonment.

In 1936, Crawford's widow, Ella leveled his former offices and commissioned architect Robert V. Derrah to design an international outdoor shopping mall and office complex called the *Crossroads of the World*.

The kitsch stucco fantasy was self-promoted as America's *first* outdoor mall. The principal building resembles an ocean liner surrounded by a small village of cottage-style bungalows. Ella Crawford's intention presumably was to commemorate her husband's contribution to progress within Los Angeles. Instead she erected a testament of shame now weathering poorly and as archaic as influence peddling and derailed political machines.

The Crossroads of the World complex today hosts numerous entertainment industry production and publishing company offices. Like Charles Crawford, it symbolizes an individual that Los Angeles historians would prefer to forget. It is safe to conclude that most people already have.

The Widow's Atonement, The Crossroads of the World Complex

Warren Gamaliel Harding: The Poisoning of a President?

The Presidential Suite of San Francisco's Palace Hotel, Room #888 requires significant financial substance to reserve. Unassumingly positioned amidst the eighth-floor opulence, its role in American history is often forgotten.

The Presidential Suite was the death site of 29th American President Warren Harding under mysterious circumstances. Harding coined the memorable quotation: "I have no trouble with my enemies. I can take care of my enemies in a fight. But my friends, my goddamned friends, they're the ones who keep me walking the floors at nights!"

Amidst more innocent times and media absence, Harding's phrasing became one of his few memorable utterances during an unremarkable presidency. Perhaps he should have taken more care looking over his immediate shoulder with regard to his personal affairs.

Scarcely known, the Republication Party chose Harding, an Ohio Senator, as an inoffensive candidate during their hopelessly deadlocked 1920 convention. Following World War I, two terms by then incapacitated Democrat Woodrow Wilson and a strong minority progressive movement within the Party, Harding became the best compromise for the Republican conservative wing. American voters agreed, electing him by a significant margin of 60% to 34% over Democratic Ohio newspaper publisher James M. Cox.

His campaign slogan of a *return to normalcy* after the fatigue of global warfare was popular amongst voters seeking isolationism and a stronger internal economic focus. This philosophy ultimately ushered in seven years of prosperity, rampant financial speculation and accompanying corruption.

Harding lavishly showered his friends, contributors and associates with powerful government positions. They rewarded his fidelity with previously unimaginable levels of graft and corruption. The most sensation political disgrace of the era, the infamous Teapot Dome Scandal forever tainted him.

Barring John F. Kennedy, Harding cultivated the most prolific Presidential reputation as an obsessive womanizer and philanderer, but only after his death. The accusations were published his detractors posthumously. He was rumored and alleged to have had extramarital affairs and sexual encounters with numerous women. One writer, Nan Britton, a 22-year old campaign volunteer, thirty years his junior, claimed in her 1927 book, *The President's Daughter*, that Harding had in fact fathered her daughter. Published DNA results testing in 2015 confirmed his paternity.

Other reports of trysts surfaced including some within the confines of the White House under the guard of U.S. Secret Service agents. Unsubstantiated claims of orgies, counter claims of Harding's sterility and troves of discovered intimate letters fueled a myriad of conjectures. None shed even minimal insight into a man many observers claimed was pathetically shy, especially around women.

Following stints as a teacher, insurance agent, and lawyer, Harding established his reputation as a newspaper publisher before his successful entry into politics. In 1891, he married Florence Kling DeWolfe, the daughter of his newspaper rival Amos Kling DeWolfe. She was a divorcee, five years Harding's senior and the mother of a young son. She reportedly pursued Harding until he reluctantly proposed. Her acute business sense, social standing and ambition made the marriage a preview model of noteworthy political liaisons to follow. She was reputed to have maintained a red book filled with notations about individuals who had offended her.

Florence Harding was clearly not a woman to be trifled with nor publicly humiliated.

The workings of the federal government and the geographical location of Washington D.C. in 1923 was isolated from the western United States. Transcontinental airline travel, radio and television were nonexistent. In June of 1923, Harding launched an ambitious westward cross-country *Voyage of Understanding* to connect with Americans and elaborate through public speaking and informal talks, his political agenda and policies. During this trip, he became the first President to visit the Alaskan territories and Canada when he toured Vancouver, British Columbia.

Rumors of his declining health had persisted since the fall of 1922 with speculation that he was suffering from chronic exhaustion and coronary disease. The stress behind the rampant corruption within his administration and possibly his marital infidelities had radically affected his sleeping patterns and recuperative powers.

Harding's tour following Vancouver traveled by train through Seattle to Portland. He canceled his speech in Portland and his train continued to San Francisco where he checked into the Palace Hotel Suite, then numbered 8064. En route, Secretary of Commerce Herbert Hoover wired his personal friend Dr. Ray Wilbur to meet, examine and personally evaluate the President.

At the Palace, Harding, severely exhausted, was diagnosed with a respiratory illness believed to be pneumonia. He was given digitalis and caffeine that apparently helped relieve his heart condition and sleeplessness.

On Thursday evening, August 2nd, Harding's health had appeared to improve. His pulse was normal and lung infection subsided. This apparent recovery enabled his presiding doctors the luxury of leaving him unattended while they dined together.

The account of this subsequent period was the basis for fueling later speculation and controversy. Unexpectedly during their absence, Harding shuddered and died in the middle of a conversation with his wife. Some accounts have her reading by his side a previous weeks article from the influential Saturday Evening Post about him entitled *A Calm View of a Calm Man*. At 7:35 p.m. he was pronounced dead and the national news wires reported the event fifteen minutes later.

The majority of attending doctor's examinations concluded that Harding had died of congestive heart failure. One, Dr. Sawyer, a homeopathic friend of the Harding family suggested he had succumbed to a fatal stroke. Consensus was mixed and an official press release stated the cause of death was some *brain evolvement*, probably an apoplexy. Many close observers to Harding would have argued that throughout his professional career, his inflexibility and limited thinking capabilities would have inhibited any significant brain evolvement.

What immediately followed his death would seem inconceivable with today's social media frenzy and disclosure-obsessed society. Mrs. Harding refused to allow an autopsy and her request was respected. This evasiveness in determining an exact cause of death and his abrupt demise before only a single witness aroused immediate questions. Certain questionable sources suggested that poisoning by a jealous, embarrassed and vengeful spouse artificially prompted his death. Suicide was also speculated. Both theories have been essentially discounted over the years due to Harding's documented medical condition preceding his death.

His political reputation proved so damaged from the scandals, his sudden death only intensified unanswered questions involving both his knowledge and involvement in the illegalities. Florence Harding donated less than 20% of his personal papers for posterity due to his fractured reputation. Subsequent President Herbert Hoover in 1931 categorized the Harding legacy as one of *tragic betrayal*, absolving the man of intimate insider knowledge or direct participation. History however does not always sustain nor validate a single individual's opinion.

Speculation remains a popular American pastime, particularly when multiple potential motives exist for murder. Infidelity and mediocrity stimulate conjecture and the imagination. Only Florence Harding knew for certain what happened during their time alone on the fateful evening of August 2nd.

A four-day eastward procession returned Harding's casket to the East Room of the White House pending a state funeral. Millions lined the tracks in cities and towns to pay their respects and mourn an individual they had minimal prior contact with. Published reports at the time indicated he was genuinely liked and admired despite his leadership failings.

Calvin Coolidge succeeded Harding. His low profile, stoic and aloof personality reflected his administration's governing policy. His policies (or lack of them) were ultimately blamed for enabling business abuses due to almost nonexistent government regulation.

Coolidge became the first President to ultimately integrate the emerging media of radio into his public communications. *Silent Cal's* personality and bland delivery failed to arouse passion with the American public. Satirist writer Dorothy Parker upon being informed that Coolidge had died, famously remarked, *How can they tell?*

Many attribute the casual and negligent policies of the Harding and Coolidge administrations for sowing the seeds of the 1927 stock market collapse and ensuing Great Depression. Their successor, Herbert Hoover inherited the impending catastrophe and its repercussions dominated his legacy.

Hoover was an eminently more competent businessman and administrator than his two predecessors. The accumulated malaise from rampant financial speculation and world economic stagnation however proved overwhelming for his leadership capabilities.

Warren Harding's popularity has historically stagnated in

comparison to the varying fluctuations of his contemporaries. This indifference towards his legacy has made the demand for concrete explanations behind his death marginal. Adventurous guests and visitors to the hotel do not have access to the suite but may view an oversized scrapbook maintained by the hotel regarding Harding's ill-fated stay.

The cost for immediate and direct communication with his departed spirit is exorbitant. The room rate reportedly exceeds $3000 per night and remains unpublished on the hotel's website.

Cohabitation with posterity, no matter how morbid, does not come cheaply.

Palace Hotel Presidential Suite

Ned Doheny and Hugh Plunkett: The Greystone Mansion Killings

Greystone is a Tudor Revival style structure located within 18-acres of splendor in Beverly Hills. Architect Gordon Kaufmann designed the palatial estate in 1928. In a moneyed community obsessed by competing architecture, Greystone reigns distinct with its spacious elegance.

The main residence resembles an ostentatious English manor influenced by American tastes. The 55-room mansion includes a bowling alley with hidden bar, walls made of leaded glass, a main hall of checkered Carrara marble, a personal switchboard, secret passageways and grand rooms filled with European antiques. The grounds included an automated 80-foot waterfall, stables, riding trails, a swimming pool, kennel and Renaissance inspired Cypress Lane designed by landscape architect Paul Thiene.

The building is an ideal setting for mystery and intrigue. The estate has been often utilized in filming productions and is publicly accessible. Few visitors realize the tragic double homicide involving the original owner and his personal secretary.

The mansion was originally a gift bestowed by West Coast oil tycoon Edward Doheny to his son, Edward *Ned* Doheny, Jr. and his family.

The gift came amidst the chaos and political skirmishes involved with the national Teapot Dome Scandal. The scandal involved oil leases in Teapot Dome, Wyoming that were awarded to favored associates of Secretary of the Interior Albert Fall without competitive bidding. The fallout tarnished the presidency of Warren Harding and exposed an unprecedented level of corruption between one of his Cabinet members and moneyed oil interests. Both Dohenys and Ned's personal assistant Hugh Plunkett were questioned regarding their participation.

Edward faced indictment regarding a documented *loan* he had given to Fall, a former business associate. Ned and Hugh Plunkett had physically delivered the financial documents as functionaries.

The relationship between Doheny and his secretary Plunkett was unusual. They were considered close friends despite their class differences.

Ned lived a comfortable and affluent existence with all of the privileges of his aristocratic status. Plunkett originally worked at gas station owned by Ned's father-in-law and was later hired as a chauffeur for the Doheny family. Both men served in World War I. Upon their return, Plunkett became Ned's personal secretary, traveling as part of the family entourage.

Hugh married and lived modestly. Ned and his wife Lucy lived in extravagant excess bankrolled by his father's millions.

The consequences of legal entanglement for Plunkett could have been ruinous. His fate was left entirely in the hands of the Doheny legal team, whose priorities were clearly with their employer. During 1929, he and Ned were scheduled to be called in to testify on bribery charges concerning the loan. Their social division became evident when Ned was promised immunity from prosecution and Plunkett was not.

While Ned remained with his father and the legal team in Washington D.C., Plunkett oversaw the construction details involved with the family residence. Ned, his wife and their five children moved in during the final months of 1928. At the family's first Christmas celebration, the combined stress of the impending hearing and fatigue from the construction project stimulated a nervous breakdown by Plunkett.

By mid-February, family members noticed that his normal placid personality was unraveling. He refused their offer of a rejuvenate stay at a sanitarium. Plunkett's eleven-year marriage was dissolving. He couldn't sleep and was developing an unhealthy dependence on sleeping pills.

On the evening of February 16, 1929, Ned Doheny and Hugh Plunkett were shot to death by single bullets to each head. Tracing a plausible motive became as elusive as determining who fired the responsible weapon.

The Los Angeles police forensic director later published a book disputing the media accepted version that Plunkett had shot Doheny and then turned the gun on himself. Newspapers created a scenario where Ned had died attempting to help a *troubled* friend suffering from nervous exhaustion.

The controversially published evidence offered numerous conflicting facts. Investigator had found a smoldering cigarette in Hugh's lifeless fingertips, extraordinary for someone committing suicide. The gun used in the murder lay conveniently *under* Plunkett's body. The weapon was hot as though it had been heated in an oven.

The family doctor, under hostile investigative questioning, testified that Ned was still alive and breathing when he initially burst into the room. However, he was already slipping into unconsciousness and delirium.

Ned Doheny appeared to have been shot at very close range. Plunkett was not. The forensic expert conjectured that the actual sequence and responsible party had been reversed from the publicly delivered account.

Still another theory suggested that Ned's wife Lucy had caught the two men together in a compromised position and shot both fatally. Rumors of a sexual liaison circulated following the killings based on the their close relationship but have never been substantiated.

Before the era of mass media exposure, wealthy family

indiscretions remained hushed. The details behind Doheny and Plunkett's deaths evaded public scrutiny. The Los Angeles District attorney promised publicly a sweeping investigation. During this period, justice and disclosure within Los Angeles was for sale due to the unsavory influence of the *City Hall Gang*.

Edward Doheny had both the resources and contacts to effectively silence the investigation. The district attorney abruptly closed the inquiry before arriving at a resolution.

Both men were cremated and buried 100 feet apart at Forest Lawn Cemetery. Ned's ashes were interned in the magnificent temple of Santa Sabina, which once housed the bones of a second century Italian saint. Plunkett's were buried underneath the sod on Sunrise Slope. Hundreds attended Doheny's funeral while Plunkett's ceremony was modestly attended the following day. Lucy Doheny sent a huge floral arrangement to Plunkett's funeral and two of her brothers served as pallbearers. Scandal, animosity and disclosure were sealed permanently.

Lucy remarried and remained at Greystone until 1955. She sold the mansion and estate to Chicago based development interests. The new owners attempted to subdivide the property and demolish the mansion. The Beverly Hills city council prevented their plan. The city purchased the property in 1965 and ultimately converted it into its current public and private uses.

Both Dohenys and Plunkett were ultimately cleared of any criminal intent involved in their dealings with Albert Fall. The Interior Secretary's legacy concluded less favorably. He was convicted of conspiracy and bribery charges for accepting the loan, stripped of his Cabinet post and jailed for a year. In retribution for his greed and the ensuing complications, Doheny's corporation foreclosed on Fall's New Mexico home due to *unpaid loans*.

The owed sum turned out to be the identical amount that originally launched the Teapot Dome Scandal inquiry.

The Former Doheny Estate

Mary Ellen Pleasant: A Civil Rights Pioneer With a Lengthy Shadow

Mary Ellen Pleasant was literally one of San Francisco's most colorful yet sublime personalities of the late 19th century.

Helen Holdredge's biography *Mammy Pleasant* written in 1953 vilified Pleasant, yet Mary Ellen still emerged as a forceful and mythical character. Holdredge's fanciful writing emphasized Pleasant's involvement with black magic, mysticism and extreme manipulative tactics to attain her objectives. The author implied that Pleasant was directly responsible for the death of her business partner and rumored lover Thomas Bell, a renowned banker and proprietor of the mysterious Bell Mansion located at 1661 Octavia Street in San Francisco.

Author Holdredge's sources were predominately diaries she had acquired from Teresa Bell, Thomas' estranged wife from a marriage Pleasant had arranged. Theresa Bell was later institutionalized and had a major falling out with her mentor Pleasant.

Mary Ellen Pleasant was a Creole born entrepreneur and financial speculator. During that era, these depictions did not exist for members of her race or gender. Light-skinned, she could pass for Caucasian and was officially known for running exclusive men's eating establishments. Her exposure to insider investment information at her lavishly catered meals enabled her and Bell, initially a clerk with the Bank of California, to amass a substantial fortune in excess of $30 million.

Mary Ellen's life however was far more expansive and impressive than simply financial trading. She worked on the Underground Railroad across many states and helped bring it to California during the Gold Rush era. She was a friend and financial supporter of John Brown and well recognized within abolitionist circles.

After the Civil War, Pleasant publicly changed her racial designation from *White* to *Black* in the city directory. She further began a series of court battles to fight laws prohibiting blacks from riding trolleys and other such abuses. In 1866, she successfully sued and won money damages against two separate railroad companies for racial discrimination when she and two other women of color were ejected from local streetcars.

She became the conduit for the African-American community within San Francisco. The majority of job placements, arranged marriages and favors were coordinated through her. This actual and implied power stirred up resentment and inevitable gossip.

The 30-room Thomas Bell mansion, constructed in 1879, was designed and furnished by Pleasant who managed the household and the all of the Bell couple's arrangements. This control and orchestration included all financial, entertainment, clothing, employment and even social agenda decisions. Throughout this period she maintained a low profile and was frequently dismissed as merely a housekeeper. Pleasant rarely socialized within Caucasian circles but everyone knew *Mammy* Pleasant, a designation she despised.

The Bell's lived separate lives and Pleasant served as their mediator. Rumors of voodoo, blackmail, prostitution and even trafficking infants were circulated about the operations of the manor. Given the remote geographical distance from downtown, such gossip wasn't surprising.

On the late evening of October 15, 1892, Thomas Bell mysteriously fell to his death from the top of a staircase twenty feet to the basement. Only Pleasant and Fred Bell, his eldest son were home. Speculation abounded that Bell had been drugged with mulled wine and pushed to his demise.

Naturally, Mary Ellen Pleasant was the prime subject and has remained so for over a century later.

The coroner ruled the death accidental. Bell had apparently been ill for the prior two months. There was accepted speculation that he may have woken up disoriented and simply fallen. Teresa Bell in her diaries thought otherwise. She elaborated on a gruesome tale that Pleasant had hastened Bell's death an hour after the fall by probing into an open skull wound with her index finger. No one has been able to confirm or conclusively dispute the imaginative account, particularly the author.

Later in life, a series of court battles with Sarah Althea Hill, Senator William Sharon, and Teresa Bell damaged Pleasant's reputation and cost her resources and wealth. Pleasant died in San Francisco on January 4, 1904 in poverty and was buried in the Tulocay Cemetery in Napa.

Sorting out fact and rumor has proven impossible. The 30-room Octavia Street mansion burned down in 1925 and was replaced in 1927 by Green's Eye Hospital. Six remaining eucalyptus trees that Pleasant planted and a historical marker have been designated by the city of San Francisco as Mary Ellen Pleasant Memorial Park.

The truth about Mary Ellen Pleasant remains as elusive and enigmatic as the woman herself.

Site of Pleasants Mansion...Trees Planted by Her

The Unexplainable Sunday Morning Sniper Attack

At approximately 8 p.m. on Saturday, April 24, 1965, 16-year-old bespectacled Michael Andrew Clark drove his parent's car from their Long Beach home without their permission. He headed north along the coastal Highway 101 through Santa Barbara County. He took his father's credit cards, Swedish Mauser military rifle equipped with a telescopic sight, a pistol and large quantity of ammunition removed from a locked gun safe.

His father, Forest Clark was a Long Beach businessman, a veteran of two wars, an active member of his church and father of three children. His mother was a housewife and schoolteacher.

Michael was reportedly an average 11th grade student and considered friendly, quiet, neat, a member of both Boy Scouts and Sea Scouts. He liked music, dances and sports and played saxophone in the high school band. He regularly attended church with his family, did not use drugs or alcohol, got along well with everyone and had never been in trouble with school authorities.

Both parents considered him a well-adjusted child and hadn't in the past displayed emotional instability or ever intentionally harmed anyone.

Forest Clark had taught Michael how to properly operate the scoped rifle at a shooting range and on a hunting trip. The location of the key to unlock the gun safe was kept in his father's dresser drawer. Both Michael and his younger brother were acquainted with the location.

At 6 a.m. the following morning after a three-hour drive, Michael mounted a hillside just south of Orcutt that overlooked the highway. He positioned himself comfortably shrouded on the incline. He experienced a cloudless sunrise and then methodically began opening fire on passing motorists.

His shootings resulted in two fatalities, 21-year-old Charles Hogan and 28-year-old Joel Kocab, five wounded shooting victims and six individuals injured by glass fragments. The men were killed attempting to assist others trapped in vehicles clipped by gunfire. The shooting continued uninterrupted until Santa Barbara County Sheriff's deputies could encircle his position. As they closed in, Clark turned the rifle on himself and committed suicide. The following day, five-year-old Kevin Dean Reida died from his wounds elevating the fatality count to three.

Nothing appeared foreseeable or coherent about Clark's intent or actions.

The Reida family sued Clark's parents for negligence in the proper raising of their son and enabling him access to a rifle. At the trial, a psychologist who had never met nor interviewed Michael, concluded that through his research and readings he had suffered from paranoid schizophrenia. The Reida's lost their suit.

In 1968, Peter Bogdanovich directed a film entitled *Targets* loosely inspired by the shooting. Actor Boris Karloff appeared in the film, one of his last, despite his rapidly declining health, immobility and need to wear an oxygen mask throughout his five days of filming.

The killings would foreshadow a darkening trend amongst teenage rampage shooters that would be acted out in schoolyards across America during the upcoming decades. Michael Clark merely fired the first shot.

Highway 101 Sniper Shooting Site

Fatal Hillside Perch

Miles Archer: San Francisco's Only Murder Site Commemorative

Burrit Street is a small alleyway flaring off from Bush Street in downtown San Francisco. Prominently mounted is a plaque that could easily be mistaken for a notation of historical importance. Ironically, it is the sole commemorative marker in the city of a murder site.

The plaque reads, *On Approximately This Spot, Miles Archer, Partner Of Sam Spade, Was Done In By Brigid O'Shaughnessy.* Of course Miles Archer, Sam Spade and even Brigid O'Shaughnessy are not historical characters. They were fictionally invented by author Dashiell Hammett for the book and film, *The Maltese Falcon.*

This alleyway is only a few blocks away from Hammett's actual apartment at 891 Post Street. Since Hammett habitually blurred reality into fiction, it is of little surprise that Sam Spade coincidentally lived at the same address.

Burrit Street Plaque

Eastside Salinas: An Invisible War Rages Streetside

Nowhere does the axis of gang proliferation and violence converge within Northern California as Eastside Salinas.

The annual crime statistics are both frightening and revealing for a population center of approximately 150,000. The city's comparative statistics noticeably exceed the state and national averages for violent and property crimes. Nationally, the homicide rate averages between 4.7 to 5 victims for every 100,000 residents, a steep decline of almost 50% since 1992. Salinas averages 16 homicide victims for every 100,000 and this figure has fluctuated minimally over the past two decades.

More telling, the majority of the killings are gang affiliation related. Amidst Salina's eastside barrios and lower middle class neighborhoods, murder is concentrated and the threat, relentless. The victims are typically Hispanic males between the ages of 18 and 29. The shootings are done on a street or sidewalk, as opposed to inside a house or business. The victim generally knows his assailant either as a family member, friend or rival gang member.

The gang culture flourishes by the collective elements of poverty, overcrowding and school dropout rates within the Hebbron Heights quarter of East Salinas. The battles lines are clearly drawn. The two defining rival gangs are the Nortenos (Northerners) and Surenos (Southerners, originating from Bakersfield southward). Their roots date back to the late 1960s and the U.S. Federal and California prison gangs Nuestra Familia (North) and La Eme (South and better known as the Mexican Mafia).

Salinas' northerly location originally accommodated a majority of Nortenos but the two-gang populations are near equality today.

The divisions, symbolisms, apparel and antagonisms are deeply divided between the warring factions. Their traditional sources of financing remain identical: the lucrative trafficking of illegal drugs, stolen goods, weapons, prostitution and American border crossings from Mexico.

Eastside Salinas serves as a depressing blueprint for the future of the disenchanted and economically left behind.

Youth gang involvement continues to expand beyond its traditional frontiers and illicit activities. Their enterprises will eventually (if not already) extend into cyberspace and more lucrative and untraceable white-collar crime.

As with most enduring vendettas, the shooting escalations typically involve retribution. The warfare litters the streets with forgotten casualties amidst a battleground without end. As the statistics have spiraled over the decades, the tally scorecards have included innocent and random killings. All of the accumulated damage remains senseless resembling an internally generated race war of extermination.

It would be simplistic to categorize each opposing group's objectives as simply fury, intimidation or competition between rivals. Chaos never adheres to predictability or structure. Many gangs have a decentralized hierarchy at the most basic street level. These factions within factions share only violence, funeral processions and revenge in common.

Media scrutiny of the ongoing tragedy has been predominantly regionalized. Sadly, many Californians living in the more populous cities of the State tend to remain ignorant and indifferent towards the plight and challenges of the central agricultural belt. As the violence continues to protrude outside of the poorer barrio confines of the Central Valley and Coast regions, attention will be unavoidable.

California and America's population composition continue to evolve. The separation between the haves and the have-nots widens with every economic surge and bubble. Urban and suburbanites note the changes and continue to grapple with adaptation.

Salinas has become a prototype for these changes. Historically a rural agricultural core, the community has swelled into suburban expansion. Monotonous furrowed vegetable fields co-exist with fresh housing developments. The rural enveloping periphery creates a disarming presence to motorists passing daily on the adjacent California Highway 101.

Not every Eastside Salinas resident has surrendered to the inevitability of gang domination.

Prayer vigils, city funded anti-gang participation billboards and well-attended anti-violence rallies strike chords of humanity and compassion amidst the disarrayed insanity.

Proactively frequent and collaborated multi-city police sweeps through gang-infested neighborhoods regularly send a message of intolerance towards illegal activities. Optimistic resolution, however, remains remote within the bleak neighborhoods.

For the young, born and seemingly confined within the neighborhoods of East Salinas, there lingers a hovering shadow of fatalism. They are liberated residents of California but imprisoned within the futility of warfare without a vision of someday ending.

Clausen Park, Site of Numerous Executions

Cesar Gonzalez, 17, Gunned Down By Three Men in Van on East Market Street

Jose Vasquez Shot In Wheelchair
Corner of Del Monte and Orchard

Jose Delores Salazar Shot At
8 p.m. on 700 Block of Holly

The Isolated Unexplainable Roadway Slaying of Ennis Cosby

Before he was publicly disgraced as an accused sexual predator and hypocrite, William Henry *Bill* Cosby enjoyed global esteem and respect as an entertainment industry icon and social justice pioneer. His legitimate acclaim had afforded him the admiration and legitimacy of credible social commentary. His once immaculate public and professional perception sadly has come into conflict with his private sexual demons.

During the early morning of January 17, 1998 at approximately 1:25 a.m., Bill Cosby assumed another role reluctantly as bereaved father. In the stillness and dimming of insufficient street lighting, his only son 27-year-old Ennis was shot to death at close range while attempting to change a flat tire on his late model Mercedes convertible.

Ten minutes earlier, he had telephoned a female friend who he was intending to visit, to arrive at the intersection of Mulholland Drive and Sepulveda Boulevard. He had requested her help to illuminate the surrounding background. His appeal proved farsighted but tragically too late. In the interim between his call and her arrival, 18-year-old Ukrainian-born Mikhail Markhasev approached him.

The conversation between the two men has never been publicly reported. It may be presumed that the armed Markhasev demanded either money or the expensive vehicle to carjack. Perhaps no words were actually exchanged and the single fatal gunshot was simply a random killing. Cosby was in the midst of loosening lug nuts. His spare tire was tilted against the dark green car body. His emergency flashers were blinking.

Markhasev was apprehended within three months after the killing. Following his conviction the following year, he was sentenced to life in prison without the possibility of parole. Five years after the shooting, Markhasev withdrew an appeal over his conviction as an act of admitting his guilt and contrition towards the Cosby family. He remains currently incarcerated at Corcoran State Prison.

Today, a modified well-lit intersection is easily accessible from the 405 Freeway. The paving, sidewalks and linings have been upgraded. The corner is situated below the stunning Getty Museum of Art and crossed daily by thousands of cars. The improvements make such future chance tragedies less likely.

Mourners internationally grieved genuinely for the Cosby family. The intensely private family accepted their sorrow with dignity and minimal public expression. They exhibited their own act of clemency towards the killer by requesting the prosecution to avoid seeking the death penalty during the sentencing phase. It was an admirable and charitable gesture towards a stranger who had robbed them of an adored family member.

Doomed legacies would ultimately define the two Cosby males. Ironically the accumulated wealth of esteem earned by the elder would vanish equally abruptly within two decades.

Upgraded Mulholland Drive Exit

Diane Whipple: Defining Accountability With Vicious Pet Owners

A savage dog mauling that resulted in a young woman's death raised legal, liability and ethical questions as to the extent of human responsibility in raising known vicious pets

Diane Whipple was the victim of a fatal dog attack in San Francisco during January 2001. The dogs were two Presa Canario dogs owned by her third-floor neighbors in the Pacific Heights district of San Francisco.

On January 26, 2001, after returning home with bags of groceries, the monstrous dogs (weighing in excess of 130 pounds) attacked Whipple in the constricted hallway of her apartment building. The two dogs were being kept by her neighbors Marjorie Knoller and husband Robert Noel, both San Francisco attorneys. The dogs were actually owned by two life-sentenced Pelican Bay State prisoners.

The dogs were integral parts of an improbable and illegal dog-fighting business scheme formulated by the prisoner owners. Noel and Knoller had idiotically agreed to take possession of the dogs within their apartment after the dogs proved too violent in a rural environment. Noel and Knoller had originally become acquainted with the prisoners through volunteer legal work. The most bizarre element of this twisted narrative was they had legally adopted one of the prisoners as their son only a few days before the mauling.

The Pacific Heights residence where the dog caretakers and victim lived is an older multi-level Spanish style construction with very narrow hallways. Just prior to the attack, Knoller was taking the dogs up to the roof when they spied and attacked Whipple in the hallway. Whipple had no possibility of escape or defense and suffered a total of 77 wounds to every part of her body except her scalp and bottoms of her feet. She died hours later from her wounds and excessive blood loss.

Both dogs were killed following the attack. In March 2001, a grand jury indicted Knoller and Noel. Knoller was indicted for second-degree murder and involuntary manslaughter. Noel was indicted for involuntary manslaughter. Both faced felony charges of keeping a mischievous dog.

At trial, Knoller argued that she had attempted to defend Whipple during the attack. Her claim was marginalized due to multiple witnesses testifying both caretakers repeatedly refused to control the dogs. The accused pair was villainized by the media as arrogant and unsympathetic figures for their refusal to even publicly apologize for the attack.

Ultimately, the jury found both Noel and Knoller guilty of involuntary manslaughter and owning a mischievous animal that caused the death of a human being. They found Knoller guilty of second-degree murder. Their convictions were based on the argument that they knew the dogs were aggressive towards other people and that they did not take sufficient precautions.

California suspended their law licenses. Follow-up appeals to the definition of their convictions clouded the final verdict before California appeals courts finally allowing Knoller's second-degree murder conviction to stand. Knoller is currently serving her sentence at Valley State Prison for Women in Chowchilla. Noel was convicted of involuntary manslaughter and after serving a four-year sentence is currently living and working in Solano County. Whipple's domestic partner, Sharon Smith succeeded in suing Knoller and Noel for $1.5 million in civil damages.

The debate continues as to the degree of liability pet owners should be mandated to maintain with known vicious pets.

Pacific Heights Apartment Building

Narrow Corridor. Elevator Front Left

Haing Ngor: An Extended and Consequential Journey Curtailed By A Random Killing

There are profound ironies so confounding amidst the chaos of life. Explanation and understanding become impossible. For Haing S. Ngor, to have undertaken an arduous 13,000-mile journey with death as your constant companion and then to die randomly amidst sanctuary seemed too bizarre to be possible.

Ngor was known principally for winning the 1985 Academy Award for Best Supporting Actor in the film *The Killing Fields*. In the movie, he portrayed a Cambodian journalist and refugee fleeing the mass genocide of dictator Pol Pot's Khmer Rouge. He became the first male Asian actor to win an Oscar and only the second non-professional.

Although the role was his debut performance, the plot and circumstances were familiar. Ngor was trained as a surgeon and gynecologist and practiced medicine in the capital, Phnom Penh. In 1975, the Khmer Rouge seized control of the country and a forced mass exodus was initiated by the regime. The genocide march expelled thousands of urban residents into concentration camps for social re-education.

Ngor was obliged to conceal his education, medical skills and even eyeglasses due to the regime's hostility towards intellectuals and professionals. He and his wife My-Huoy were expelled from the capital. While on their journey on foot in one of the camps, his wife died while giving birth to their child. Ngor was unable to perform her required Caesarean section. Such an act would have exposed his medical skills and certainly provoked a death sentence for father, mother and infant.

The Khmer Rouge government fell in 1979. Ngor was able to work as a doctor in a Thailand refugee camp. In 1980 he immigrated to the United States with his niece. He was unable to revive his medical practice and did not remarry.

He was cast as a journalist named Dith Pran in *The Killing Fields*. He was reluctant to act, lacking experience but relented based on a promise he had made to his late wife to accurately portray the Cambodia tragedy to an indifferent world. The film and story impacted millions. His award became a crowning achievement for a necessary message.

Following his Academy award, Ngor acted sporadically and lived frugally in a modest periphery neighborhood of Los Angeles' Chinatown.

On February 25, 1996, three members of a local gang shot Ngor dead outside of his apartment in a bungled robbery. A Rolex watch and gold locket containing his wife's picture inside were the only two personal items missing. $2,900 in cash was left in his pant pocket. Due to the ineptitude of the thieves, there was initial speculation the killing might have been revenge motivated by sympathizers of the Khmer Rouge.

In 1998, the three habitual criminals, Tak Sun Tan, Indra Lim and Jason Chan were sentenced to extended sentences with Chan singled out as ineligible for future parole. Tan is currently incarcerated at the Salinas Valley State Prison. Lim is interned at the Correctional Training Facility in Soledad. Chan is imprisoned at the California State Prison in Lancaster.

Following Ngor's death, a significant number of acquaintances emerged from the shadows to assert financial claims upon his estate. The bulk of his American assets were squandered in legal fees defending each frivolous claim. A more worthwhile Haing S. Ngor Foundation was established in 1997 following his death as a charitable organization oriented to promoting human rights worldwide and Cambodian history and culture.

Ngor in many published interviews following his academy award recognized the timelessness of his performance. His three insignificant killers could not conceive nor diminish the luster of an enduring legacy that graphically portrayed a catastrophe humanity had chosen to ignore. The power of cinematic exposure remains a powerful educational tool for influencing perceptions and reconstructions of history.

Apartment Complex Where Haing Ngor Was Slain

Huey P. Newton: A Tarnished Messenger with Feet of Clay

On the morning of August 22, 1989 at approximately 5:15 a.m., Huey P. Newton's life ended abruptly on a sidewalk in the Lower Bottoms neighborhood of West Oakland. Newton, the self-titled Minister of Defense for the militant Black Panther Party of Oakland met his ignominious death with certainty. He resolutely faced his killer, half his age. He probably understood at that instant the cycle of violent confrontation he had publicly espoused would ultimately claim his own life.

Various media accounts melodramatically reported that he taunted his murderer Tyrone Robinson by quoting prophetically, *You can kill my body, and you can take my life but you can never kill my soul. My soul will live forever!* Robinson responded by shooting him point blank multiple times in the face. Newton, the enigmatic messenger was dispassionately erased from the streets of his adopted Oakland.

The 1400 block of Ninth Street, the crime scene, was not Newton's Oakland residential neighborhood. He frequented the vice-plagued area habitually. Decaying but statuesque Victorian houses visually softened the prevalent drug trade and prostitution. As neighborhood residents related in published reports then, one sealed their front doors when the evening gunshots echoed into the darkness.

Over twenty-five years later, real estate speculation has superficially freshened and gentrified the neighborhood. The effect has not eradicated the shadows of a violent past. One does not linger or loiter in this neighborhood without consequence.

Newton's fate was prompted by a chance encounter following his exit from a Ninth Street crack cocaine house. Tyrone Robinson, then twenty-four years old was already an ex-convict and reputed drug dealer. He was a member of the Black Guerrilla Family, a prison gang founded in 1966 by George Jackson while he was incarcerated at San Quentin. Jackson had met his own violent demise at San Quentin and his attempted release was the motivation for the 1970 Marin County Courthouse shootout.

Robinson claimed Newton's killing was self-defense, maintaining that the victim had pulled a gun on him demanding cocaine when the two converged on a nearby street corner. Newton's gun was never recovered. Robinson was convicted of the murder in 1991 and sentenced to 32 years in prison. He began his sentence at San Quentin and was later transferred to Pelican Bay, then Corcoran and currently at the California State Prison in Sacramento, obscured and disregarded. He added the name Kambui to his in 2016. His identity and role were inconvenient aspects of the martyrdom that would later shroud Newton's mythology. His role has become largely antidotal over twenty-five years after the act.

Huey Newton was cremated and his ashes reportedly interred at Evergreen Cemetery in Oakland, the same location where 412 unclaimed bodies of the Jonestown mass suicide are buried. Various interpretations of his life and struggles have been reinvented and interpreted for iconic literature, cinema and political commentary involving American race relations. The reality of his life and actions are far more complicated.

Was he a legitimate freedom fighter or simply a sociopathic street thug repeating revolutionary slogans he had not authored?

Newton served as a willing symbol for the radical Black Panther Party, a group he co-founded while still a student at Merritt College in October of 1966. Newton epitomized the best and worst elements of the social consciousness movement. Charismatic, charming and articulate, his forceful personality energized a movement bent on confrontation.

The Black Panther Party became an armed political organization oriented towards African-American rights. Discarding the non-violent protest tactics of the southern Civil Rights movement, the Panthers advocated that violence and/or its impending threat would expedite social change.

Their leadership from its inception understood the propaganda impact of media manipulation and public spectacle. A contingent of Black Panthers once entered the California Legislature chambers fully armed in order to protest a gun bill being debated. Their on-site street provocations included interrupting arrests and other police activities when they presumed that African-American citizens were being intimidated. Their organizational leaders and members were targeted, harassed and under regular surveillance by law enforcement authorities.

The tenor of the times and mutual provocation ultimately provoked violence between the Panthers and law enforcement agencies. Newton's destructive seeds were sewn deeply. He exhibited violent tendencies and reckless impulsive behavior behind his flamboyant public veneer. Death accompanied his turbulent cult of personality in the form of inconvenient witnesses, peers and street acquaintances. The most prominent homicide was his voluntary manslaughter conviction of Oakland Policeman John Frey in 1968. Frey was killed while arresting Newton, shot with his own gun. The responsible weapon was never located.

Newton's repeated altercations with the legal system, his peers and stretches of imprisonment become depressing reading. He chose exile in Havana, Cuba between 1974-77 due to pending murder and assault charges against him. He returned to imprisonment and public trial. A succession of mistrials released him but his social consciousness rhetoric became perceived as opportunistic and insincere. In 1982, Newton was accused and tried on embezzlement charges involving a Black Panther founded Oakland Community School. He pleaded no contest to a single allegation and served a six-month jail term.

The vibrancy and urgency of violent racial militancy waned by the conclusion of the 1970's. The movement had disintegrated into contending factions and the founding Black Panther Party was disbanded in 1982. The leadership abuses had undermined the constructive community works of the party.

During the final year of Newton's unraveling life, he spent 90 days incarcerated at San Quentin Prison for possessing drug paraphernalia, a violation of his parole from one of his earlier cases. The climatic confrontation on Ninth Street seemed inevitable. His narcissism, personal demons and downward personality spiral had already sabotaged his social change relevance.

Today, a solitary sapling and handicapped parking sign identify Newton's earthly exit. When viewed from the east, the trees shadow resembles a prone and sprawled body silhouette. From whatever prism one views Newton's legacy, his death became another senseless urban casualty. An estimated 1000+ mourners at his Allen Temple Baptist Church funeral service lavished accolades and tributes upon him one week following his murder. The forgotten and dishonored prophet was resurrected as an icon of the protest idealism of the 1960s and 70s.

Huey P. Newton, the deeply flawed, charismatic and intelligent individual becomes indecipherable. Twenty-five years later, the measure of his influence remains as elusive as our full understanding of the protest era. Time and perspective may one day make coherent sense of the period and the man.

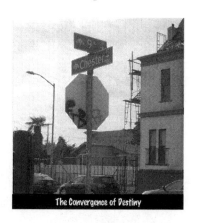

The Convergence of Destiny

The Murder Stretch of Sidewalk

The Location of Huey Newton's Fall

Johnny Stompanato: A Fatal Attraction

Johnny Stompanato was born in the Midwest into an immigrant middle-class family, the youngest of four children. His mother died six days after giving birth and his father soon remarried.

He attended the Kemper Military School in Boonville, Missouri and following graduation, like most of his generation, joined the military in the midst of World War II. He became a Marine and served in the Asian and the South Pacific theatre. He was discharged from the Corps in March 1946.

Like many returning veterans, his homecoming into civilian life proved complicated. For Stompanato, discerning good from evil entanglements was no longer simply a matter of fighting a hostile enemy. Relocating to Los Angeles, he opened and managed a gift shop selling inexpensive crude pottery and woodcarvings. The enterprise became a front for his primary activities as a bodyguard and enforcer for gangster Mickey Cohen. Cohen's enterprises controlled the majority of Los Angeles' vice activities.

The emergence of organized crime expanded into major metropolitan cities post-war. A surplus of unemployed and trained war killers was available for mob employment.

Stompanato was known for his handsome appearance, rashness and bodybuilding physique. In 1956, he began a romantic adventure with actress Lana Turner. Turner had reached a critical decline in her career. She had recently turned forty, appeared in a succession of box office flops and lost the financial security of her contract with MGM Pictures. Her liaison with Stompanato would prove toxic for both parties.

Their relationship was consistently stormy, punctuated by arguments, aggression and his frequent beatings.

Turner took advantage of an acting opportunity by appearing in an English film *Another Time, Another Place*, co-starring an emerging young actor Sean Connery. Connery successfully seduced Turner during the filming and the international press explicitly reported their sightings together and flowering relationship.

Stompanato became livid with jealousy and impulsively flew over to England. With customary impatience, he stormed the film set and threatened Connery with a gun. Connery, who would cement his future acting reputation in the role of James Bond was unimpressed. Towering over Stompanato and also a bodybuilder, his own formation from the Fountainbridge tenements of Edinburgh made a pointed weapon an irritating distraction. He reportedly bent back Stompanato's hand forcing him to drop the weapon. He then leveled him with a right hook prompting his assailant to flee the movie set.

The account still reads well decades later and may even be true.

Stompanato was immediately deported from the United Kingdom for weapon possession. The film was completed without further incident and released with modest acclaim. Several similar version remakes would follow. Lana Turner returned to the United States with a stalled career and more abuse at the hands of an enraged and humiliated Stompanato. Turner's fourteen-year-old daughter Cheryl Crane silenced his anger one evening.

On April 4, 1958 during yet another confrontation between Turner and Stompanato, she impaled him fatally with a carving knife. She maintained at her trial that he was in the act of violently attacking her mother. A jury agreed and returned a verdict of *justifiable homicide*.

Not everyone applauded the decision. The Stompanato family filed a $7 million damage suit against Lana Turner. Mickey Cohen threatened Connery during his first filming visit to the Los

Angeles area. Connery prudently lingered under the public radar briefly. During the 1960s, he emerged in films as 007, a suave and worldly British secret agent.

Turner's career briefly resurged following the murder and a return to the public spotlight. The film industry has never been charitable to aging actresses and her roles steadily lessened. Her career lapsed into a forced semi-retirement. She died at the age of 74 in 1995.

Cheryl Crane's life followed a circuitous path after the murder. She published a book in 1988 detailing the trauma of living within her mother's turbulent household and her eventual emotional recovery following the trial. She ultimately relocated to Palm Springs with a stable partner and a less dramatic existence.

Lana Turner's Residence and Murder Site

Barbara Graham: A Sympathetic Film Portrayal Masking Reality

Barbara Graham was a genuinely calloused and doomed figure while she lived. She earned the notorious distinction of becoming the third woman in California to be executed in the gas chamber in 1955. She became the inspiration for an Academy Award portrayal by actress Susan Hayward in the 1958 film *I Want to Live!* and a later 1983 television remake.

The film portrayed Graham as a sympathetic and innocent victim caught up in a male orchestrated botched robbery that resulting in the violent death of Mabel Monohan. Monohan received no compassionate treatment by her perpetrators. She was mercilessly dispatched for being an uncooperative object of erroneous prison gossip.

There was little about Graham's biography or attributed quotes that suggested that she was *innocent* or merited compassion. Her life was a succession of poor choices.

She was born to an unmarried mother in 1925 and life's misfortunes accelerated from that inauspicious beginning. At two, her teenager mother was condemned to reform school. Graham followed her example throughout her teenage years eventually attending the identical institution after being arrested for vagrancy. She exhibited little inclination or ambition to complete her education and didn't.

She made a superficial attempt at reformation. In 1940, she married a US Coast Guardsman, had two children and enrolled in a business college. After three years, she abandoned her studies, marriage and the constraints of a conventional life. She lost custody of her two sons, a nearly impossible outcome from that era.

Her failed lifestyle experiment resulted in a new and predictable occupation. She became a *seagull*, nicknamed for prostitutes

159

flocking near naval bases. During World War II, she serviced a Pacific Corridor clientele including ports in Oakland, Alameda, Long Beach and San Diego. Her attractive appearance, flaming red hair and engaging personality made her desirable. She earned a distinction for working briefly in one of famed San Francisco Madame Sally Sanford's brothels. Sanford would augment her own legend by later becoming Mayor of Sausalito.

Graham's life of prostitution introduced her into associations with hardened criminals, gamblers and drug abusers. She mirrored their excesses. She spent portions of the next decade in jail and crowned her free fall by a marriage to bartender Henry Graham in 1953. With Graham, she had another son and found her soulmate, a hardened anti-social personality and drug addict.

Barbara embraced two friends of Graham, Jack Santo and Emmett Perkins. Consistently in character, she began an affair with Perkins, who confided with her about a story the pair had overheard in prison. The tale centered around Mabel Monohan, a 64-year-old widow who allegedly kept large amounts of cash hidden in her suburban Burbank home. The stash was stored on behalf of her gambling former son-in-law, Tutor Scherer.

In March 1953, Barbara Graham, Santo and Perkins teamed up with two associates, John True and Baxter Shorter (a professional safecracker). The loosely assembled gang schemed to loot Monohan's house one evening. Graham's role was to gain entry into the house by posing as a distressed victim experiencing car trouble. She innocently asked to use the widow's telephone. The ruse worked perfectly and enabled the other gang members to rush inside the house.

It was the singular aspect of their plan that succeeded.

The five demanded money and jewels from Monohan who stubbornly refused to divulge anything. She understood the desperate nature of criminality but underestimated their capacity for impulsive violence.

Graham (or another member) pistol-whipped Monohan for her obstinacy, cracking her skull. Her accomplices then suffocated the prostrate woman, silencing the sole source for locating the object of their break-in. The robbery attempt was futile as nothing of value was recovered despite a thorough ransacking of the house. What the team of imbeciles were rumored to have overlooked was nearly $15,000 in jewels and valuables concealed in a purse within a closet near the prone body of Monohan.

The murder and absence of motive seemed incoherent to investigating police. Desperate for suspects, five career criminals, including three former associates of gangster Mickey Cohen were arrested. Cohen's gambling operations had once been entrenched in the nearby Toluca Lake district and protected by the Burbank Police Department. In 1951, a California Crime Commission investigation into their comfortable arrangement resulted in the resignation of the police chief, mayor and a councilman.

One of the random five arrested was the safecracker Baxter Shorter. He was the sole individual actually present at the aborted robbery and murder. Shorter panicked over the prospects of facing the death penalty alone and immediately recounted a version of the events.

He embellished details to minimize his role. He confessed that he'd been used only as a lookout and had witnessed the pistol-whipping by Perkins and not Graham. He was *horrified* to have been associated with a murder. He elaborated that he had called the police department within hours following the tragedy in the hopes of saving the dying Monohan. A dispatcher error led a summoned ambulance to a nonexistent Los Angeles address instead of Burbank.

Shorter potentially may have avoided prosecution for the murder. His duplicity hadn't escaped the notice of his partners once police released him. He was promptly kidnapped by Perkins and Santo from his downtown Los Angeles apartment and relocated to a grave in the San Jacinto Mountains. His body was never recovered.

Lacking a principal witness, the prosecution for the murder stalled. Perkins and Santo were arrested for Shorter's kidnapping after being identified by his widow. Barbara Graham was equally occupied during the same span. She was arrested for passing over $250 worth of fraudulent checks.

Perkins and Santo were released due to the lack of body, but immediately detained by Burbank Police for Monohan's murder. By June 1953, a fragile case was being constructed against Perkins, Santo, Graham and True for Monohan's murder. The fabric was based principally on hearsay evidence by a periphery ex-con.

Fortunately for prosecutors, John True cracked under the strain of suspicion and agreed to turn state's evidence. With all of the potential defendants locked up, he opted to accept the identical terms Shorter was offered for his testimony.

Graham, who protested her innocence throughout, undermined her credibility by attempting to purchase an alibi from an ex-con associate. She was unaware that her potential alibi was working in conjunction with investigators. Their conversations were recorded. The press during the sensational trial labeled her *Bloody Babs* for lack of a more imaginative moniker.

John True's substantiated testimony and circumstantial evidence ultimately enabled a jury to convict Graham, Perkins and Santo of all the murder and robbery charges. True disappeared from public view following his controversial testimony.

Graham, Perkins and Santo were sentenced to death and their simultaneous executions were scheduled for June 3, 1955 at 10 p.m. Perkins and Santo were expediently dispatched without protest. Graham's execution was delayed for nearly two hours as her attorneys vainly petitioned California Governor Knight for clemency. The pause proved ideal for her screenplay martyrdom and notable quotations.

The negotiations prompted agonized outbursts from Graham beginning with her first. *Why do they torture me like this? I can't take this. Why didn't they let me go at ten? I was ready to go at ten.*

Once the governor conclusively denied her petition, she was led into the gas chamber. She begged for a blindfold and was given a sleep mask by an attending jail matron.

Her second public utterance evaded any semblance of remorse or request for forgiveness. Instead she condemned her accusers. *Good people are always so sure they're right.*

The irrepressible Graham capped her defiance when one of the men in charge of her execution offered her advice on making the passing easier and quicker for her by inhaling deeply. She responded, *How the hell would you know?*

The insolent murderer had miraculously assembled a literate body of proponents during her trial and following her execution. Their wrath over injustice apparently found the realities accompanying her life inconvenient additions to their indignation. Critics of capital punishment rallied behind her cause, employing the manipulative vehicles of motion pictures and books to eulogize her as a dupe of male victimizers and media sensationalism.

The question more appropriately asked should be ultimately who *duped* who?

Mabel Monohan's Burbank Residence

Marvin Gaye: A Visionary Dishonored Within His Household

Singer Marvin Gaye understood the capricious world of music industry popularity. His sheer talent and stage charisma had vaulted him into international stardom. A mid-career lapse, accentuated by family and personal demons had once consigned him into tax exile and potentially career oblivion. At the peak of an improbable comeback, the man responsible for his birth felled him cruelly.

During 1978, amidst a career crater, he had divorced his wife Anna Gordy, the sister of Motown Record owner Barry Gordy. Motown was Gaye's record label and tantamount to his early success. As a partial payment towards her alimony settlement, Gaye recorded a bitter divorce tirade of an album *Here, My Dear*. The album was a commercial failure. Gaye vanished into a professional hiatus.

Scaling rapid unimaginable heights only to plunge into their accompanying precipices became a familiar pattern for Gaye. The relationship with his minister father, Marvin Gay, Sr. endured similar extremes. As Pentecostal performers, their accompaniments were brilliant. Offstage during his teenage years, Gaye, Jr. was disciplined often and frequently kicked out of his father's house. He discontinued his high school studies and enlisted in the Air Force. He was later discharged for insubordination.

Marvin Jr. was restless but musically brilliant.

Following his return to hometown Washington D.C., he performed with touring vocal groups. His growing reputation expanded his exposure as a desirable background session singer for established music acts. These assignments attracted the attention of Barry Gordy and his fledging Motown Records.

Under Gordy's tutelage and Motown's rise, his career, stage presence and songwriting capabilities flourished. His diversified skills earned him paid assignments to play drums in recording sessions and with touring groups.

The emotional rift with his father did not entirely heal with time and distance. He added an "e" to his surname to distance himself from his father's influence and the accompanying homosexual slang references. As international tastes discovered the Motown sound, Gaye prospered as one of its most marketable acts. His career and exposure skyrocketed.

He teamed with singer Tammi Terrell on successful duets. She collapsed in his arms during a 1967 performance and was diagnosed with a malignant brain tumor. Her career was finished. She died three years later from brain cancer.

Gaye's trajectory accelerated. His simplistic love ballad recordings during the late 1960s were surpassed by his finest work in 1971. He released his classic *What's Going On*. The album featured the probing depth and timeless societal questioning. The theme was inspired by Gaye's insightful and stark observations of police brutality during anti-war rallies in Berkeley.

The masterpiece severed an introspective nerve in the listening public elevating previously catchy love compositions into a more sustained and complicated pleas towards social consciousness. His lyrics still achingly resonate and reverberate with truth. The lyrics uniquely crossed color lines and illuminated society's sense of estrangement and desperation. The timely songs issued a call towards collective action and healing that remains mute to much of society.

He followed up this commercial breakthrough with the albums *Let's Get It On* and a motion picture soundtrack for the film *Trouble Man*. He began touring internationally and receiving his due acclaim as a substantive voice. His live concert album sales substantiated his stellar performance credentials.

At the absolute pinnacle of commercial success, the adulation and praise shifted. His contentious divorce, rampant cocaine use and a shift in popular music towards disco, temporarily made his own works too sobering for public consumption. His attempts to replicate the senseless dance rhythms of a trending fad proved futile. Marvin Gaye, like so many of his soul music peers, could not evolve in reverse gear. By the conclusion of the decade, social consciousness was no longer in vogue and rampant consumerism was the replacing deity.

Gaye relocated to London to avoid potential imprisonment for back taxes exceeding $4.5 million. His cocaine dependency worsened and his life spiraled into freefall.

Amidst a wreckage of despair and self-loathing, he returned to his elemental strengths. In 1981, he relocated to Ostend, Belgium and began recording new compositions. He curtailed his drug use, began exercising rigorously and performing again. He had fallen into the abyss and clawed resolutely back.

During the subsequent year, CBS records negotiated his contractual release from a willing Motown Records. Within the process, he negotiated a workable settlement with the IRS for his debt. The terms offered a short reprieve and enabled Gaye's return and re-appreciation.

Regaining professional traction, he released possibly the most robust comeback album in history with *Midnight Love* and featured single *Sexual Healing*. The album in January 1983 rejuvenated his career, returning him to elite concert status and opened the window to widely exposed performances and events. Audiences *rediscovered* Marvin Gaye. His earnings were once again flowing and his legitimacy confirmed by substantial music industry awards.

His career was progressively healing but his soul remained troubled.

Returning to the Los Angeles environment that had once nearly destroyed him, he resumed his cocaine dependence and an exhibition of paranoia-oriented behavior. He sought refuge in his parent's West Adams district home. He had purchased their house from his career earnings. The location is adjacent to the Santa Monica Freeway, concealed by a concrete barrier and strategically planted foliage. The neighborhood is comfortable and unpretentious, but borders the more turbulent South Central Los Angeles battlefields across the freeway.

On Christmas Day 1983, Gaye unwisely presented his father with an unlicensed .38 caliber pistol intended for protection against potential intruders. The volatile relationship between father and son was reignited living within close quarters. Old quarrels resurfaced and painful recollections of a strained coexistence tainted both men. His father's stinging criticisms of his son's secular themed music and previous years of purported physical abuse created a contaminated environment.

His temporary sanctuary became his tomb.

Although Marvin Jr., had experienced the highest strata of professional acclaim, achievement and recognition, within the household, he was merely regarded as his father's defiant son. Family members witnessed his re-ascension into chaos fueled by drugs, erratic behavior and suicidal tendencies.

Family conflicts are rarely straightforward. Each member's personal interpretation even less so.

On the morning April 1, 1984, his parents quarreled over an apparently misplaced insurance policy letter. Marvin Jr. intervened. The son sided with his mother. Threats and shouting escalated. Words were replaced by shoves, kicks and violence. Was the childhood victim turning upon the aggressor?

Shortly after noon, Marvin Gay Sr, terminated the dispute. He entered his son's room with the drawn and loaded .38. He targeted his son's heart and fired twice. Marvin Gaye, Jr. died instantly. He was 44-years-old.

Most of the family members rallied around their father's actions. At trial, one of his brother's confided that the killing was Marvin's suicidal wish. An autopsy concluded that Gaye had traces of cocaine and PCP in his system. Gaye's father claimed self-defense and wept uncontrollably when notified he had slain his son. A month and a half following the shooting, a benign tumor was discovered and removed from the base of his brain. Had the tumor contributed to his own erratic response?

A plea bargain agreement to voluntary manslaughter enabled the father a suspended six-year sentence and five years of probation. He did not serve a jail sentence. His wife reportedly filed for divorce the day following the shooting although she posted his bail for release. He died fourteen years later of pneumonia in a Long Beach retirement home, his own ministry long abandoned and forgotten. He publicly expressed remorse for the shooting until the end of his life.

The world lost a talent with perhaps more to contribute by his senseless killing. Sadly even Jesus Christ remarked that a prophet is never honored in his homeland. It is possible Marvin Gaye, Jr. had additional profound works left to provoke and inspire listeners into greater levels of enlightenment.

It is equally likely that his own drug usage had emptied his message. The visionary may have been exhausted and had nothing of consequence remaining to compose.

The Gay Family Residence

Phil Hartman: The Shocking Murder and Suicide From An Unanticipated Source

Actors, performers and especially comedians often lead divergent double existences between their public persona and private lives.

Phil Hartman had established impressive credentials in each of these genres and international exposure for his eight seasons on the *Saturday Night Live* television series. Born in Ontario, Canada, Hartman moved to the United States at ten and graduated with a degree in graphic arts from Cal State University Northridge. He was credited with designing album covers for prestigious rock bands before evolving into comedy circles.

For all of acclaim he had accumulated professionally, his private life proved less stable. His third marriage to Brynn Omdahl in 1987 was mired in turbulence. They had two children together. Omdahl, a former model and aspiring actress could never contend with the success of her husband. Her personal demons escalated into drug dependence and violent mood extremes.

On the evening of May 27, 1998, Brynn Hartman shared dinner with a film industry friend at a nearby Encino restaurant before returning home. A heated and extended argument ensued with her husband regarding her drug use and his threat to leave the marriage. He ended the dispute by going to bed and sleeping soundly.

At 3 a.m., intoxicated and fresh from a snorting bout of cocaine, she entered his bedroom with a .38 caliber handgun. She fatally shot him twice in the head and once in his side. Erratically she drove to the home of a friend and confessed. He initially did not believe her. The two drove back to her residence in separate cars. Her friend discovered the body and immediately telephoned police at 6:20 a.m. Upon arrival, the police escorted her friend and the two Hartman children from the house.

Brynn Hartman locked herself in the bedroom and committed suicide by shooting herself in the head.

The shock, disbelief and subsequent tributes paid to Phil Hartman revealed a man genuinely liked and respected for his enormous talents. Notably absent was an anticipated sense of the impending tragedy. The telling observation was that Phil Hartman the individual was the man that nobody truly knew.

The Former Hartman Encino Residence

Phil Spector: The Crumbling Foundation of a Musical Genius

It appears unthinkable that a music industry icon such as Phil Spector would have squandered fame, prestige and freedom for the haphazardly impulsive killing of Lana Clarkson on February 3, 2003.

The story remains a disjointed puzzle with little coherence or logic.

What has been publicly published is that Lana Clarkson accompanied Spector to his Pyrenees Castle residence that evening out of fascination, curiosity or interest in making a recording industry contact. Her body was found by police, slumped over a chair with a single gunshot wound to her mouth and broken teeth scattered over his carpet. Spector had been observed excessively intoxicated earlier in the evening.

At trial, Spector's driver testified having viewed the fateful gun in his employer's hand and heard a rambling confession to the act. Spector maintained that Clarkson had *kissed the gun* in an accidental suicide. The prosecution introduced evidence from four women that Spector had previously pulled guns on them before while intoxicated when they had refuses his sexual advances.

The jury agreed with the prosecution's contention that his actions were a consistent pattern. He was convicted of second-degree murder in 2008 and sentenced from 19 years to life in prison. He is currently jailed at the California Health Care Facility in Stockton.

Spector pioneered a distinctive production technique incorporating deeply layered tracks of music to create a *Wall of Sound*. This background would pulsate with energy behind the vocal tracks. The technique has been widely emulated and employed by subsequent generations of musicians and producers. Spector legitimately earned the label of *genius* and *innovator* for his musical vision and unique production arrangements. His audio fingerprint remains ingrained on popular music spanning in excess of fifty years.

As a cruel irony, reports since his prison internment have indicated that he has lost his voice permanently due to laryngeal papillomas of the throat. His former home, Pyrenees Castle has also suffered injury with his absence.

The Alhambra based residence was completed in 1927 for the Dupuy family as a retreat funded by their investments in real estate and oil. The property, designed by local architect John Walker Smart rises clandestinely above the squat Alhambra stucco residences. The 8,600 square foot castle features a red tile roof, Italian marble foyer, 10 bedrooms, 8 1/2 baths, secret passages, wine cellar and a host of innovations.

In 1998, Spector acquired the mansion following decades of decay, abandonment and vandalism. The sprawling estate enabled Spector the seclusion he desired and an isolated outlet for his addictions and eccentricities. Imposing foundation slippage and cracking currently has destroyed one of his primary retaining walls. Like Spector's fortune, the crumbling is emblematic of a life that extended past its legacy.

The wall will ultimately be repairable. The lives and fates of Lana Clarkson and Phil Spector cannot.

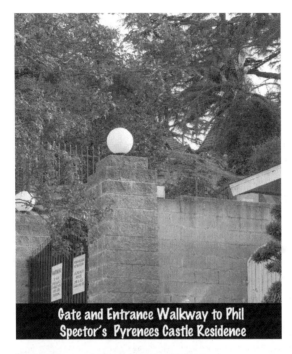

Gate and Entrance Walkway to Phil
Spector's Pyrenees Castle Residence

The Cracking Foundation of Spector's
Pyrenees Castle Foundation

Ramon Novarro: The Gruesome Torture of a Closeted Screen Idol

Ramon Novarro entered the infant silent film industry in 1917 playing small roles. By 1923, his roles became more prominent and he was touted as a rival to Rudolph Valentino as the screen's dominant *Latin Lover*. Upon Valentino's abrupt death in 1926, he ascended to an elite level eclipsed only by actor John Gilbert.

He was considered one of the great romantic lead actors appearing and seducing leading actresses such as Joan Crawford, Norma Shearer, Greta Garbo, Myrna Loy and Lupe Velez. He successfully made the transition into speaking parts with talking films but MGM studios did not renew his contract when it expired in 1935. He continued with minor inconsequential roles into the 1960s as his fame receded.

Novarro was born Jose Ramon Gil Samaniego to a well respected family who had emigrated from Durango, Mexico to Los Angeles in 1913 to escape a revolution in their country. His ancestry was traced back to the small Castilian town of Burgos.

He was one of thirteen children from a devout Roman Catholic family. Three of his sisters became nuns. His Catholic background created troubling conflicts with his lifestyle. His screen image as a dashing ladies man was fabricated. His closet homosexuality, while not novel in the film industry, traumatized him and influenced a directly attributed alcoholism.

He invested wisely in a Hollywood Hills residence, designed in 1927 by Lloyd Wright, the son of his more renowned architect father. He maintained a comfortable lifestyle with his former earnings. The man and his legacy became largely forgotten until his violent death.

Novarro became a frail and lonely alcoholic. On October 30, 1968, he hired two brothers, Paul and Tom Ferguson, aged 22 and 17, from a sex agency for services. What transpired that evening involved a severe beating administered by the brothers to Novarro when he failed to provide $5,000 presumed to be hidden on the premises. Novarro died by asphyxiation from his own blood.

The brothers were arrested and convicted to extended prison terms, but released on probation during the mid-1970s. Each would return to prison for a variety of offenses. Tom Ferguson committed suicide in 2005. Paul Ferguson is currently interned at the Crossroads Correction Center in Cameron, Missouri due to a 1989 conviction for rape and sodomy.

The disclosure of alternative sexual orientations amongst leading male actors has significantly evolved within mainstream cinema. Acceptance hasn't become universal. Novarro was rightfully protective of his reputation and public legacy. The ultimate selection of his paid companionship proved fatal.

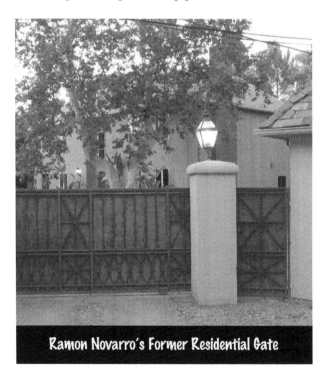

Ramon Novarro's Former Residential Gate

Ronni Chasen: When Two Divergent Worlds Collide

The divergent universes of motion picture publicist Ronni Chasen and unemployed felon Harold Martin Smith rudely collided shortly after midnight on November 16, 2010.

Smith's vehicle (or potentially bicycle), sidled up to Chasen's late model Mercedes-Benz from the passenger side at the popularly traveled corner of Sunset Boulevard and Whittier Drive in Beverly Hills. It is presumed that Smith intended to rob Chasen who was returning from a film premier. What transpired during the exchange may only be speculated. Chasen probably attempted to drive off and was shot point blank with five hollow-pointed bullets, an unusual form of ammunition employed by someone nearly destitute.

After being shot, her car veered towards a curb and toppled over a concrete streetlight. Investigators found Chasen slumped over in her seat with the steering wheel airbag inflated. She had blood flowing from her nose and chest area. The front passenger side window was shattered from the shooting.

Speculation initially concentrated around various motives for her homicide including a contract killing. None made sense, as she hadn't cultivated any discernable enemies. Smith was a habitual criminal with a background in burglary and drug possession. He had been discharged on parole the previous year. He had confided to neighbors that he was the responsible party for the killing and claimed had done so for money. Police ultimately discounted his claims as simple boasting.

Harold Smith was fingered as a possible suspect based on a tip generated from an *America's Most Wanted* television emission. When investigators approached Smith at his East Hollywood apartment, he turned a gun on himself and committed suicide. The gun was identified as Chasen's murder weapon.

In the end, investigators concluded the killing was the consequence of a randomly botched robbery.

Even amidst the lush atmosphere of wealth and opulence, the divide between rich and impoverished, respectable and criminal is illusionary. For all of the security insulation a life of achievement and compensation brought Ronni Chasen, unforeseen fate intruded into her carefully constructed life.

The Fateful Intersection of the Shooting

The Telephone Pole Which Chasen Crashed Into

Sal Mineo: A Career Comeback Suddenly Curtailed

Sal Mineo's acting career had reached a plateau and decline by the age of 37. He had earned significant praise for his film roles in *Rebel Without A Cause*, *The Man in the Gray Flannel Suit*, *Tonka*, *Exodus* and a variety of television role performances. He had even recorded a record album that featured two top-forty singles.

His exotic appearance and acting skills initially elevated him into matinee idol status with women. His later reputation for homosexuality often precluded his consideration for leading roles. Mineo, like many in his profession was well recognized, but not successful enough to guarantee him prominent career sustainability.

The decline in his public popularity began with his own aging. His most famous roles were based on teenage parts. He acquired enough post-teen acting credits to sustain his credentials, but wealth did not accompany. The apartment complex where he resided was located a block below Hollywood's Sunset Strip, but in a neighborhood that no one would confuse with Beverly Hills.

On February 12, 1976, Mineo was playing the role of a bisexual burglar in a comedy theatre production of *P.S. Your Cat is Dead*. The play had attracted a popular following during its San Francisco run and the cast was preparing for the Los Angeles production.

Arriving at his apartment following a rehearsal, Mineo was approached by Lionel Ray Williams, a pizza deliveryman in a robbery attempt. He was stabbed to death on a spot where his rear driveway intersected with the sloping pathway to his apartment entrance. The knife blade lodged into his heart inducing immediate and fatal internal bleeding. A year after Mineo's death, a similar fatal stabbing occurred in the neighborhood claiming the life of actress Christa Helm. The case remained unsolved until Williams was arrested for the crime.

In 1979, he was tried and convicted for the murder along with ten other robberies in the same area. He was sentenced to 57 years in prison. He was paroled within thirteen years. He would return to familiar incarceration later for assorted crimes. Williams is currently removed from the California prison rolls and presumed living.

Mineo's career may have been resuscitated by his theatre role. The debate is pointless. The entertainment industry habitually has a notoriously short memory span for actors and actresses that have the audacity to age.

Mineo Was Slain Where The Shrubbery Meet The Walkway

The Abrupt Departure of a Soul Music Legend In His Prime

In the winter of 1964, Sam Cooke was an established international star enthroned atop the popular music industry. Between 1957 and 1964, he had registered thirty American top 40 hits. His most renowned compositions and distinctive renditions of *You Send Me*, *Cupid, Wonderful World*, *Chain Gang* and *Twistin' the Night Away* still stir emotional sensibilities.

His pioneering publishing, business acumen and performance contributions directly influenced the rise and sustainability of soul music legends Aretha Franklin, Bobby Womack, Al Green, Stevie Wonder, Marvin Gaye, Billy Preston, Curtis Mayfield, Otis Redding and James Brown.

In his prime at 33, this handsome and charismatic performer had not only established an enduring legacy, but also possessed the ambition, talent and capacity to distance and surpass his contemporaries. He was prolifically creative, inspired and directly involved in every aspect of his production arrangements.

By late 1964, he was twice married and once divorced. He had three children by his second wife although one had died at the age of two.

On the evening of December 11, 1964, Cooke attended a Los Angeles nightclub and shared time with Elisa Boyer who he'd met there. Instead of escorting her home as she claimed to have repeatedly requested, he checked both of them into the seamy Hacienda Motel on South Figueroa Street. The property has varied minimally over the ensuing decades with the exception of name and ownership changes.

Varied accounts and chronologies of events have differed over each participant's role, intent and fault in the subsequent tragedy. Each version has stimulated dispute and even more questions.

Boyer's versions indicated that upon his use of the bathroom to take a shower, she accidentally grabbed some of his intermingled clothing with hers while attempting a hasty flight from the property. She testified at a preliminary inquest, she feared Cooke was intent on raping her. Other versions suggest that she had deliberately enticed him to the motel to steal his wallet and belongings.

Cooke reportedly raced furiously down the staircase into the manager's office apparently wearing only a sports coat and his shoes. He assumed that Boyer was hiding in the office despite manager Bertha Franklin's denials. Franklin claimed Cooke exhibited intimidating and violent behavior that escalated into an ensuing verbal and physical struggle. Franklin retrieved a shotgun from the back and mortally shot Cooke dead in the torso.

Her claim of self-defense and Boyer's corroboration of events resulted in an inquest ruling of *justifiable homicide*. Suspicions remain over inconsistencies and the credibility of the testimony, particularly amongst family members and associates closest to Cooke. Subsequent evidence has not shed any new insight into the events.

What becomes obvious is that Sam Cooke was in the *wrong* location, with the *wrong* person at the *wrong* time.

His death became yet another tragic creative force that ending prematurely. We will never know what beauty he may have further revealed.

Original Hacienda Motel

Motel Staircase and Courtyard

Father Eric Freed's Brutal Slaying: A Lost Coast of Fractured Souls

Eureka has made inroads towards the rehabilitation of its historic center core. The seaside business district adjacent to Arcata Bay appears inviting. The extended breakwater of the Samoa Peninsula stretches protectively along its western border guarding against tidal shifts from the turbulent Pacific Ocean.

Decorative Victorian era structures are being refurbished to their former preeminence. Decorative murals create a sense of colorful vibrancy and developmental infrastructure investment is evident.

Yet something appears amiss amidst the change. The picturesque seaport touts itself as the *Lost Coast of California*. There exists a sense of defiance against conforming to the traditional seaside stylized resort. There is marginal pretense amidst this gentrified façade. Alongside the civic improvements are a prevalent street population of homeless, drug abusers and the mentally ill. The visual evidence is neither camouflaged nor likely to ever be economically eradicated.

Blame has traditionally been laid on the decades long cannabis trade cultivated within the nearby forests. Humboldt County has evolved into a recognized magnet for transients and counter-culturists.

Stronger and more lethal hallucinogenics such as heroin, cocaine, meth-amphetamines and prescription pharmaceuticals have accompanied the marijuana trade. Since late 2016, recreational use marijuana has become legal within California. Cannabis legalization has been unproven to lessen the dependence or usage of these stronger and more addictive drugs.

Violence has traditionally accompanied the illegal drug trade. The nearby Rancho Sequoia area of Alderpoint is renowned for its marijuana cultivation farms. The territory was renamed

Murder Mountain following several high-profile disappearances and homicides.

Legalized pot is unlikely to thin or eliminate the desperate individuals that stalk Eureka's downtown avenues. One such individual, Gary Lee Bullock, personified the menace of a wandering fractured soul. His lethal rage towards Father Eric Freed, Pastor at Eureka's St. Bernard Church altered both of their fates.

Bullock, a heroin and meth addict exhibited a pattern of disturbing behavior during the daytime of New Years Eve, 2013. He was familiar with a transient lifestyle. Despite only previous minor legal entanglements, nothing could replicate how he spent his final evening of freedom. Perhaps that morning, his drug addiction had finally spiraled beyond redemption.

No one except he can confirm what he had ingested that fateful morning. Around 9:00 a.m., he confined a woman against her will at a motel that his brother owned and where he had previously lived. The property was in Redway, 65 miles south of Eureka, adjacent to Interstate 101. Sheriff Deputies were telephoned about the disturbance but Bullock fled before their arrival.

By the early afternoon he had resurfaced locally and became involved in a verbal battle with another man that escalated into a physical altercation. Bullock was speaking incoherently and presumed under the influence. He again fled before apprehension but was spotted inside a nearby trailer park.

He burst into one residence but was forcibly evicted. He was emitting wild noises and gyrating erratically. After being tossed out of the unit, he attempted to conceal himself behind hedges of juniper bushes. Sheriff's Deputies finally tracked him, calmed him down and then arrested him. En route to the County Jail in downtown Eureka, he resumed his rage and attempted to kick out the windows of the patrol car.

He was booked into the jail at 3:30 p.m. but refused a medical examination despite being under the constant restraint of law enforcement personnel. He lingered in confinement for nine hours. A departmental decision-maker made a fateful and flawed determination. They released him at 12:45 a.m. onto the downtown streets of Eureka, far from where he'd begun the day.

The officer's rationale was he they had no further legal authority to continue to contain him. Yet this decision seemed to lack common sense. Why release a violently disturbed individual into the dead of night with no means of accommodations? He was reportedly instructed where he might find a homeless shelter, but left unescorted into the darkness.

Two principal one-way street arteries partition downtown Eureka. Both are segments of Interstate Highway 101. From the jail, Fifth Street heads north towards the Humboldt County coastline. Sixth Street ventures south towards the downtown. Exiting the jail stairway on Fifth Street, Bullock walked one block east on J Street. He turned right towards Sixth Street and following traffic one block further arrived at the corner of Sixth and I Streets. This intersection was the location of the St. Bernard Church and Rectory.

Churches have historically been considered destinations for sanctuary. For a deranged, desperate and disoriented individual seeking shelter on a hostile New Years Eve, he may have considered its portals his sole outlet. Within an hour after his release, the video cameras mounted on the church and rectory captured his erratic sequence of activities.

He rang all of the building's doorbells. He pounded ferociously on the front and back doors of both the church and rectory. He attempted to try doorknobs and isolate vulnerable window openings without success. Either the sole occupant Father Freed was a comatose sleeper or simply used to the solicitations of unwelcome outsiders. He lived inside and lodged upstairs.

At 2:10 a.m. two uniformed security guards escorted Bullock off of the property. The problem appeared solved. Yet the problem was far from resolved. Bullock returned eight minutes later upon their departure.

He resumed his entry efforts in the patio area and found a vulnerable woman's bathroom door. He remained inside for half an hour. This location proved only a temporary solution. Another half-hour later, he was viewed dislodging an eight-foot pipe from one of the rectory's south walls. He also removed a wooden stake from the rear garden.

Bullock considered more aggressive tactics with his newly found tools. Around 3:00 a.m., another uniformed individual accosted him. This individual was presumed to be a police officer due to an apparent visible badge. Apparently unaware of what had transpired with Bullock earlier in the day, he routinely chased him off the property. Bullock's absence was short-lived. He returned to the unlocked bathroom and his familiar pattern of strolling around the building speculating on his best means of access.

At 4:00 a.m., Bullock initiated decisive action. He shattered a back window on the north side of the rectory building and crawled through. He returned outside to retrieve a portion of the metal pipe and wooden stack. By this stage, his fury became manifested into torture. Was Father Freed cognizant of the noise? If so, there was no published record that he telephoned the police for assistance.

During the next two hours, Bullock's inhuman brutality included vicious blows resulting in fractured bones throughout Freed's head and body. The blunt impact was accompanied by violent slashing from a broken cone-shaped glass vase. The macabre scene resembled ritualistic torture.

Once the massacre was completed, Bullock wrapped Freed in a blanket and doused him with liquor. He attempted to ignite the priest unsuccessfully. The rectory was ransacked and a cigar was left smoldering near a gas burner on a downstairs stove. His intent was presumably oriented towards igniting the rectory and destroying all evidence of his actions.

The cigar extinguished itself. Later, a Sheriff's deputy would turn off the gas averting a potential explosion. At 6:45 a.m., Bullock emerged from the rectory with a remote garage door opener. He stole Father Freed's car and drove back to his family's residence. En route, he stopped to dump assorted personal items of Father Freed's into the nearby Eel River. Four days later, several of these items were found beneath the Miranda Bridge including a bright red travel case, humidor and cigars, hymnal, business card and Japanese Bible. Father Freed had lived twenty years previously in Japan.

Father Freed's body was discovered by a Church Deacon New Years Day morning when he failed to show up for the 9 a.m. mass. His body was lying face up in the middle of the bedroom floor with blood spread over his face. On the afternoon of the following day, Bullock was apprehended without resistance.

Bullock's insanity plea was rejected during his 2016 trial. He was found guilty of murder, carjacking, burglary and attempted arson. He was sentenced to two concurrent life sentences without the possibility of parole and is currently imprisoned at the Pleasant Valley State Prison in Coalinga.

Blame is convenient and simplistic to spread towards law enforcement authorities in this instance. But is the blame justified for these tragic consequences?

Eureka is not the only American community with a transient substance abuse and mental illness population. Bullock's extreme actions were not easily anticipated. He has a substantial peerage loitering aimlessly amidst streets and communities throughout America seemingly ready to detonate. But where can you contain this population when mental health facilities are already overburdened and given a mandate to downsize?

The police cannot be blamed for failing to reform an uncontrollable epidemic of damaged lives from substance abuse and mental illness. They can only clean up the carnage in the aftermath and vainly attempt to patrol and moderate some form of public scrutiny and coherence.

When individuals opt to pursue their own form of regressive suicide by substance addiction, casualties are inevitable. We are not winning the campaign against drug abuse devastation by simply legalizing one. Until society's insatiable user demand ceases, the battle lines will remain in our own neighborhoods.

St. Bernard's Rectory

Entry Window

The Continued Fascination With the Black Dahlia Murder

What is it about the lurid murder and severed torso of 22-year-old Elizabeth Short that still fascinates?

On the morning of January 15, 1947, Short's nude body was discovered in two pieces on an empty lot in the Leimert Park residential complex being constructed nearby the Los Angeles Memorial Coliseum. Today, the vacant space has been replaced by a nondescript single-level house and lawn, indistinguishable from others in the neighboring tract.

Elizabeth Short's brief life was similarly ordinary. The press sensationalized her biography as a call girl and adventuress. The mundane truth is that her life was far from sensational. She had shuffled residences between her bi-coastal divorced parents. She suffered from asthma and bronchitis. She lived and worked in various West Coast cities. She was once arrested at sixteen for underage drinking.

Her juvenile arrest remains our predominant visual image of Elizabeth Short. Her black and white mugshot features a stunning symmetrical face with pronounced cheekbones, curly raven hair and haunting penetrating eyes that rivet our attention.

Frothing newspaper coverage erroneously nicknamed her the *Black Dahlia* while following her sensationalized murder. The reference came from a film noir murder mystery film released several months earlier called *The Blue Dahlia*.

Historically unsolved murders within California are not uncommon. Typically, more publicized and notorious killings prompt more creative suppositions. The search for Elizabeth Short's killer fueled paths to many suspects, purported confessions, speculations, books and film adaptations of the story. Each theory has lacked a provable ending and the fascination towards investigation continues unimpeded by the impossibility of resolution.

The shocking brutality and inhumanity of her murder eludes contemporary novelty based on a desensitized public. Modern television and film graphically depict similar visually abusive images. Digital technology has enabled us to view unimaginable horror from a detached perspective.

In 1947, despite following a cataclysmic global war with millions of innocent casualties, Americans remained susceptible to outrage and absorption about one single senseless homicide,

The continued public fascination over Elizabeth Short's isolated death still defies explanation. Sadly, justice for her killing, even over seventy years after the fact becomes more imaginative than possible.

In 1947, despite following a cataclysmic global war with millions of innocent casualties, Americans remained susceptible to outrage and absorption about one single senseless homicide,

The continued public fascination over Elizabeth Short's isolated death still defies explanation. Sadly, justice for her killing, even over sixty-five years after the fact becomes more imaginative than possible.

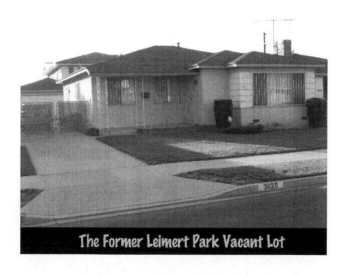

The Former Leimert Park Vacant Lot

The Silent and Senseless Murder of Lindsay Cutshall and Jason Allen

Sonoma County's Russian River empties into the Pacific Ocean through a gulch severing Goat's Rock Beach and Fish Head Beach adjacent to the town of Jenner, California. Jenner, population 136, is a slumbering afterthought wedged into the winding topography of the Pacific Coast Highway (Highway 1) as motorists pass headed towards Mendocino.

If one pauses to rest in Jenner it is doubtlessly either due to the stunning panoramic views or the sheer tedium of the drive. A few modest hotel properties service the tourist clientele. August weekends are a near certainty to be fully occupied.

The route between Jenner and Mendocino features erratic patches of sunshine, even during the summer months. Tanning is not its primary appeal, rather spectacular rock formations, elevated bluffs, crashing surf and an abundant sea lion population. Such pristine and elemental beauty invites contemplation, admiration and pause for reflection.

Like generations of precedent visitors Lindsay Cutshall, 22, and her fiancé Jason S. Allen, 26, were moved by the splendor. They recorded their impressions during the sunset of August 14, 2004 in a personal travel journal.

"The sun is going down in the horizon," Lindsay wrote. "All I see is the beams shining on the cliff face. And I know that God is awsome (sic). I look around and I see his creation all around me."

Jason wrote: "As I stir this Mac & Cheese I think to myself what a wonderful life. I've just spent two awsome (sic) days with my fiancé Lindsay. Can life ever be so perfect. Only with a person who is so great. God gives me this privilege in life and He has given me a wonderful woman to enjoy it."

Later that same evening or early the following morning, the young Midwestern couple were shot to death as they slept fully clothed in separate sleeping bags on an obscured stretch of Fish Head Beach. Their bodies were not discovered until Wednesday, August 18, when a Sheriff's helicopter was dispatched following a report of a man who was stranded on a cliff above Fish Head Beach. The helicopter spotted the bodies and notified the department.

Both Cutshall and Allen were killed with an 1894 Marlin .45 caliber long rifle, either a long colt style, or a carbine magazine. The rifle was both uncommon and too high a caliber for common use by ranchers in the area. Shell casings were not found at the scene of the crime, suggesting the killer retrieved them.

Cutshall and Allen's travel journal with their handwritten entries were found inside a secure small wooden hutch on the beach near their makeshift campsite.

Lindsay Cutshall was from Fresno, Ohio and Jason Allen from Zeeland, Michigan. The couple met in 2002 while Cutshall was a student at Appalachian Bible College in West Virginia, and became engaged six weeks later. They planned to marry in the autumn of 2004.

During the fateful weekend of their death, they had enjoyed an impromptu getaway from the Christian youth adventure camp near Placerville where they worked. Their outing included visits to Fisherman's Wharf in San Francisco, crossing the Golden Gate Bridge and climaxed by a picturesque drive along the meandering Pacific Coast highway. They settled upon their sleeping arrangements at Fish Head Beach because on the evening of August 14, all of Jenner's accommodation properties were booked. Their selected stretch of beach was secluded and guaranteed privacy.

None of Cutshall's or Allen's belongings had been taken, ruling out robbery as a motive, and neither of the campers had been sexually assaulted. Their car, a battered red Ford Tempo was parked in a pullout spot on the side of Highway 1 in Jenner and untouched. A silent, single bullet to the skull had executed each. The evening overcast, common to northern Sonoma County, masked the moon and neither likely had any advanced warning that they were not alone.

Camping and overnight sleeping is prohibited, but not uncommon amidst drifters and hitchhikers on the rural stretch of beach. Warning signage is evident on the primary path that leads from the highway to the beach below. Initial police speculation concentrated on a roaming drifter murdering the young couple and then leaving the area.

Crude Satanic and Dragonesque images and abundant profanity were scrawled and carved on some of the nearby bleached driftwood. When they were drawn was never determined. Ten years later, they remain. Were the writings symbolic of a more sinister evil or merely expressions of common adolescent angst?

Despite exhaustive efforts by detectives, the scant evidence, no apparent motive and minimal clues yielded no solid leads or suspects. Over a decade later, the case remains cold but open.

All that remain are unanswerable questions. Waves habitually pound the shoreline in their custom only to recede into repetition. Tides rise and lower as they have for centuries oblivious to human existence. The stark coastal beauty reminds us that for Lindsay Cutshall and Jason Allen, their last evening together on earth served perhaps as a welcoming prelude to the paradise that their religious beliefs anticipated.

Ignored Beach Entry Warning Sign

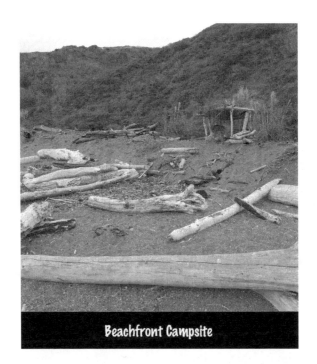

Beachfront Campsite

Driftwood Drawings

Was a 1963 Beachfront Slaying of a High School Couple a Prelude to Future Terror?

On Tuesday, June 4, 1963, the Senior Class of Lompoc High School was celebrating their traditional *cut* day. None of the students would be obliged to attend school. Over two-thirds of the graduating students had decided to congregate at a school-sponsored gathering at Goleta Beach, located slightly north of Santa Barbara.

Bob Domingos and Linda Edwards had alternative plans at a remote beach far from the assemblage and further north near Gaviota. Bob, 18, and Linda, 17, were soon graduating like the others and planning their upcoming November wedding. Private and intimate time together was scarce living with their parents. His family owned a modest 60-acre ranch on the periphery of Lompoc. Domingos was popular and responsible, being an officer in the Future Farmers of America, guard on the school's football team and working both on the family farm and for Richfield delivering gas locally.

The couple had invited one of their close friends to join them that day but she cancelled when her boyfriend was obliged to work.

As was the local custom, Domingos parked his distinctive two-tone copper and black colored Pontiac under a grove of eucalyptus trees alongside Highway 101. Their selected stretch of beach was secluded but easily accessible by crossing parallel railroad tracks and descending a sloping path lined by concealing shrubbery. The coastline as it did then, remains stark and unspoiled. It is camouflaged from a roadside view by vegetation and exotic sculptured stones shaped by the breaking waves. The topography and access route remain identical.

Assorted sized rounded stones inundate the beach with limited sand patches. The isolated spot offers privacy and is still a popular local fishing site. Such purity remains a reminder of the pristine grandeur of the vanishing California coastline.

At some point during their daytime reverie, probably the late afternoon, the couple was visited by a shadowy outside presence.

An intruder sadistically fired eleven bullets into Domingo from behind and eight into Edwards, one with the force to shatter her right leg. Physical resistance by Domingos was evidenced by his facial bruises and may have prompted the excessive shooting. Perhaps he had fought the intruder and then attempted escape. Powder burns indicated that most of the shots were fired from close range and from a .22 caliber automatic weapon, probably a pistol.

Published accounts vary slightly and conclusively on details. Some theories have suggested their killer approached them while they were absently sunbathing. Edwards was then reportedly obliged to bind Domingos at gunpoint with lengths of pre-cut narrow rope. Not all accounts have even mentioned the rope bindings. Some have suggested the weapon was a rifle. Most accounts concur that the killer was already on the beach before their arrival.

In the aftermath, the murderer methodically dragged both dead bodies an estimated thirty feet into a nearby shack that was discreetly located nearby an adjacent run off creek. The shanty was used by transients and popular with local teenagers. Its unobtrusive location might have served as the killer's own sleeping quarters the previous evening, enabling his knowledge of its existence.

The shack no longer stands and several decades of overgrowth and impassability have buried its location. Photographed adjacently piled leaves and limited wood charring evidence suggested an attempt was initiated to burn the structure afterwards. The attempt was either aborted or unsuccessful.

The killer laid Domingo face down underneath Edwards who

faced upwards. Her one-piece bathing suit had been sliced at the top revealing her breasts. Newspaper accounts were adamant in reporting that she had not been sexually molested.

The couple's two fathers, Linda's brother and an on duty California Highway Patrol officer discovered the bodies on the following evening in the pitch darkness illuminated by only a single flashlight.

Over a half century has elapsed since the double homicide and resolution remains as remote as motive. Revenge was ruled out based on the couple's popularity and acknowledged absence of enemies.

Two intriguing speculations have emerged that have never been conclusively answered.

The day before, a local stone quarrier pocketing $360 was knifed to death during a robbery involving three individuals. Two of the trio resided locally and were aware of the victim's reputation for carrying large sums of money. The third party and the killer was a transient they had picked up hitchhiking and who had participated in a few petty thefts with them. The locally residing accomplices were so unnerved by the savagery and impulsiveness of his violence that they stranded the murderer who they called *Sandy* (based on his hair color) at a nearby motel.

When the two were eventually captured, they related his role to murder investigators, which proved sustainable. Unfortunately, the time lapse between their capture and information provided about their mysterious companion were erroneous. Sandy had vanished.

Sandy's composite drawing resembled the future Northern California Zodiac serial killer, particularly his wearing horned rimmed glasses. The Zodiac's first authenticated murder of David Faraday and Betty Lou Jenson in Vallejo was still five years from occurring. Coincidentally (or not), one of the principal Zodiac suspects Arthur Leigh Allen was suspected to have lived in a nearby Lompoc trailer during the approximate time period. Other Allen related associations tease with possibility. He was later interned in the nearby Atascadero State Prison between 1975-1977 on pedophilia charges when the Zodiac written correspondence ceased abruptly and permanently.

At the height of the Zodiac pursuit during 1972, the Sheriff of Santa Barbara County announced similarities in evidence and execution with the Domingos/Edwards killings. In a press conference he concluded there was strong evidence of a correlation with the Zodiac case. The linkages were never explicitly documented and the story wilted soon afterwards. Perhaps his connecting assumption was Allen who was by 1972 an active subject of interest in the Zodiac investigation. Pragmatically his announcement may have simply been a publicity gesture to revive a cold case with zero thawing prospects.

Were the killing of Bob Domingos and Linda Edward the Zodiac's first victims? Did the couple unintentionally disturb a desperate fugitive named Sandy? Was Sandy the Zodiac?

This direction of questioning will never find a sustainable conclusion. The most maddening aspect of an unsolved murder investigation is that each puzzle piece collected results in an even murkier task of assembling it into the proper context.

For the unexplainable and apparently motiveless killing of Domingos and Edwards, resolution became permanently and irrefutably swept out with the tide.

Pathway to the Beach

Probable Murder Site Beach Stretch

Rugged but Stunning Coastline

The Santa Rosa Hitchhiking Murders: Preying on the Innocent

It is inconceivable to imagine an era when hitchhiking was an acceptable alternative for those who either did not have automobiles or were underage to drive. People debate whether we are more secure or vigilant today based on statistical decreases in violent crime. Perhaps we've simply become less trusting and vulnerable than during the early 1970s.

The San Francisco Bay Area then was a hub for mass murderers and none were more repulsive than the Santa Rosa hitchhiker killer. He preyed upon predominantly teenage girls thumbing for rides on Interstate 101 and the backroads of northern Sonoma County.

Sonoma County has long been renowned as a wine production belt and during the early 1970s, the landscape was predominantly rural and unpopulated. Today, housing and commercial developments have supplanted much of the geography.

The killings began on February 4, 1972 when two middle school students Maureen Sterling and Yvonne Weber, both 12, were returning home following an evening of ice-skating at the Redwood Empire Ice Arena (since renamed after Peanut's creator Charles Schultz). The girls disappeared at approximately 9 p.m. and were last seen hitch
hiking on Guerneville Road. Both bodies would be found tossed together ten months later on a steep embankment. The cause of death could not be determined due to the deterioration of the remains.

Exactly one month later, Santa Rosa Junior College student Kim Allen, 19, was given a ride by two men from her job at a natural foods store in San Rafael and dropped off at the Bell Avenue entrance to Highway 101. She was carrying a large wooden soy barrel with red Chinese characters on it. She was discovered the

206

following day on a creek bed between Santa Rosa and Glen Ellen. She had been bound, raped and slowly strangled. The two men who had provided her original ride were discovered but ruled out as suspects after passing a polygraph test.

On November 11, 1972, Lori Kursa, 13, disappeared while shopping in Santa Rosa with her mother. She had a reputation for both running away and hitchhiking. Her frozen remains were discovered a month later in a ravine northeast of Rincon Valley in Santa Rosa. She had not been raped but had died from a broken neck. A witness indicated he saw two Caucasian males earlier shoving a young woman into a van and drive towards the direction where she was discovered.

Carolyn Davis, 14, ran away from her home in Shasta County in early February 1973, but officially disappeared July 15, 1973 after being dropped off by her grandmother at the Garberville Post Office. She was last seen that same day hitchhiking from a Highway 101 exit ramp in the city. Her body was discovered two weeks later at the identical location as Yvonne Weber's and Maureen Sterling's. She was killed by strychnine poisoning apparently a week before her death. There was no conclusive evidence she had been raped.

The only victim who had reached the age of majority, Theresa Walsh, 23, was intending to hitchhike to Garberville from Zuma Beach in Malibu to visit her family for the Christmas holiday. She was last seen on December 22, 1973 the day she had departed and was found six days later, partially submerged in Mark West Creek by kayakers. She had been tied up and sexually assaulted. She was determined to have been dead for approximately one week. There was speculation due to heavy seasonal rains that her body may have drifted several miles.

With the media attention focused on higher profile killers such as the Zodiac, David Carpenter and Edmund Kemper, the Sonoma County killings did not generate the same level of attention. Each of these killers was investigated as suspects but their involvement was never substantiated.

Instead, six young woman and doubtlessly more were victims of a maniac due to their basic lack of transportation and discernment in choosing an outlet.

Kim Allen's Body Location

Therese Walsh's Body Discovery

Location of Yvonne Weber, Maureen
Sterling and Carolyn Davis' Bodies

Raymond Washington: A Cycle of Senseless Violence Devours A Former Leader

It was fatalistic that the patriarch who elevated Los Angeles gang warfare should be eliminated by one of his descendants.

On August 10, 1979 at approximately 10 p.m., 25-year-old Raymond Washington was gunned down on the corner of South San Pedro and 64th Street in the South Central district of Los Angeles. He was the victim of yet another drive-by shooting. He appeared familiar with his killers. A passenger leveled him fatally with a sawed-off shotgun as he approached their vehicle. He died two hours later. There was no clear motive, no suspects and once again, no coherence behind the slaying.

Washington's notoriety was based on being a founding member of the violent African-American *Crips* street gang recruited from the housing projects of Watts. Their lethal feuds with another gang, the *Bloods* from Compton and other affiliated gangs became legendary urban lore. Their rivalry was visually differentiated by distinctive apparel colors, graffiti symbolism and hand gestures.

A disintegrating cycle of violence and death encircled Washington's brief life ultimately strangling him. He was the youngest son of four from a broken home. He spent the second half of the 1970s in prison and detachedly observed a transformation in the scope of gang operations. Neighborhood gangs were initially organized under the guise of neighborhood *protection* and *security*. Their orientation changed.

Washington's forte was his intimidating muscular physique, meanness and proficiency in fistfights. During his incarceration, the rival conflicts escalated into weaponry. By the time of his release, Washington had no more control over the gang he founded than keeping the violence contained. Lucrative drug distribution and extortion had altered the financial orientation of gangs and infighting became inherent between competitors.

Washington's prison stay had effectively relinquished any control he might have once commanded. Aside from his expressed interest in consolidating the various regional gangs into a united organization, he was adamantly opposed to infringing immigration into his controlled neighborhood environment. Organized street gang membership and illicit activity has since spread internationally.

A life constructed on blood feuds typically can have only a singular outcome. There are no memorials commemorating Raymond Washington's life within his neighborhood or death site. Instead, graffiti, discarded furniture and a pronounced absence of urban Los Angeles economic vitality remain.

A variety of diverse ethnicities have since infiltrated South Central Los Angeles necessitated by economics. The poor and disenfranchised are obliged to pay cheaper rents with compromised security. The terrain is terrifying to outsiders and an incentive for the ambitious raised there to vacate when circumstances allow.

Could Raymond Washington's life been redeemed or transformed? Two of his top associates, Stanley *Tookie* Williams and Gregory *Batman* Davis initiated efforts via children's books and non-profit organizations to combat movements they helped pioneer. Williams' was executed at San Quentin in 2005 for killing four individuals in two separate armed robberies.

Any moral behind his death has been obscured behind the grim statistics of subsequent senseless fatalities. Lifestyle glorifications through popular films, music and clothing trends have created a gang fashion *chic*. The horrifying realities reveal a more severe and sobering scenario.

Buoyancy is a fragile commodity for the young men and women of South Central Los Angeles. Their odds of violent death multiply the longer they reside on their vicious streets and choose to participate in an affiliate gang.

Raymond Washington helped create the monster that ultimately devoured him. Other ambitious successors wait their turn.

The Fatal Shooting Location

David Nadel: The Death of a Man and Rebirth of a Performance Icon

The Ashkenaz Club is Berkeley's most renowned live world music club venue. Many of the organization's supporters claim Ashkenaz was *multicultural* before the term was even coined.

Performance artist David Nadel founded Ashkenaz in 1973 after relocating from Los Angeles to attend UC Berkeley. Nadel began the center as a collective with a dance troupe and expanded into the present location on San Pablo Avenue. The organization drew its name from his Ashkenazi Jewish ancestry and resembles an Eastern European synagogue.

On December 19, 1996, an unruly patron, Juan Rivera Perez was ejected from the club. He returned a half hour later knocking on the front door. Nadel answered and was greeted by a handgun shot to his head. He died two days later.

Perez was reportedly enrolled in an *English As A Second Language* program and was attending the nightclub as part of a graduation program. He reportedly fled to his native Mexico, which historically has been uncooperative in extraditing violent criminals back to the United States.

He remains at large today.

In the wake of Nadel's murder, a group of Ashkenaz patrons purchased the building and re-opened the club six months later. It continues to operate today.

Nadel was renowned as a global activist and supporter of numerous and varied causes. One might dispute his political leanings, but no one challenged his generosity and passion. Nadel's death widened the base of ownership participation but sadly his killer will probably never face accountability for his murder.

Ashkenaz Front Entrance

Geneva Ellroy: The Transference of Tragedy Into Literary Expression

Reading author James Ellroy's *My Dark Places* is an exercise in observing the lingering and consequential effects of an unsolved murder in the life of a survivor.

On the late evening of Saturday, June 21, 1958, Ellroy's mother, Geneva (Jean) was viciously strangled with a cotton cord and one of her stockings. She was dragged on asphalt and dumped in an acacia and ivy thicket. The location was a lane known as Kings Row, behind the Arroyo High School football stadium in El Monte. She was a redheaded 37-year-old divorcee and registered nurse.

Pearls from a broken necklace led to the body. According to newspaper accounts, she was disheveled in a torn blue dress with no undergarments. A navy blue coat covered the nude half of her lower body and one stocking was pulled down to her ankle. Her brassiere had been removed.

Her murder was the fourth committed in El Monte up to that point in 1958. Her killer was never identified. Unlike the other three homicides, which were followed by quick arrests, Ellroy's killing lacked substantive leads, motive and witnesses. Police sought for questioning an unidentified blonde woman with a ponytail. The two women had been sighted together the evening before at a local cocktail bar. Ellroy's car was located in the parking lot on the day following her murder.

The crime generated local coverage briefly, but the urgency behind the investigation withered.

For 10-year-old son James Ellroy, the consequences proved both devastating and pivotal towards the shaping of his personal and professional direction.

He candidly documented his adolescent and adult demons in his autobiography *My Dark Places*. The book traced the author's decent into depression, anti-social behavior, alcoholism and drug addition. He detailed much of his personal decline towards his mother's abrupt absence and the blunt trauma behind her death.

His own personal devastation eventually was productively channeled into writing. His globally popular crime novels included *The Black Dahlia*, *The Big Nowhere*, *LA Confidential* and *White Jazz*. Speculation is widespread that his writings about the Black Dahlia's (Elizabeth Short) unsolved murder may have been directly influenced by his own mother's less publicized killing.

My Dark Places documents his own research and successful effort to reopen his mother's cold case. The time lag, absence of remaining evidence and living references made the case irresolvable.

Jean Ellroy, like many divorcees of her era was stigmatized and obliged to seek dubious outlets for sexual partners. Her violation and death by presumably one of her partners would have generated minimal empathy. The pattern of personality disintegration by her son was not unusual in instance of violent killings.

The acacia thicket no longer remains. The dumping site is a uniformly paved and lined unassuming parking lot. For the three baseball coaches who discovered the body and one impressionable young man, the site would remain unforgettable. The three coaches, then middle-aged are since deceased. The ten-year-old boy remains permanently tainted.

Despite an unsatisfying solution due to the passage of time, one positive element emerged. Ellroy's skill of detailed writing has subsequently fascinated and educated readers into the intricacies behind criminal acts. His own personal agony was transcribed into a genuine voice.

His legacy of tragedy gifted a written expression of clarity.

The Presumed Former Location of the
Acacia Thicket and Ivy Dumping Patch

Another Perspective View

Roscoe "Fatty" Arbuckle: Ten-Minute Disputed Sex Scandal

Imagine ascending to the apex of your profession as the highest paid entertainer in the world. Imagine losing it all based on being condemned for a disputed ten-minute action with no actual witnesses.

In 1921, Roscoe *Fatty* Arbuckle signed a three-year contract with Paramount Pictures for $1 million, an unprecedented figure at the time. Arbuckle had been a performer since his teen years traveling the West Coast on the vaudeville circuit. In 1913, at the age of 26, Arbuckle became renowned when he signed with Mack Sennett's Keystone Film Company in the role of one of the Keystone Kops. By Labor Day weekend 1921, he had arrived at his career pinnacle, set apart from his peers.

To celebrate just having finished three pictures at the same time and his new contract with Paramount, Arbuckle and a couple of friends drove up from Los Angeles to San Francisco on Saturday, September 3, 1921 for some weekend revelry. Arbuckle and friends checked into the St. Francis Hotel in San Francisco. They stayed on the twelfth floor in a suite that contained rooms 1219, 1220, and 1221 and overlooked downtown Union Square.

Over the course of a raucous three-day party at the suite, a young actress, Virginia Rappe became severely ill and died four days later. Newspapers nationally sensed a story and went ballistic. Headlines insinuated that popular silent-screen comedian Fatty Arbuckle had killed Rappe, 26-years-old with his weight while savagely raping her. It was Hollywood's first sex scandal.

To this day, no one is certain what happened exactly at that party and specifically in room #1219. Two distinct versions of events have emerged.

Maude Delmont, a renowned blackmailer became Arbuckle's principal accuser citing remarks he presumably made about Rappe before closing the door to room #1219. Partygoers heard

Rappe's screams. She was found by some accounts *naked* and by others *fully clothed and bleeding* when Arbuckle opened the door. He was fully clothed. Delmont was never compelled to testify under oath with her accusations.

Arbuckle claimed that when he retired to his room to change clothes, he found Rappe vomiting in his bathroom. He then helped clean her up and led her to a nearby bed to rest. Thinking she was just overly intoxicated, he left her to rejoin the party. When he returned to the room just a few minutes later, he found Rappe on the floor. After putting her back on the bed, he left the room to get help.

Other party attendees claimed that when they entered the room, they found Rappe tearing at her clothes (something that has been claimed she did often when she was drunk). Party guests tried a number of strange treatments, including covering Rappe with ice, but her condition only worsened.

The hotel staff was contacted and Rappe was taken to another room to rest. With others looking after Rappe, Arbuckle reportedly left for a sightseeing tour and then drove back to Los Angeles.

Rappe was not taken to the hospital on that day and her condition continued to deteriorate. For three days, no one bothered to transfer her to a hospital based on their assumption that her condition was due simply to excessive drinking. Finally on Thursday, Rappe was taken to the Wakefield Sanitarium, a maternity hospital known for giving abortions. A medical examination reportedly found no evidence of sexual assault.

Virginia Rappe died the following day from peritonitis, caused by a ruptured bladder. It was the identical death suffered by matinee idol Rudolph Valentino.

Upon her death, Arbuckle was soon arrested and charged with the murder of Virginia Rappe. Newspapers exploited the story because it sold copies. Some articles had Arbuckle crushing her with his weight and others had him raping her with a foreign object. The newspaper accounts spared no imaginative details or graphic speculations.

In the newspaper accounts, Arbuckle was presumed guilty and Virginia Rappe was an innocent 26-year-old girl. The papers excluded reporting that Rappe had a history of abortions, with some evidence indicating that she might have had another a short time before the party.

The public reaction to Arbuckle was fierce. Perhaps even more than the specific charges of rape and murder, Arbuckle became a symbol of Hollywood's immorality. Movie houses across the country immediately stopped showing Arbuckle's movies. The public was angry and used Arbuckle as a target.

Arbuckle was charged with first-degree murder, eventually reduced to manslaughter. With the scandal as front-page news on almost every newspaper, it was difficult to get an unbiased jury.

He was tried on three separate occasions, twice to hung juries. Finally he was acquitted. Public condemnation prevailed. His friends deserted him en mass. He was briefly blacklisted and his legal debts from the trials were staggering.

For the next twelve years, Arbuckle had trouble finding work. For the remainder of his career, he followed a perpetual comeback trail. The oddest of ironies was that Arbuckle signed a film contract with Warner Brothers on June 28, 1933 to act in some comedy shorts. The day after, he enjoyed a small one-year anniversary party with his new wife. Arbuckle went to bed and suffered a fatal heart attack in his sleep. He was 46.

The mystery remains whether he was the perpetrator of a violent crime or himself the victim. The only know facts during the ten decisive minutes on September 3, 1921 was that Arbuckle and Rappe ended up together in a bedroom which proved poor timing for both. Reportedly Rappe did utter the words that would damn Fatty: *He did this to me*. In the end, the interpretations of these words sealed two fates; his for his immediate career demise and hers as a trivia anecdote.

St. Francis Hotel Top Floor Penthouse

Fateful Room #1219

Kym Morgan: Death By Classified Advertisement

Decades before the era of social media websites and online listing services, individuals seeking employment, accommodations or selling unwanted items opted for newspaper classified advertising.

On the morning of April 28, 1985, Kym Morgan received a telephone response to an ad that she had placed in a local newspaper. She was seeking to barter doing light chores in exchange for a room in coastal Santa Barbara.

The response and caller's subsequent offer seemed ideal. A home in picturesque Montecito awaited merely her inspection and approval. A timely acceptance was imperative and arrangements were finalized to meet at a local market parking lot that same afternoon. The male caller had suggested that she meet his children at his mother-in-law's nearby house.

Morgan was 24-years-old and nearly six feet tall. She was a photography student at the Brooks Institute in Santa Barbara and supplemented her studies part-time as a model.

She was sighted in the parking lot that afternoon with a male having a dark complexion and wearing a conspicuous Hawaiian short, blue pants and two-inch elevator shoes raising his physical stature to approximately 5' 6".

She entered into his car and was never seen again.

Four days later, a man scavengering aluminum cans on mountainous East Camino Cielo Road discovered a female body part. The expanse of East Camino Cielo offers an idyllic view of the Santa Barbara coastline in the distance. More gruesome findings were to follow strewn over the roadside foliage. The remains were identified as Kym Morgan.

Her own 1962 white Chevy Corvair remained in the grocery

store parking lot unoccupied and unlocked.

The brazen brutality behind the killing stunned the community. What magnified the irony was that this was the second violent attack on Morgan within six years. The probability of two extreme aggressions within such a close period of time seemed incalculable.

When Kym was 19, an unknown assailant abducted her from a Los Angeles discotheque. He beat, raped and left her for dead. The violence was so extreme only her mother was capable of identifying her based on a small freckle between her middle and ring fingers to law enforcement investigators.

Miraculously she survived following four months of hospitalization. During this period, she relearned how to speak, walk and feed herself. She suffered from amnesia regarding the event. Her full rehabilitation required several years.

The search for Kym Morgan began the day after her disappearance prompted by calls to police from her anxious roommates. Despite a composite drawing of the man she had met in the parking lot, no credible suspects were ever arrested. Several known area serial killers were discounted due to their incarcerations. A lone suspect of interest was never charged and immediately relocated to the East Coast away from local scrutiny.

Kym Morgan's case remains open but decidedly cold. To have survived a preliminary near-fatal assault only to be murdered the second time is the cruelest irony. No connection to her killing was ever linked to her initial attacker.

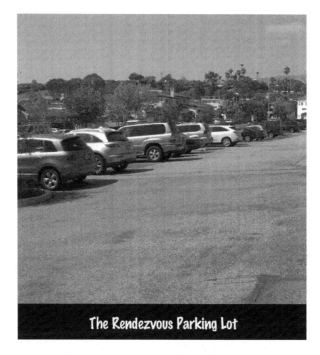

The Rendezvous Parking Lot

The Body Dumping Grounds
on East Camino Cielo Road

**The Resolute Will To Keep William Desmond Taylor's
Murder Unsolved**

William Desmond Taylor was discovered on the morning of
February 2, 1922 dead inside his bungalow at the Alvarado Court
Apartments in the trendy Westlake Park district of downtown
Los Angeles. In his pocket was a wallet holding $78 in cash, a
silver cigarette case, pocket watch, penknife and locket bearing
the photograph of actress Mabel Normand. A two-carat diamond
ring remained on his finger.

Missing was an undisclosed large amount of cash he had shown
to his accountant the day before, a motive and ultimately an
incentive by police to resolve the mystery.

The original officiating doctor indicated that Taylor had died of a
stomach hemorrhage. When police investigators rolled the body
over, it became obvious that Taylor had been fatally shot in the
back at least once. The doctor's identity was never revealed and
he was never heard from again.

Between 1914-1922, Taylor acted in 27 and directed 59 silent
films. The film industry was exploding and money following.
Prosperity proliferated but shadows were darkening the horizon.
The year previously, Roscoe *Fatty* Arbuckle had been accused of
murder and moral degradation involving the death of actress
Virginia Rapp.

The scandalous murder of Taylor, widely respected within the
industry, threatened to crumble the fragile golden pillars of
lucrative commerce. There remained only one prudent course of
action: inaction. The City Hall Gang controlled Los Angeles'
municipal government and a scaled down investigation or silence
could be assured by graft.

National newspapers found murder investigation an inventive
sport. Numerous suspects emerged convictable in print. All
seemingly had murderous motives. None were arrested.

The suspects included: Edward Sands (Taylor's former valet and a former convict), Henry Peavey (Taylor's current valet who found the body and another former convict), Mabel Normand (a love interest who Taylor attempted to cure of cocaine addiction), Charles Eyton (General Manager of Paramount Pictures seen removing compromising items from Taylor's bungalow), Mary Miles Minter (an underage actress and sexual liaison), Charlotte Shelby (Minter's mother), Ross Sheridan (a reputed blackmailer) and Margaret Gibson (never an official suspect but she confessed to the murder on her 1964 deathbed).

A neighbor, Faith Cole MacLean claimed to have viewed an intruder who appeared in costume and was possibly a woman disguised as a man. Numerous subsequent publications speculated wildly on the puzzling case that refused to be solved.

Taylor was reputedly raised from Anglo-Irish gentry. His polish and manners endeared him to the industry elite. He entered the armed forces as a private at the age of 46 to fight in World War I. By the time he arrived in France ready for combat, the conflict was completed. He was ultimately promoted to the temporary grade of lieutenant before he was discharged.

His death provoked shock amongst the film colony. His former four-year fiancé, Neva Gerber typified him as the *soul of honour, a man of personal culture, education* and *refinement*.

None of these endearing qualities prevented his killing.

The Alvarado Court bungalows were long ago leveled to accommodate a small retail shipping center parking lot. The downtown Los Angeles film colony relocated to Hollywood and then dispersed globally. Mabel Normand's scandals and tuberculosis forced an early retirement from films and premature death at only 37 in 1930.

In 1924, her own chauffeur would shoot to death millionaire oil broker Courtland S. Dines with her pistol. Dines was romantically involved with Normand's friend and Taylor's other next-door neighbor Edna Purviance. Normand was the last person to reportedly see Taylor alive and wept inconsolably throughout his funeral ceremony.

For all that William Desmond Taylor appeared to be missed. It seemed equally desirable for his killer to remain unknown.

Former Location of the Alvarado Court Apartments in Westlake

Ted Healy: The Suspected Homicide of the Fourth Stooge

Ted Healy is credited as being the creator of the Three Stooges act and a style of slapstick comedy that has increasingly lessened in popularity due to its overt sexism and violent tendencies.

Healy was originally a successful vaudeville performer and considered the highest paid performer during the 1920s. The original concept behind his creation of the Stooges was to invite planted cast members (stooges) and hecklers from an audience during a *serious* acrobat routine and encourage improvisational mayhem.

Audiences adored the unforeseen results and his show became wildly successful.

Moses Horwitz (known as Moe Howard) was Healy's childhood friend and initial recruit. Moe's brother Shemp joined the act in 1923 and Larry Fine was added in 1928.

The chemistry onstage disintegrated backstage. Cast members quit, returned and the group frequently quarreled and reorganized. In 1929, the quartet appeared in several Broadway productions. Wider exposure came with their appearance in the 1930 film *Soup to Nuts*.

The success of their subsequent films ultimately diminished Healy's control. The Howard brothers and Fine separated from Healy's troupe over contract disputes. The trio began performing apart and established their own professional identity. Healy sued them for using his gimmickry and routines. The Shubert Theatre Company owned the copyrights to the show and produced the trio's work. Healy was frozen out of the proceeds,

He attempted to replicate his own competitive version of the Stooges and the other original members frequently collaborated with him despite their legal dispute. Curly Howard replaced his brother Shemp and by 1934, the Howard brothers had

229

professionally parted ways with Healy entirely. Healy appeared in a succession of films integrating new *Stooges* into the cast.

His personal life was as chaotic as his on stage character. He twice married impulsively, divorced, reconciled and later fathered a son John Jacob with his second estranged wife. Ted would die four days before his birth celebrating at the famed Hollywood Trocadero nightclub. He was 41-years-old.

The circumstances behind his demise on that December 20, 1937 evening have never officially been verified. He was initially presumed to be the victim of a heart attack. The controversy surrounding preceding events prompted the treating physician's refusal to sign his death certificate.

At the Sunset Strip club, a heated argument escalated between Healy and three reported *college- aged boys*. There have been subsequent but unconfirmed suggestions that the *boys* were actually actor Wallace Berry and two film producers. The younger men knocked Healy to the ground and proceeded to kick him in the head, ribs and abdomen. He was clearly injured, bloodied, and incoherent after the beating and returned by taxi to his apartment.

He expired the next morning. Autopsy findings revealed that Healy died of acute toxic nephritis and chronic alcoholism. The external wounds from the fight were specifically ruled out as his direct cause of death.

Not everyone was convinced by the findings. No one however was ever arrested.

Despite his earnings, Healy flagrantly overspent and died destitute. His friends and colleagues established a trust fund to financially support his widow and son.

His son would later change his name to Theodore John Healy in honor of his late father. He lived a more conventional lifestyle in the Atlanta area. He joined the U.S. Naval Academy, served a tour of duty in Vietnam, married, became a schoolteacher and later a financial planner. He passed away in 2011

Today the Hollywood Trocadero nightclub site is integrated into a sequence of shops and restaurants. The Hollywood of yesteryears has vanished. The Three Stooges are unknown to most individuals under the age of forty. Their infrequent telecasts are consigned to extreme late night television viewing.

Ted Healy is rarely mentioned in the same conversation as the Howard Brothers. Hardcore fans and archivists exclusively remember his contribution. Many viewers today with society's modified social consciousness question why people ever considered violent slapstick to be funny in the first place.

Former Site of the Hollywood Trocadero Nightclub

The Visalia Ransacker and Potential Nightstalker Connection

Between the Spring of 1974 until late 1975, in excess of more than eighty unsolved burglaries plagued Visalia. The serial burglar typically targeted single-family dwellings during late night hours. He would ransacked his target's interiors and generally steal only small insignificant items.

This baffling string of break-ins was climaxed with the invasion of Claude Snelling's home on the late evening of September 11, 1975. Snelling heard an inside disturbance and upon exiting his bedroom discovered a masked intruder attempting to kidnap his daughter. The burglar opened fire on Snelling and fled. Snelling, a journalism professor at the nearby College of the Sequoias died from his wounds.

Three months later police patrols staked out neighborhoods where the intruder had been previously active. A suspect was stopped for questioning. Before his interrogation, he pulled out a handgun and shot at the detective. The bullet shattered the officer's flashlight, but he survived. The shooter escaped into the darkness and likely out of the Visalia area.

The strange break-ins abruptly ceased. Shortly afterwards, a more violent series of night entries, violence and rapes began in the Sacramento area. This *East-Bay Rapist*, also called the *Original Night Stalker* terrorized northern California for nearly a decade and also evaded capture. Were these two individuals the same person?

No announced suspects of interest have emerged about the identity of the *Visalia Ransacker*. Did a seemingly isolated small town murder tie into a much broader rampage of terror?

Professor Snelling's Visalia Residence

The Vindictive Rage of Elliot Rodger

The shooting and stabbing rampage of University of Santa Barbara student Elliot Rodger on May 23, 2014 earned him a recognition and notoriety, which had eluded him throughout his 22-year life. He understood fame and the companion gifts bestowed upon those it favored due to his father's prominence within the film industry. Despite being raised in privilege and affluence, the emptiness and social disfunctionability that tormented his core culminating in explosive fury. His wrath killed six and wounded fourteen innocent victims on a sultry Friday evening towards the end of the school term.

His attack was clearly premeditated based on incendiary texts and uploaded rationale videos he had posted on social media outlets preceding and in the midst of the carnage.

Certain details still remain sketchy regarding the chronology of events. Most have been publicly documented. The terror presumably required months of advanced planning, fueled by intense hatred and despair. What factors ultimately triggered his final breakdown remained entombed within the mind of Rodger who ended his life with a self-inflicted gunshot. His suicide followed an eight-minute homicidal rampage through the constricted streets of Isla Vista.

The diminutive village of Isla Vista is adjacent to the University of California at Santa Barbara (UCSB), headquartered in Goleta. UCSB is the third oldest general education campus within the University of California system and advertises a student enrollment of nearly 24,000. The institution is most academically renowned for its influential public research center. The Pacific Coast beachfront location softens a traditional perception of academia. It is reasonable to conclude that Isla Vista and Goleta are twin identities but the former is a separate unincorporated community composed predominately of transitory residential students.

Isla Vista resembles more of a vacation beach resort than campus satellite accommodation. The atmosphere is relaxed and festive. Elliot Rodger felt and exhibited a deep seeded alienation and resentment towards a casual existence that intermingled study with social partying and liberal sexuality. He was the uninvited spectator enraged that he still remained an uninvited participant, despite his affluence and self-perceived refinement.

Within the village of Isla Vista, the majority of student traffic remains on foot and is confined to a universe of principally six square blocks. For an individual seeking a shooting gallery, the potential for damage is unlimited. Within this claustrophobic maze, Elliot Rodger had innumerable targets but few outlets for escape.

It was reported that during the afternoon and early evening of May 23rd, Rodger fatally and repeated stabbed his two roommates, Cheng Yuan Hong and George Chen along with one of their friends, Weihan Wang, who picked that unfortunate weekend to visit. The sequence and timetable of each slaying has never been publicly clarified, but the responsible weaponry included two long fixed-bladed knives and a machete. The resulting carnage stained the apartment walls, which Rodger attempted to sanitize, presumably to conceal each roommate's death from the others before ambush.

Rodger exhibited a history of contemptuous behavior towards prior roommates. Reports circulated following his rampage that both of his roommates had earlier attempted to transfer due to Rodger's behavior. Nearly a year after their son's deaths, the three victim's families sued the Santa Barbara County Sheriff's department citing claims of negligence and inactivity despite substantial evidence of an impending threat. The menacing factors included Rodger's apparent cache of weaponry and ammunition in his room and social media outbursts. Deputies had reportedly visited the residence on previous occasions due to reported disturbances.

Rodger's mental health became a focal point based on a reported diagnosis of Aspergerger syndrome and sensory processing disorder. He had undergone significant counseling and therapy for erratic behavior, but not classified as a dangerous risk or prone to violence. His published online correspondence and posted videos raised questions regarding these professional oversights posthumously.

Blame becomes simplistic to widely distribute. Who may ultimately prevent an unhinging personality except the perpetrator? Warning signs may go unheeded until catastrophic consequences accentuate them.

After killing the trio in his apartment, Rodger concluded that time was no longer his ally. Neighbors had neither heard nor reported any unusual disturbance within the complex.

Rodger methodically sat in his car in the apartment parking lot for approximately 45 minutes uploading his final video correspondence and an email manifesto from his laptop computer. He had resolutely determined the next and final stage of his attack would be focused on exacting maximum casualties. His principle rage was oriented towards the female gender he had felt most estranged from and rejected by. He had no exit strategy. He was armed for combat with nearly 600 rounds of ammunition, two pistols and two knives.

He drove four blocks north from the parking lot to the Alpha Phi Sorority House, exited his car and began aggressively knocking on the front door. He anticipated that an opened door would liberate a perceived lifetime of rejection. Instead he was met by a familiar response: silence. No one bothered to answer. He returned to his stylish black BMW coupe alone once again.

Simultaneously strolling along the western wall of the Alpha Phi building, a group of sorority sisters became his secondary targets. He fired at them through his car's lowered window. These strangers symbolized his lifetime sense of rejection. At short range, he killed Veronika Weiss and Katherine Cooper, while wounding Bianca DeKock multiple times. The women could neither resist nor flee.

His eight-minute suicidal binge was nearly half completed.

Heading south, he fired indiscriminately into a coffee shop window that fortunately was closed. A cluster of friends heard the shooting in the distance and ducked into a nearby deli market. Christopher Michaels-Martinez viewed the approaching black coupe from the doorway and was felled by a stray fuselage from Rodger's gun. Michaels-Martinez became simply one more stranger and another dead victim. He was also Rodger's last fatality and accurate lethal shot.

During the final course of Rodger's insane weave-and-fire driving, he shot unsteadily and randomly at more pedestrians, wounding another dozen. He swerved his vehicle to purposely strike several. Time and space were constricting him. The claustrophobic one-way avenues of Isla Vista hemmed in his mobility and law enforcement personnel were armed, in pursuit and minimizing his maneuverability rapidly.

The hunter had become the prey. Rounding the southern extremity of local Perfect Park, he exchanged gunfire with four strategically positioned officers. He was wounded in his hip and then accelerated into a bicyclist. The cyclist flew headlong onto the car, smashing his front windshield and prompted a collision into a parked car. The chase was complete. Apprehended alive, he would have to publicly explain and atone for his actions. As with the majority rampage killers about to be captured, he opted for an abrupt termination absent of explanation.

In the interim following the crash, two sheriff deputies cautiously approached his car. Rodger concluded the drama by firing a bullet into his temple. His personal purgatory had ended. For his victims, the sobering realization and consequences of his actions were just beginning. The deputies pulled the slumped over Rodger out of the vehicle to handcuff him. Instead of resistance, they dislodged a lifeless cadaver.

His abrupt suicide incited significant later speculations. No one could adequately explain what actions might have prevented the tragedy.

Immediately following, prayer vigils and campuswide solidarity marches provided temporary balm and respite. The behavior of university-aged populations tends towards resiliency. Remembrance is fleeting. Commemorative banners hung across the street from Rodger's suicide crash site throughout the following fall term. Few other remembrances by then were visible.

Over time, Elliot Rodger will revert to becoming as invisible and forgotten as he perceived himself while living. The party and festive environment of Isla Vista lulls students into the attractions of the temporal. There remains only limited space for a successively fresh batch of participating underclassmen.

Despite or because of his background of privilege, Elliot Rodger felt distinctly remote and rejected from this seemingly superficial setting. Most of us have experienced the role of observing spectator reluctantly in our lives. Why Rodger chose to deprive others of their own preference and experience remains the sole mystery.

Elliot Rodger's Apartment

Parking Lot Where He Uploaded His Video

Alpha Phi Sorority Front Door

Location of His Final Fatality

Rounding the Corner Wounded, Rodger Crashed
Into a Parked Car Near Telephone Pole

Suicide Location in Crashed Car

Memorial Banner Across The
Street From Suicide Spot

The Helzer Brothers: Children of Thunder

A lethal cocktail mix of drug use, schizophrenia and religious fanaticism manifested into a series of monstrous killings by the Helzer Brothers.

Justin Helzer and Glenn Helzer, (who went by his middle name Taylor), murdered five people as part of a bizarre blackmail scheme. Taylor Helzer was a stockbroker and self-prophesied prophet. An important element of his doctrine included raising money for a religious movement oriented towards bringing Jesus Christ's return to Earth. As the figurehead of his organization of three, he orchestrated a sequence of killings driven by inner voices and spirits.

Following high school graduation, the Helzer boys fulfilled a two-year Mormon missionary requirement of service. Taylor's mission was in Brazil and Justin's in Texas. Upon their return to northern California, Justin became a cable installer and Taylor a stockbroker in downtown San Francisco.

Taylor followed a traditional suburban lifestyle upon his return, marrying and fathering two daughters. The façade endured three years before he wearied of the restraints of being a proper husband and Mormon. He rebelled against the strict religious living code and began liberally indulging in drugs and sexual relations outside of marriage. During this stage of mutiny, he began wearing exclusively black clothing and neglecting his personal hygiene.

The Mormon Church reportedly excommunicated him for his profane behavior.

His erratic behavior and drug use intensified during 2000. He initiated a delusional campaign to take over the Mormon Church involving a variety of criminal schemes to facilitate his designs. He founded a self-help group called Impact America and recruited his impressionable younger brother Justin and an acquaintance Dawn Godman as participants. Godman moved into their rental house in Concord.

From the outlet, fraud and killing in God's name were accepted cornerstones agreed upon by the trio in their strategic planning.

Among the money raising ploys debated included recruiting underage Brazilian girls as prostitutes for wealthy businessmen that could evolve into blackmail revenue. Another tactic considered was to adopt Brazilian orphans who would be trained to assassinate the top Mormon leadership in Utah. The subsequent void would pave the entrance for Taylor to assume leadership of the institution.

In 2000, the conspirators officially called themselves *The Children of Thunder*. To fuel their ambitious agenda, Taylor ultimately resorted to more common means of fundraising. He decided to extort some of his elderly former clients with the goal of obtaining in excess of $100,000 seed money.

Taylor at the same time began dating 22-year-old Selina Bishop, the daughter of musician Elvin Bishop. Her designed role in his plot was to open a checking account enabling him to launder money he intended to extort from his former clients. This account Taylor reasoned would remove his name from all illicit activities exposing only Bishop. She was infatuated by him and completely unaware of the implications involved by opening the account (at least initially). She later became expendable.

The initial target of his extortion plot was a former client (from a list of five) who lived in Walnut Creek but was not home during their visit on Sunday, July 30. Their second choice, Ivan Stineman, 85, and his wife, Annette, 78, completely trusted Taylor having been acquainted as both clients and friends over the years. Reportedly, the same or the following day, both Helzer brothers, wearing suits and carrying briefcases, knocked on their door and escorted them over to the their Concord residence.

During the ensuing hours, Annette Stineman reportedly phoned the manager of the Concord branch of her stock brokerage nervously indicating she wished to liquidate her investments. Although the request was unusual, the manager honored it.

Prosecutors speculated that the trio then forced the Stinemans to drink Rohypnol, a sedative and known *date rape* drug, and made them write out two checks, one for $33,000, and the other for $67,000 to Selina Bishop. Taylor thought the retirees would overdose on the Rohypnol and die, but they didn't. Instead the brothers in front of a horrified Godman savagely killed them. The following day Godman deposited the checks into Bishop's account.

On August 3rd, the murderous siblings accompanied by Godman, killed Selina Bishop in their home to silence her after she collected the money from the account on their behalf unaware about the homicidal plot. The bodies of Selina Bishop and the Stinemans were dismembered and stuffed into nine black duffel bags, which were later fished out by divers from the Sacramento-San Joaquin River Delta.

During the pre-dawn hours of August 4, Taylor shot dead Bishop's mother, 45-year-old Jennifer Villarin, and her boyfriend, James Gamble, 54, for fear that they would go to police once her daughter was reported missing. Jennifer Villarin had once met Taylor Helzer and knew that he had been dating her daughter. Helzer had a spare key to her daughter's studio apartment where her mother was housesitting and had entered undetected.

The brother's attempts to hide the crimes unraveled quickly. On Monday, August 7th, sheriff's deputies drove to the Helzer's rental house with a search warrant. They wanted to look for the gun that was used to kill Villarin and Gamble. All of the tenants were home when they knocked on the door. When the deputies swept through the house, they found ecstasy, hallucinogenic mushrooms, and drug paraphernalia, but no gun, according to the police report. The cops arrested the trio on drug possession charges.

Later that day, the first two duffel bags, one containing a human head, the other a torso, floated to the surface of the Mokelumne River. After the rest of the bags were recovered, experts at the Contra Costa County Crime Lab used DNA analysis to identify the victims, which confirmed preliminary findings made using dental records.

Authorities charged all three roommates with 18 felonies, including murder, extortion, and kidnapping. It would require four more years for juries to sort through the tangled details of the case and sentence the last of the trio for crimes they'd committed.

Faced with solid evidence against all three, Godman struck a deal with prosecutors. In exchange for pleading guilty to five counts of murder and testifying against the Helzer brothers, she avoided the death penalty and got a sentence of 38 years to life in prison. She is currently incarcerated at the Central California Women's Facility in Chowchilla.

In March 2004, Taylor Helzer entered a surprise guilty plea, and his attorney relayed Taylor's impromptu confession to a stunned courtroom. On June 16, a jury convicted Justin Helzer of 11 counts, including murder, extortion and kidnapping for his role in the killings. He pleaded not guilty by reason of insanity.

On April 16, 2013, Justin Helzer, 41, was found dead in his single cell at San Quentin Prison. Helzer used a sheet tied to his cell bars to hang himself. An earlier suicide attempt two years earlier had left the death row inmate blind when he stabbing himself repeatedly in the eye with pens and pencils. Glenn Taylor Helzer remains on death row at San Quentin, a dishonored prophet in exile.

Helzer Brothers' Rental House

The Christmas Eve Massacre by a Santa Impersonator

The lone vacant lot at the end of a Covina cul-de-sac remains peculiar within the vibrant suburban neighborhood. Another real estate valuation bubble has inflated pricing and once again prompted renovation, refurbishment and renewal with the intent for resale.

An empty lot defies entrepreneurial opportunity. Fencing has surrounded the vacant parcel for nearly seven years exhibiting only an expansive lawn, uniformed backdrop trees and a drained swimming pool with accompanying slide. These traces are the sole evidence of former life on the property.

On Christmas Eve 2008, nearing midnight, Bruce Jeffrey Pardo adorning a disarming Santa Claus outfit, knocked on the front door of his former in-laws residence. Pardo was toting a gift-wrapped package and four concealed pistols. A party of 25 people was enjoying the holiday festivities including Pardo's recently divorced wife and family.

Pardo's eight-year-old niece rushed excitedly to answer the door. Uncle Bruce met her attempted embrace with a point-blank gunshot to her face. She miraculously survived. The faux Santa then discharged one of his 9mm semi-automatic handguns randomly into the terrified assemblage. The horror escalated.

Pardo unwrapped his present. The package contained a homemade flamethrower, with which he sprayed racing fuel gasoline around the house in order to set it ablaze. Simultaneously he began executing selected individuals with his handgun. The shootings and inferno ultimately killed nine people and wounded three.

He concentrated his rage exclusively towards his ex-wife's family. The dead included his ex-wife, Sylvia Ortega-Pardo, her mother Alicia Sotomayor Ortega and father, Joseph Ortega. Other fatalities included Sylvia's two brothers, Charles and

James Ortega and their wives Cheri Lynn Ortega and Teresa Ortega. Sylvia's sister, Alicia Ortega Ortiz and son Michael Andre Ortiz were also killed,

The intensity of the fire seared most of the victims beyond recognition and entirely destroyed the house. Flames elevated 40-50 feet into the Christmas skyline. Identification of the victims could only be completed via dental and medical records.

The genocide singed the source as well. Pardo suffered third-degree burns before his exit with the Santa suit adhering to his skin and defying removal.

His original planned escape strategy was to Canada. He had taped a significant sum of cash to his body and purchased an airline ticket. The physical agony sustained from the burns likely proved unbearable and altered his plans.

Instead of reinventing a fresh existence, Pardo drove thirty miles to his brother's empty house in Sylmar. He emptied a bullet into his head as a final act of defiance. Before pulling the trigger, Pardo had rigged his rental car for detonation and parked it a block away from his brother's house. It was a symbolically demonic ending for a man with no prior criminal past. Yet he was a man convinced that he had lost everything.

His motives were later traced to a contentious divorce settlement confirmed one week prior to the attack. The massacre was intended to address a litany of grievances and bitterness that had doomed his marriage of only one year. He had been recently fired for fraudulent billing practices as an electrical engineer.

Simmering beneath a conventional surface, Pardo was a troubled individual ready to detonate. He had stored a significant cache of weapons and incendiary devices in his Montrose home. Their ultimate intended use might have later proliferated into a more expansive expression. The shadows darkening his existence found an initial outlet.

The emptiness of the vacant lot summarizes the vacancy branding his life. Bruce Pardo obliterated an entire family and their residence, but in the process his own identity as well.

The Lifeless Empty Lot

The 101 California Building Rampage: Victims of Chance by a Deadly Rampage

At 2:57 p.m. on July 1, 1993, 55-year-old southern California mortgage broker and unsuccessful real estate speculator Gian Luigi Ferri entered the high-rise office building at 101 California Street in San Francisco. Dressed in a dark business, carrying an attaché case and wheeling a lawyer's case on a dolly, he resembled one of the building's practicing professionals and associates. Ferri resolutely entered an elevator to the 34th floor and the offices of the law firm of Pettit and Martin.

Exiting the elevator on the 34th floor, his intentions were precise and oriented towards combat. Ferri donned a pair of ear protectors and removed his sports coat. His battle armaments included multiple semi-automatic pistols and hundreds of rounds of ammunition including dozens of magazines carried in his lawyer cases. It was certain he had no personal exit strategy except death.

Without uttering a word, he entered the law offices and indiscriminately began firing at anyone and everyone in his sighting. He exited the office and after roaming the 34th floor, he then moved down one floor through an internal staircase and continued shooting. The carnage continued as he descended several floors.

Eight people were killed and six others injured during his shooting spree. Over 110 San Francisco police offices responded and shut off the alarms, which ultimately trapped Ferri between the 29th and 28th floor. He viewed his own demise with officers mounting the stairs and fired one shot into his chin killing himself instantly.

Ferri had been a client of Pettit and Martin over a dozen years prior to the shootings. He nursed an irrational grudge against the firm over their advice provided on certain real estate purchases regarding several trailer parks in Indiana and Kentucky. He had apparently no further contact with the firm since then. His life had steadily unraveled and he was deeply in debt. Two of his victims were lawyers with the firm Ferri blamed for his financial downfall. Neither had anything remotely to do with that advice.

His other victims were all unknown to the killer. None of the dead or wounded was on a personal hit list he carried in his attaché of more than 30 names. The list was composed reportedly of criminals, rapists, racketeers and lobbyists. A rambling letter found on Ferri's body bemoaned his perception of being victim to a system out to crush him. Aside from his blame towards Pettit and Martin, the four-page typed letter included rants about monosodium glutamate, the Food and Drug Administration, and the legal profession.

The dead included Deborah Fogel, a secretary for the law firm Davis, Wright and Tremaine, four employees of Pettit and Martin: John C. Scully, an associate lawyer in the firm, Allen J. Berk, a law partner, David Sutcliffe, a summer legal assistant, a secretary, Shirley Mooser and Donald Michael Merrill, whose reason for being in the building were unclear. Injured in the attack were Vicky Smith, Sharon Jones O'Roke, Brian F. Berger, Deanna Eaves and Charles Ross. John Scully was mortally wounded while heroically thrusting himself in the line of fire in front of his wife Michelle, who was also shot in the arm.

The shootings renewed calls nationwide for tighter gun control. The publicity from the senseless killings was followed by a number of legal and legislative actions. In the immediate aftermath, a California judge repealed a law that had given gun manufacturers immunity against lawsuits from shooting victims and their relatives. The victims of the massacre filed a collective lawsuit again the Florida based gun manufacturer of Ferri's weaponry.

Eight hushed years later, with the bloodstains long washed away and the bullet holes repaired, the California Supreme Court ruled against gunshot victims (and their survivors). Further, future victims were prohibited from suing gun manufacturers for injuries done to them by someone using one of their weapons. Another team of faceless and victimless lawyers had ultimately prevailed in these proceedings. The debate continues amongst a divided nation, still unresolved. Gun abuse continues to reign legally within the United States.

The Pettit and Martin law firm has long ceased operations at 101 California, unable to recover from the notoriety. Another law firm leases and operates from their suite. Visitors to the 101 California office building circulate freely throughout the lobby with security in evidence. Daily many enter elevators without scrutiny. Business has returned to normal.

Massacre 34th Floor Entrance Door

101 California Street Building

The Disintegrating Mind and Schoolyard Entrance Massacre by Brenda Spencer

Brenda Spencer existed in squalor with her separated father in a middle-class San Diego neighborhood amidst an environment destined to bear damaged fruit.

Absent of parental guidance and example, adrift in school, the sixteen-year-old Spencer slept on a single mattress on her living room floor surrounded by empty beer and whiskey bottles throughout the house. The warning signs of her mental instability were flagrantly raging.

During the summer of 1978, she was arrested for burglary and shooting out windows at the Cleveland Elementary School with a BB gun, directly across the street. She was known for hunting birds for sport in her neighborhood.

In December, a psychiatric evaluation arranged by her parole officer recommended her admission to a psychiatric hospital due to clinical depression.

Her father refused. He compounded her escalating mental deterioration by giving her as a Christmas present, a .22 caliber rifle with telescopic sight and 500 rounds of ammunition. When asked why such an unusual gift, Spencer suggested it was an incentive to encourage her own suicide.

One month later on Monday, January 29, 1979, she fell off from her teetering precipice into an irreparable darkness.

Spencer began firing arbitrarily at children waiting outside of the locked admission gate of the Cleveland Elementary School. In the course of her shooting spree, she wounded eight children before killing an assisting school principal Burton Wragg and custodian Mike Suchar as he was attempting to pull the wounded Wragg to safety. She also shot a responding police officer in the neck upon arrival to the scene.

She returned inside her house and barricaded herself after having emptied thirty rounds of ammunition. A local journalist was able to engage her in a telephone conversation during her stand off with police. When asked the inevitable question as to why she had opened fire on innocent children, her flippant response was *I Don't Like Mondays*.

Hours later, she surrendered despite threatening to stage a final rampage,

A series of evasive responsibility denials would follow. Claims of intoxication during the act were disproved by drug and alcohol testing immediately afterwards. Other contributing factors cited by her included beatings and sexual abuse by her father, which were never proven. Her mental instability made separating fact from fancy difficult.

Poor parenting appeared obvious. Poor parenting, however, never makes murder justifiable or is cause for evading personal responsibility. Each act of parental irresponsibility, indifference and negligence shoved the mentally disturbed Spencer towards a reprehensible fatal action. Brenda Spencer ultimately pulled the trigger and knew she was wrong for doing so.

A popular rock song entitled *I Don't Like Mondays* followed later in the year and a television documentary was produced seven year later on the event. The school was shuttered in 1983 due to declining enrollments. It has since been leased by the San Diego School District to a variety of different charter and private schools.

Brenda Spencer is currently incarcerated at the California Institution for Women in Corona where Mondays perpetually remain as monotonous as weekends.

Brenda Spencer's Residence Across the Street From the Cleveland Elementary School

Former Gated Entrance to the Cleveland Elementary School

Dr. Victor Ohta: The Execution and Incendiary of the House on the Hill

The fulfillment of the American dream represents many interpretations from differing perspectives. For some, the evidence is materialistic accumulation. For others, it is symbolized by an absence of such trappings and the capacity for freedom of expression.

Dr. Victor Ohta and John Linley Frazier's lives remained polemic until their fatal intersection on October 19, 1970.

Ohta, then 45, had become a success story beginning from his humble origins as the son of a Japanese immigrant farmer in rural Montana. He studied medicine at Northwestern University and became a major in the Air Force after joining in the mid-1950s.

By 1970, he had become a very successful eye surgeon in Santa Cruz and was widely respected for his philanthropic activities. He was lavishly compensated for his progressive accomplishments. He was renowned for his extravagant spending and generosity, represented symbolically by a maroon Rolls Royce and sprawling mansion estate overlooking Monterey Bay in the oceanfront resort of Soquel.

Trapped on the other end of the spectrum, John Linley Frazier's life had never amounted to a great deal during his first 23 years. Despite a reportedly normal upbringing, he dropped out of high school. He enrolled in a trade school, married and became an auto mechanic. His modest trajectory unraveled during the spring of 1970 with his LSD use and subsequent drug addiction.

His marriage disintegrated, he quit working and embraced the counterculture existence of the era. Like many, he grew his hair long, ceased shaving and began a brief period of communal living. His LSD use prompted him towards apocalyptic visions, mysticism and obsessions towards an ecologically sparse

258

lifestyle. His personality paranoia ultimately made him incompatible with the passive lifestyle adopted by his peers.

He relocated into a six-foot-square shack in the Soquel woods with an imposing view of Dr. Ohta's overhanging mansion. Their clash of values seemed inevitable. Charles Manson's cult had exterminated five members of the Beverly Hills bourgeois class only fifteen months earlier. The Vietnam War and accompanying protest movement were raging uncontrollably. Class revolution and anti-materialistic rhetoric was the Mantra of the young and disenfranchised.

John Lindley Frazier hallucinated into imagining himself as a self-appointment leader of the coming revolution.

It was a workday afternoon on Monday, October 19th. Virginia Ohta, Victor's wife was the only person home when Frazier scaled the steep hillside and invaded the vulnerable mansion with a .38 revolver. He was familiar with the property's layout having months before broken into the house and stolen a pair of binoculars. His rigid condemnation of their lifestyle had disgusted his own idealistic purity making their lives expendable.

Victor Ohta epitomized everything Frazier was not nor ever likely to become. Frazier bound Virginia's wrists with one of her expensive silk scarves. Soon, Dorothy Cadwallader, Victor's secretary, arrived with one of the two Ohta sons (Derrick and Taggart). Victor himself arrived with their second son unaware of their impending disaster. Frazier tied the captives together at gunpoint and relocated them to the outside swimming pool.

He initiated a lecture about the evils of materialism and the destruction of the environment. Victor Ohta was disturbed and in disagreement with his tormentor's rant. Frazier demanded that Ohta assist him in burning down his prized mansion as a rite of purification. Ohta refused. Frazier shoved the bound doctor into the pool where he emptied three cartridges into his body.

Frazier then simultaneously executed each hostage including the family cat. Each victim floated lifelessly on the surface of the pool. He entered the house and typed a terse note proclaiming the beginning of World War III and a rambling warning against individuals misusing the natural environment. The note was left symbolically under the windshield wipers of Ohta's Rolls Royce.

As a final stroke against materialism, he blocked the two dirt roads leading to the house with the Rolls Royce and another of the Ohta's cars, a Lincoln Continental. He left their expensive jewelry, photography and electronic equipment untouched. He then torched the house by igniting fires in diverse locations creating an accumulated inferno.

Aaron Green, an internationally recognized architect and associate of Frank Lloyd Wright, had designed the 3,800 square feet single-floor mansion on a 10-acre ridge of the Santa Cruz Mountain Range. A naturally shaped swimming pool and Japanese garden were sheltered between the house and an extensive garden wall of stone and redwood. The structure was accentuated by masonry trim but predominantly sided by rough-sawn redwood paneling and red cedar roofed shingles.

The distinctive landmark's smoke and flames pierced the late October evening. Firefighters were impeded by the blocked access. By the time the roads were cleared and fire extinguished, the house was burnt beyond repair. The discovery of the floating corpses compounded the nightmare.

Frazier had escaped his bloody rampage by stealing the family's third car, a green station wagon. It was recovered the following day, burned and abandoned in a Southern Pacific railroad tunnel approximately twenty miles away.

Frazier eluded capture for only four days. His erratic behavior and violent outbursts made him an obvious suspect to his associates. Without hesitation, they fingered him as a probable suspect. He was arrested asleep in his secluded shack with the stolen Ohta binoculars.

His first of three trials ended with the jury convicting him of first-degree murder after only five hours of deliberations. The jury condemned him with the death penalty on December 30, 1971. His timing proved opportune because California repealed the death penalty in 1972 and 107 Death Row inmates, including him, had their sentences commuted to life in prison. Throughout his trials, Frazier played the insanity plea card, but unsuccessfully. He attempted every theatrical ploy within his limited repertoire including shaving half his hair, beard and eyebrows and muttering incessantly to himself throughout the proceedings.

His crazed appearance and antics provoked only disgust from his unimpressed audience. Following decades of imprisonment, he ultimately became eligible for parole. Each request was routinely denied.

In August 2009 following thirty-five years of incarceration and several parole denials, Frazier hung himself in his small cell at Mule Creek State Prison in Iona, near Sacramento. Just before his final exit, he had been transferred out of an intensive mental health program into the general prison population.

Suicide would cast a lingering shadow on the Ohta family. Victor Ohta's mother and one of his daughter's Taura would kill themselves within seven years following the massacre. A sole remaining daughter, Lark, would remain the only survivor to his successful legacy abruptly destroyed.

John Lindley Frazier's Daily View
of the Ohta Mansion

Entrance Gate to the Ohta Residence

Edward Allaway: The Questionable Case For Cured Insanity

Can the criminally insane ever be cured, rehabilitated and released harmlessly back into society?

The question has been elevated into public discussion and policy in the case of Edward Charles Allaway.

On July 12, 1976, Allaway ruthlessly gunned down seven people and wounded two others in the California State University Fullerton library's first floor lobby and basement media center. The dead included Seth Fessenden, Stephen Becker, Paul Herzberg, Bruce Jacobson, Donald Aarges, Frank Teplansky and Deborah Paulsen.

Allaway was a custodian at the library and offered a delusional motive that the victim's were pornographers forcing his estranged wife to appear in their films.

After the shootings, he fled the campus and visited a nearby Anaheim hotel where his separated wife was employed. He telephoned a confession to the police and meekly surrendered.

Years prior to the attack, he had seriously injured a co-worker at a Michigan plant and just before, he had threatened his wife with a knife and subsequently raped her. He had a history of mental illness, which included suicide attempts, institutionalization and electro-shock therapies.

At his trial, he was diagnosed as a paranoid schizophrenic by five different mental health professionals and convicted by a jury on six counts of first-degree murder and one count of second-degree murder. During the sentencing phase of the trial, the jury deadlocked on the state of his mental capacities and the judge ruled him *not guilty by reason of insanity*. He was committed to the California state mental hospital system commencing at Atascadero State Prison avoiding a prison term. He was subsequently transferred to Napa State Hospital before arriving at his present residence at Patton State Hospital continuing ongoing medical treatment.

No one will ever mistake a mental institution for a maximum-security prison. Inmates have significantly more freedom, space to stroll and direct contact with others including the opposite sex. The law stipulates that convicted defendants found insane must remain institutionalized until they are found sane. The question persists, then what?

In 2009, officials at Patton State Hospital were prepared to release Allaway due to their conclusion that he was no longer suffering from schizophrenia and had been adequately weaned off his medication.

The condition regarding the hospital administrators' own collective sanity and judgment were questioned by then California Attorney General Jerry Brown and Governor Arnold Schwarzenegger. Vehement opposition was voiced by each of the victim's living relatives. They still remain suffering daily from the searing trauma of their loss. The Patton State Hospital administrators withdrew their recommendation for release. In July 2016, he was quietly transferred to Napa State Hospital.

Allaway has on multiple occasions petitioned for his right to be returned back into society.

An imposing question remains as to whether an insane person can be cured? If cured, should he then stand accountable for his heinous actions? Many of the victim's families publicly doubted his insanity claim from the outset. They claimed his violent past was evidence his staged responses were merely a performance.

The ultimate issue however transcends the question of curable mental illness. Is the risk of releasing a mass murderer justifiable to society? Precedent suggests strongly against such a perilous decision.

The New Library Lobby Built Over The Former

The 1977 Golden Dragon Massacre: The Gang Who Didn't Shoot Straight

San Francisco throughout the 1970s was a magnet for racial tension, which sporadically manifested itself into violence. No example proved more spontaneous and deadly than the September 1977 gang related massacre at the Golden Dragon restaurant in Chinatown.

Contemporary Chinese gangs trace their lineage from tongs, secret collectives and societies common to southern China. Tongs resemble the clandestine organizational structure of western culture Masonic organizations but are often motivated by more sinister objectives. Their formation initially was influenced by immigrant's needs to band together in combating ethnic exploitation.

Tongs ruthlessly governed Chinatown's criminal activities during the late nineteenth century. Many were disbursed and lost influence following the 1906 earthquake, which obliterated the sector. Some sources insist their presence and influence has never dissipated. Not all tongs are considered disreputable or affiliated with criminal influences. Many of the more established provide essential recognized services such as immigrant counseling, Chinese schools and English classes for adults.

The word Tong translates into hall or gathering place. During the late evening of September 3rd, which had spilled into Sunday morning by 2:40 a.m., a hundred Asian and Caucasian diners remained in the popular Golden Dragon restaurant. The Chinese habitually enjoy an *Hsiao Yeh* (little snack). Chinatown restaurants often accommodated these preferences until a traditional closing time of 3:00 a.m. Amongst the Labor Day weekend dining crowd were ten members of the Wah Ching gang including their leadership. They were affiliated and sometimes allied with another faction, the Hop Sing Boys, whose tong owned the restaurant. Members of the Hop Sing Boys were also present that evening.

A rival group, the Joe Boys (Chung Ching Yee) was alerted by one of its members, Carlos Jon, who worked at a downtown hotel of their presence. Within a brief span, numerous members of the Joe Boys assembled at the home of a Pacifica tattoo artist to launch a surprise assault on their rivals. They distributed firearms including a sawed-off shotgun, conventional shotgun, . 45 automatic rifle, .38 handgun, ammunition and nylon stocking masks. They drove to Chinatown in an automobile stolen by gang member Peter Cheung.

Blood had been spilt two months earlier in a gun battle at the Ping Yuen Housing Project between the Joe Boys and Wah Ching. Four members had been wounded and one killed, 16-year-old Joe Boys' member Felix Huey. Retaliation was inevitable and a congested restaurant the ideal opportunity, preventing escape.

The intention behind the attack was to seek out and systematically eliminate the Wah Ching members. The plan deviated immediately. Four of the Joe Boys randomly sprayed gunfire into the crowded concentration of patrons, employees and tourists. Perhaps the gunmen had panicked anticipating return fire. The shooting spree lasted less than sixty seconds before they fled. The bedlam resulted in five fatalities and eleven wounded.

Not a single Wah Ching member was injured. The intended victims were lodged in the rear of the restaurant. Upon sighting the Joe Boys entrance and viewing the drawn weapons, they ducked and tipped over their tables for protection, concealing themselves during the fuselage.

Chester Yu had remained in the car and was reported to have driven the group back to Pacifica where they spent the night with other gang members. Another member of the gang and a suspect in the murders, Sai Ying Lee, was never apprehended. His escape from later arrest failed to clarify his exact role in the killings although he was also rumored also to be the getaway driver.

Chester Yu and Tony Szeto were responsible for dumping the employed weapons into the San Francisco Bay near an airport location. The gang members reportedly sawed the guns into bits before dumping them. Yu later escorted police during their investigation to the site where the guns were recovered.

One week later the Wah Ching gang would retaliate with the slaying of Joe Boy Yee Michael Lee in his Richmond district residence. Mark Chan, another gang member was wounded nine times but miraculous recovered. His gang affiliation resulted in another ambush two years later. He ultimately left San Francisco due to his target status.

One of shooting survivors although not injured, Hop Sing Boys' member Raymond *Shrimp Boy* Chow later became one of Chinatown's most notorious gangsters. Once apprehended, he was convicted, imprisoned and a key prosecution witness in the trial against more reputed international crime boss Peter Chong and his tong Wo Hop To. His testimony earned him an early release in 2003 and a subsequent reputation as a reformed gang member, speaking often and publicly against his former lifestyle.

Not everyone was convinced of his redemption and transformation. Chow was arrested in March 2014 during an FBI raid in connection with an investigation into official corruption by California State Senator Leland Yee. In 2016, Chow was found guilty on 162 counts including racketeering, robbery, aiding and abetting the laundering of drug money and conspiring to deal in the illegal sales of goods. For these crimes and arranging the 2005 execution style slaying of Allen Leung, a prominent Chinatown businessman, he was sentenced to life in prison.

The five innocent fatalities from the Golden Dragon shootings included Denise Louie (20s), Calvin Fong (18), Paul Wada (25), Donald Quan (20) and Fong Wang (48), a Taiwanese waiter at the restaurant.

The Joe Boys gang ultimately disbanded. Four confirmed shooters were eventually arrested and convicted for the massacre. Additional gang members were convicted for accomplice roles and given reduced sentences based on their cooperation with investigators.

The shooters included:

Tom Yu, the attributed leader of the attack, was convicted of five counts of first-degree murder, 11 counts of assault and one count of conspiracy to commit murder. He appealed his conviction all the way to the United States Supreme Court. He is presently incarcerated at the California State Prison in Vacaville.

Peter Ng was convicted of five counts of first-degree murder and 11 counts of assault. He is also presently incarcerated at the California State Prison in Vacaville.

Melvin Yu was convicted of five counts of first-degree murder and 11 counts of assault. In 1995, a Los Angeles Times article profiled his incarceration at the Deuel Vocational Institution in Tracy. He is no longer listed on the California prison rolls under this name and presumably has been released.

Curtis Tam, also known as Stuart Lin, claimed to have accompanied the shooters under duress and aimed his shotgun away from diners. He was an immigrant from Hong Kong who was then 18 and attending Galileo High School. He was the first arrest in the case. He was convicted on five counts of second-degree murder and 11 counts of assault. He is no longer listed on the California prison rolls and presumed released.

The accomplices:

Chester Yu served two years in the California Youth Authority at Stockton. He was released in 1980 and moved out of California.

Carlos Jan, who placed the original call informing the gang of the Wah Chin's presence was given immunity for his testimony against Tom Yu and relocated out of California.

Peter Chung, who'd stolen the car used to transport the gang from Pacifica cooperated fully with the police investigation and testified in several of the trials. He served less than one year at the California Youth Authority at Stockton. In 1980, a passing truck accidentally sideswiped him at night as he sought help on foot for his disabled vehicle on Interstate 580.

Tony Szeto was convicted for two years in state prison for his assistance in dumping the murder weapons. California's first appellate court reversed the conviction due to insufficient corroboration. The prosecution team was successful in reinstating the conviction before the California Supreme Court. That decision became a leading precedent case for laws involving accomplice corroboration.

Writer Brockman Morris in his book *Bamboo Tigers* was a major source in relating the fates of many of these participants. His most ironic portrayal was the one written about Gan Wah *Robert* Woo. Woo received a $100,000 reward offered by the City of San Francisco for his information leading to the apprehension, arrest and conviction of the perpetrators. He had reportedly declined to participate in the killings but knew intimate details about them, which he revealed to investigators. A career criminal, he was detained at various facilities throughout his life and became a visible target once his role as star informant was revealed.

He ultimately relocated to New York where he planned to resettle and marry. In 1983 he abruptly vanished. He resurfaced and was shot fatally by police during a botched December 20, 1984 gang heist of the Jin Hing jewelry store in Los Angeles' Chinatown.

The paradox behind the involved parties was that each were young, physically slight, barely spoke English and recklessly impulsive in their preparations and ultimate execution of their plan. Despite their age, they were hardened killers and criminals already involved in stolen property, extortion and illegal drug trade.

The Golden Dragon restaurant, despite the carnage, continued operations the same evening of the shootings with notable damage. In 1981, the Golden Dragon and its owners Jack Lee, B. Hong Ng and the Hop Sing Tong paid a reported $450,000 out of court settlement to two wounded survivors and families of the three of the murder victims. The restaurant continued in business until 2006 but ultimately closed after a failed health inspection and failure to pay their employees for numerous months.

The Imperial Palace restaurant has since resumed operations in the popular location.

The San Francisco police department established the Asian Gang Task Force following the massacre. The killings had been preceded by a reported thirty-nine murders during the decade by drive-by shootings and assassinations. The task force today has been credited with having contained many potentially explosive situations but their presence is incapable of restricting society's transformation.

Tong societies remain active in Chinatown. The legend of the reticent Chinese wall of silence remains intact. Southeastern Asian gangs within San Francisco have proliferated. The Imperial Palace restaurant now closes promptly at 10:00 p.m. nightly.

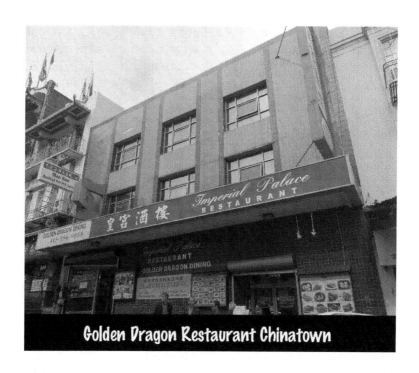

Golden Dragon Restaurant Chinatown

Scott Dekraai: The Mad Rampage and Excruciating Slow Justice

A contentious and extended child custody battle involving a couple's 8-year-od son provoked a deadly shooting rampage in a Seal Beach hair salon on October 12, 2011.

The Meritage hair salon became an execution chamber for berserk shooter Scott Evans Dekraai armed with three handguns. The attack, which lasted approximately two minutes, killed six within the salon (two died the day following from their wounds). The victims included Randy Lee Fannin, the shop owner, Michelle Fournier, the killer's ex-wife, Lucia Kondas, Victoria Buzzo, Christy Wilson, Michelle Fast and Laura Webb. Webb's mother, who was having her hair done by her daughter was critically injured by the shootings but survived. Two of the fatalities were customers.

To cap his descent into madness, Dekraai shot David Caouette to death through the front windshield and passenger window of his parked vehicle outside the salon. He had apparently visited a restaurant adjacent to the salon and had no connection to the other victims.

Dekraai's outburst was motivated by an adverse custody decision against him the day before and an argumentative conversation with Michelle Fournier earlier that morning. He methodically shot each victim in the head and chest and would have killed more had several patrons not been able to exit the building or remained hidden in the back room.

Upon storming the salon, owner Fannin attempted to calm the determined Dekraai by pleading, *Please don't do this. There's another way. Let's go outside and talk.*

Words could not placate an individual intent on blood. Carnage was Dekraai's response. He was arrested less than a half mile from the scene in a pick-up truck clothed in body amour. He did not attempt to resist a superior armed police force.

The shock and disbelief within the community resulted in a candlelight vigil the following day and donations to a substantial victim's aid fund. Seal Beach had only one solitary murder during the four previous years preceding the rampage.

The public outrage did not result in swift justice. Later in the month, Dekraai was indicted on eight counts of murder with special circumstances and one of attempted murder. The prosecutor expressed his intention publicly to seek the death penalty. Nearly three years later Dekraai was convicted based on a *guilty* plea.

The sentencing phase, which would have normally followed, was delayed due to a ruling by an Orange County Superior Court judge in March 2015. The judge cited evidence that Dekraai's constitutional rights had been violated while imprisoned at the Orange County Central Men's Jail. A jailhouse informant had been placed in an adjacent cell to his.

Dekraai was either incredibly indiscreet with his remarks or the informant was exaggerating his access to informed comments. The informant claimed in testimony that the killer had bragged about the homicides in conversations between the two. Whether the placement of the informant was intentional or coincidental, the testimony should have seemed irrelevant considering the magnitude of the act. The judge's ruling indicated his conclusion that the placement of the informant was deliberate.

In the interim, the California Attorney General's office has been designated to assume the duties from the county prosecutors. The ruling does not affect the verdict, but may influence whether Dekraai is given a death sentence or life imprisonment. The sorting out process has continued in limbo since without a sentencing declaration.

Whether Dekraai is sentenced to death or life imprisonment, his own life will be extended indefinitely. This option was never available to his tragic victims.

Even opponents of the death penalty should find that scenario troubling.

The Meritage Salon

Mel and Elizabeth Grimes: The Consequences Behind a One-Ton Stone

A stone escalated the feud out of control. The offending rock was neither a valuable gemstone nor polished rounded river stone. John Franklin Kenney paid a nursery to deliver a common boulder weighing one ton. The sizeable sandstone was strategically lowered behind his neighbor's parked Volkswagen bus blocking access to their carport.

Within the terminology of real estate law, an easement is a common inconvenience when two property owners legally share access to a single parcel of land. John Kenney and his next-door neighbors Mel and Elizabeth Grimes had been obliged to share an access road to exit both properties for over seven years.

An insignificant segment of the road, approximately 4' wide by 10' long came into eventual dispute. Visibly, it was located on Kenney's property, but on the Grime's side of the road, which had to be crossed to access their carport. Common sense would assume this patch would be considered a portion of the easement and insignificant to quarrel over.

Not to John Kenney.

The dispute over the insignificant stretch became lethal and the most notorious homicide in the history of the Carmel Valley. Carmel Valley village is often confused with Carmel-by-the-Sea, the coastal resort lining the Pacific Coast and renowned Pebble Beach. The valley is sublime pastoral lowland nestled into the Santa Lucia Mountain Range. Oak and sycamore trees line serpentine roads with accompanying grasslands, savannas and vineyards. The village is located approximately 12 miles from the more famous resort.

Local residents prefer the idyllic natural serenity to the stress of transient motorists and shoppers.

The aggressive act by Kenney towards his neighbors crystallized years of resentment. A reported initial dispute over the payment towards a repaired crossing bridge several years before escalated into a nightmarish set of claims and counter claims between dueling neighbors. Vengeance, accelerated hatred and mutual inflexibility were articulated through the legal system via mutual restraining orders, multiple claims of building code violations and physical altercations.

John Kenney was approximately fifteen years older than his neighbors, but age was not the defining element of the conflict. In effect, the dispute became the divergence between one neighbor who insisted upon uniformity and symmetry and another pair who could have cared less.

John Kenney was a petroleum engineer, consultant and former college professor with an impressive pedigree. He split time between his Carmel Valley residence and Nancy, France with a wife and two adopted daughters. His Carmel Valley residence was modest, but trim and meticulous.

Mel Grimes was a locally based attorney and his antithesis. His home, which he owned since 1995 and shared with wife Elizabeth, reflected his personal eccentricities and multiple impulsive fancies. Habitually overgrown foliage, excess vehicles, unchained parading pets, planted surfboards, stray signage, and a small discarded sailboat defined his aesthetics. His décor resembled an eyesore and fire hazard to Kenney. Others interpreted the mess as his unique personality expression.

Both of their houses were predominantly camouflaged to outsiders due to the rustic foliage, but not to each other.

Their relationship symbolized the incompatibility of order confronting cluttered chaos on a daily excruciating and grinding basis. Neither party felt obliged to leave.

The intention behind the boulder was clearly meant to provoke the Grimes. The stated intention based on John Kenney's attorney's advice was to protect his perceived property rights. A simple title search could have legally resolved the issue. Research after the conflict climaxed into tragedy confirmed the parcel was indeed a portion of the easement. Mel Grimes certainly knew this fact when he purchased the house and property in 1995. John Kenney likely knew it as well but feigned ignorance and demanded possession.

On January 29, 2007, Kenney anticipated the turmoil his actions would provoke. Both parties had just returned from vacations. The Grimes arrived from Hawaii and Kenney from France. That morning, Kenney had contacted the local Sheriff's office anticipating a hostile reaction from his neighbors upon the placement of the boulder. Sheriff's deputies did arrive in the mid-afternoon as the delivery truck was leaving. The cargo was deposited without incident. Mel and Elizabeth Grimes were not at home.

The couple arrived home at approximately 5:30 p.m. separately and simultaneously. As Kenney anticipated, both were furious. Mel Grimes immediately located a sledgehammer and shovel from his tool shed and began to smash the boulder repeatedly still attired in his business suit. Elizabeth Grimes telephoned 911 to request assistance because she sensed trouble. Mel Grimes suffered from a heart condition that his frenzied stone bashing was likely to aggravate.

During his trial, John Kenney claimed that he felt intimidated by Mel Grimes wielding a sledgehammer. He further asserted Elizabeth Grimes was in the act of menacing and attacking him. He had made a similar claim against her several months previously in a deposition.

As the sole witness to the event, his testimony might have sustained credibility were it not for the recording of Elizabeth Grime's 911 call. Grimes had been speaking with an emergency operator and her exchanges with her husband were vehement and heated. She confirmed to him that a sheriff deputy was en route and pleaded for him to cease his exertions.

During her conversation, John Kenney exited his house, contrary to his attorney's advice. Perhaps this was his intention from the outset. He approached the couple armed with a loaded semi-automatic .45-caliber pistol. The eerie 911-telephone call recorded a brief but terse shouting exchange between Kenney and Elizabeth Grimes. He demanded her to vacate his property.

What followed was a rustling noise, accompanied by two gunshots and Mel Grimes moaning from the fatal discharge. Kenney then turned the gun towards Elizabeth and two more shots were discharged. Five shots were fired with one missing his target. The second shot into Elizabeth was while she lay prone on the ground. The couple had the presence of consciousness to exchange *I love yous* to each other. Mel Grimes expired and Elizabeth Grimes would shortly follow as she was medically airlifted to a nearby hospital.

Neither victim had anticipated their ruthless execution.

John Kenney's jury at trial rejected his self-defense claim. He pitifully reiterated the menace and vulnerability sensed by the justifiably enraged couple. He was convicted of the second-degree murder of Mel Grimes and first-degree murder of Elizabeth Grimes because of her prone positioning during the second round he shot into her. He expressed no remorse at the sentencing phase of the trial.

His behavior remained predictably anal and pathetic during the months and years to follow.

Six months after the double murder and before he was tried, Kenney sued the deceased Grimes for pain and suffering, disability and severe emotional distress based on a previous battery claim against Elizabeth Grimes. The lawsuit predictably stated no mention that the defendants were dead or that the plaintiff was the responsible party. The suit was dismissed.

His defense attorney was deeded Kenney's one-acre property as payment for his unsuccessful legal services in October 2008. The home was immediately placed on the market and presumably sold with proper disclosure. The status on payment for the legal fees involved with the ill-fated boulder advice remained unpublished. Kenney lost an appeal of his murder conviction in 2011. The Grimes home sold in November 2011.

John Franklin Kenney's permanent residence is currently the RJ Donovan Correctional Facility in San Diego. He likely maintains an immaculate and pristine cell.

The Grimes Former House

The Graduate Students Rage Against His Perceived Academic Tormentors

Frederick Martin Davidson was a 36-year-old mechanical graduate student at San Diego State University in 1996.

The engineering department faculty had rejected his initial master's thesis. He was convinced that the entire department were involved in a conspiracy against him.

He simmered in anger against three specific faculty members.

He was bitter and resentful towards his faculty advisor Chen Liang, who he felt had exploited his long working hours within the departmental laboratory. The projects given to him in his mind amounted only to mundane tasks with absolutely no relationship to his thesis. Preston Lowrey III had labeled him a *cheater* in conversations with other faculty members. He was certain Constantinos Lyrintzis had inhibited his prospects of finding permanent employment.

Perhaps unaware of his bitterness towards them, the three faculty members agreed to sit down with Davidson at 10:00 a.m. on Thursday, August 15, 1996 and review his thesis. Davidson had a surprise waiting. Three student observers were invited for morale support.

Davidson began the proceedings by heightening the stakes. He handed Liang an email printout from an employer offering him a job should he pass his thesis defense. He did not anticipate the faculty members reversing their earlier opinion.

In the silence that followed the transfer of the printed email, Davidson silently walked over to a first aid kit mounted on the wall. He removed a loaded 9mm handgun and five additional magazines of ammunition. He immediately turned around and began firing. He struck Liang fatally who was seated. He clipped the other two professors who were attempting to scatter.

281

Lowrey attempted to escape via the sole access door to the hallway. He never made it. Davidson gunned him down repeatedly until he expired on the floor of the doorway.

Lyrintzis was trapped. With no exit to freedom, she slipped into an adjoining classroom and hid futilely under a table. Davidson reloaded another magazine into his handgun and relentlessly tracked her down. For her, the moment their eyes locked certainly created an eternity of pure terror.

He ruthlessly shot her to death while she crouched under the table. The overall carnage resulted in 23 rounds being fired at the three professors with 16 direct hits.

Each of the student observers was allowed to flee without incident. They notified the third-floor faculty and student members to evacuate. Davidson telephoned the police to confess.

He had originally intended to commit suicide after the shootings having composed an explanatory note. He meekly and tearfully surrendered to police still holding his handgun. His cowardice had betrayed his determination to make a defiant statement.

In July 1997, Davidson was convicted under a plea-bargaining arrangement that spared him the death penalty. He was sentenced to three consecutive life terms without the possibility of parole and is currently interned at the California State Prison in Lancaster.

The three slain professors were honored by a *L3 Memorial Park* commemorative adjacent to the engineering building. As the tragedy has receded from public recognition, the discreet memorial seems oddly diminutive in proportion to the flagrant and odious loss.

San Diego State Engineering Building

Engineering Building Classroom

The L3 Memorial Park

Memorial Plaques For Three Slain Professors

Lynwood *Jim* Drake: A Loose Wire Springs A Rampage

Lynwood C. Drake III did not fit the typical profile of a methodical serial killer despite the planned sequential order of his killings on the evening of November 9, 1992. *Crazy Jim* as labeled by Morro Bay locals had scores to settle for a life that simply had unraveled.

He was an embittered, unemployed construction worker and bartender who snapped following months of accumulated financial reverses and gambling losses. He had the distinction of having appeared in the film *The World According to Garp* but ultimately became closer identified as San Luis Obispo County's first recognized serial killer.

He hunted down and killed six people and wounded another in three separate towns before killing himself.

The killing rampage began over a dispute between Drake and his former landlord regarding his eviction from a Morro Bay rental. The diminutive residence was distinctively designed as a windmill. Drake had failed to pay rent for several successive months.

His landlord and initial shooting victim, Andrew Zatko, 80, was a prominent local citizen and live-in companion of the actual house owner, Gladys Walton, a former silent film actress. Walton, whose son wrote a memoir detailing her ten-year love affair with Al Capone was known in films as the *Glad Girl*. She would pass away the following year at the age of 90.

Morro Bay in the early 1990s was a community with a miniscule crime rate. Citizen's sense of invulnerability was reinforced by a significant number of residents habitually keeping their front doors unlocked and keys dangling from car ignition switches. Drake walked into Zatko's home through the unlocked front door and shot him in the neck with a .32-caliber pistol killing him instantly.

He continued his rampage against Norman Metcalfe, 37, who'd assisted Zatko in the eviction process six months earlier by testifying against Drake and helping to remove his belongings. He callously shot Metcalfe between the eyes at his home and during an ensuing struggle for his gun, killed Danny Cizek, 32, and wounded Jeffrey Sidlin, 27, friends of Metcalfe.

The killings were motivated by Drake's presumption that his eviction had destroyed his life and family stability. The eviction had prompted his common law wife and daughter to relocate to North Dakota. He was purportedly living out of his car at the time of his spree. Drake suffered from a variety of debilitating physical ailments leaving his employment prospects scant. His dual reputation for erratically unstable behavior made desirability to hire him impossible.

Immediately following the homicides and while being sought by police, Lynwood Drake addressed a second grievance by driving 40 miles to a Paso Robles card room, the Oak's Card Parlor (now defunct). He had been reportedly banned from the establishment for unruly behavior and cheating. It was reported that two days before the rampage, he had gambled away his remaining funds there.

For these shootings, he armed himself with a 12-gauge shotgun. His initial victims were dealers David Law, 41, and Joe Garcia, 60, in the back of the facility. He then killed a patron, Kris Staub, 31, trying to exit the building. An additional ten terrified and panicked customers remained vulnerable begging him to spare their lives. He relented. There were additional slights and individual to address. Reportedly, car difficulties prevented him from eliminating his pastor and one of his daughter's day-care workers.

His rampage was nearing its climax. He drove to the home of another former landlord, Joanne Morrow in San Miguel. He beat her with a blackjack and threatened to kill her. Instead he took her hostage. By 5 a.m. the following morning, police had surrounded Morrow's house and escape became impossible. Miraculously, despite his menacing rants, he spared her life. While Morrow was on the phone with hostage negotiators, Drake raised his revolver and fired a single fatal cartridge into his skull.

The carnage was complete but piecing together his motives became more beguiling. Drake left a delusional suicide note in his pants pocket bemoaning his life of persecution. He criticized an unsupportive family and associated himself with outlaw Jesse Cole Younger, a member of the Jesse James gang.

His attempt to redress his life's failings generated no empathy towards his perceived injustices or agreement towards the merits of his actions.

Morro Bay today remains an apparent oasis of tranquility and safety. The crime rate remains marginal. Doors however are now secured and locked like most contemporary American suburban and rural towns.

The name of Lynwood C. Drake III is generally anonymous to residents who have settled into Morro Bay since 1992. He is forgotten or unmentionable by choice to most long-term residents. His rampage has been relegated as an insignificant footnote in local history.

Innocence and illusions are not lost solely by a single incident such as Drake's but rather their accumulation. Inhabitants become cautious and numbed hearing the significant daily doses of bad news through their media outlets. The erosion of trust between residents, transients, neighbors and society in general has become sadly commonplace.

Restoring future trust and a comfortable sense of security may ultimately require successive generations. In truth, this loss is more likely permanent.

The Windmill House in Morro Bay

Adolescence Angst With A Gunfire Solution

Charles Andrew *Andy* Williams had just turned fifteen and had been attending Santana High School in Santee since the 2000 fall semester. His admission to the school followed his parent's separation the year before and father's relocation from Maryland during the summer.

Williams' adaptation to his fresh school environment proved difficult. He claimed that he was excessively bullied and accepted only within a small group of skateboarders. He claimed that he had attempted to speak with a guidance counselor about the abuse, but all were overwhelmed by other concerns. He perceived that a drama teacher had intentionally humiliated him in front of his class during an acting exercise.

On Monday, March 5, 2001, Williams felt he had endured enough. He arrived at school armed with his father's .22 caliber long-action revolver. At 9:20 a.m., Williams entered one of the boys bathroom and fatally shot Freshman Bryan Zuckor. He exited the bathroom and began firing indiscriminately at other students. He wounded 12 and killed another student, Randy Gordon. A student teacher and campus security supervisor entered the bathroom in an attempt to stop the disaster. Williams wounded him five times.

Students chaotically ducked for safety. Throughout his barrage, Williams would resurface from the bathroom smiling. He felt empowered by the mayhem he was generating. The euphoria was short-lived.

Police officers arrived and stormed the bathroom. Williams was discovered kneeling on the floor with the weapon in his hands. He had been unable to summon the nerve to kill himself.

In the aftermath, an investigation was conducted to determine the validity of his bullying and abuse claims. The results were inconclusive. The only definitive individuals identified as his tormentors were the small group he spent most of his time with. As an outsider, being ignored may have seemed the equivalent of being abused. A conflicting motive later surfaced that the shootings had been in response to a dare by his friends.

Were Andy Williams' claims legitimate or simply a sympathy-seeking charade?

In 2002, Williams pleaded guilty to all of the charges against him in order to avoid a public trial. A California judge sentenced him like an adult to a 50-year to life term in prison. He initially served time in a Youth Offender Program before being transferred to an adult prison. He is currently interned at the Ironwood State Prison in Blythe.

Since his conviction, Williams has cultivated a band of supporters who have advocated both a retrial and reduction in his sentence due to the severity. Multiple appeals have been denied.

Adolescence is a complicated transitional period into adulthood, with or without the added stressors of taunting and bullying. Williams' actions eliminated any opportunity for his eventual adjustment. Most distressed individuals ultimately labor and emerge through such a difficult period. The dead were not given the opportunity and the wounded will forever be haunted by his personal turmoil.

Williams's Shooting Grounds

Santana High's School Courtyard

The Oikos University Massacre: Piecing Together a Disjointed Puzzle

The underlying reasons behind rampage killings are often difficult to pinpoint. The tragic results frequently end with a self-inflicted suicide by the killers and no answers.

It is left for the media, law enforcement officials, survivors and their families to piece together explanatory motives of apparent senseless acts. The disintegration of a killer's personality and orderly identity may appear obvious in retrospect. Behind each perpetrator is a human being that was either a simmering psychopath or a tormented individual that concluded they could no longer exist or tolerate their living environment.

Does conceptually understanding the devil's motives make his atrocities less despicable?

One L. Goh does not easily classify into the definition of student rampage killer, even given the setting of his shooting spree, an educational institution. American schools have become a depressingly recurring setting for mass shootings. The motives vary, but the shooters are typically male, adolescent and fringe members of their student bodies.

At approximately 10:30 a.m. on April 2, 2012, Goh, 43, entered an Oikos University nursing class in session, lined up its students against a wall and began firing a .45-caliber semi-automatic handgun. His aim was predominantly towards female students. He killed seven and wounded another three students. Oikos University is a Korean Christian college located in a business park nearby the Oakland International Airport. The campus resembles one of the expansive wholesale and product distribution warehouses that populate the neighborhood.

Oikos offers credentials in Christian Theology, Music and Nursing, the degree he briefly pursued earlier during the 2012 Spring Semester. He had dropped out of the program after only a few months. Other sources had him expelled for unspecified disciplinary reasons. He became bitter over his departure and the school's refusal to refund him full or even partial tuition monies. The administrator, who was identified as his most likely target, publicly disputed the allegation. She maintained that he had voluntarily left the program on his own. The issue of accuracy may or may not be resolved during his impending court trial.

Dismissing his actions as straightforward mania becomes simplistic. In the eyes of the grieving innocent victim's families, there can normally be no alternative. Their profound grief attached to the loss of their loved ones leaves little space for compassion towards a cold-blooded executioner. Through most eyes, his acts were wrong, unconscionable and premeditated. Through most eyes, the culprit should be duly punished.

The sole question remaining is whether he receives a capital punishment sentence or will be permanently confined to a California mental institution.

Goh was a native of South Korea and followed his parents and two older brothers to the United States during his youth, later becoming a U.S. citizen. He initially resided in Virginia, just outside of Washington D.C. and then relocated to the rural southwestern portion of the state. He helped run a construction company until mid-2008.

The construction industry splintered nationally and collapsed with the widespread housing meltdown. By the summer of 2008, Goh had lost his income, was evicted from his apartment and creditors impounded his car. He ended up living with his father in Oakland at a housing project for senior citizens. He worked at a San Mateo warehouse, with his father at a Daly City grocery store and periodically as a mover. He had not yet surrendered hope to his diminishing prospects.

Contemporary American culture promotes an obsessive notion over the necessity of sustained forward progress or reinvention.

Anything less is perceived as failure. Viewing habitually the garish displays of wealth in the Bay Area can be a disillusioning barometer for the legions that have failed to keep pace.

Goh's financial disasters were compounded by family calamity. In 2011, his most favored brother, an Iraq War veteran and decorated Special Forces hero died in a freak head-on collision with a multi-ton boulder stationary on a Virginia road traveling at 70 mph. The news devastated his family and especially his mother. She returned to Korea and died only months after his brother's funeral.

Goh's father supplemented his son's attempt at reinvention with a $6,000 loan to pay for his Oikos nursing tuition. The investment proved disappointing with Goh's abrupt departure from the school. Numerous published reports confirmed he was widely teased for his advanced age, chubby appearance and poor English skills. Persistent bullying and physiological harassment are common ignition triggers for rampage killings.

Disillusionment with his choice of school may have influenced his decision to leave, assuming he did so voluntarily. Examining reports have condemned Oikos substandard academic and job placement track record. Was his shooting decision influenced by a bitter realization that he had chosen the wrong vehicle for redemption?

A single, several or all of these factors may have accumulated to make One L. Goh snap. His career transformation project had clearly failed with his departure from the school. Had he reached the identical dead-end conclusion many irate shooters share in common?

In the attempted analysis to understand an evil act, it is convenient but negligent to forget the victims. Killed were Tshering Rinzing Bhutia (38), Doris Chibuko (40), Sonam Chodon (33), Grace Eunhae Kim (23), Katleen Ping (24), Judith Seymour (53) and Lydia Sim (21). Wounded were Dawinder

Kaur (19), Grace Kirika (43) and Ahmad Javid Sayeed (36). Were any of his victims also his tormenters or merely the random targets of his rage?

He surrendered several hours after the shootings approximately five miles away in an Alameda Safeway parking lot without resistance.

One L. Goh clearly suffered a concentrated accumulation of reverses. Judging his mental stability and motivations are further complicated by his inability to articulate using the English language. During his upcoming trial, should it ever occur, a third-party defense team will likely distribute blame and responsibility elsewhere.

Even they may never share a public forum to vent specific causes and effect.

His setbacks however are not necessarily unique. Many individuals who've suffered worse misfortunes have coped, re-grouped and recovered in varying degrees based on their resiliency. Their struggles do not generate headline news or prompt violent expression.

Goh was arraigned two days following the murders and was charged with seven counts of murder and three counts of attempted murder. He did not enter a plea.

In jailhouse media interviews, he followed a more conventional response tactic by indicating he was *deeply sorry* for the killings, but only remembered parts of the day. Amnesia and short-term memory loss consistently plague numerous murderers performing heinous acts.

Following his initial court appearance and interviews, he went on a hunger strike losing twenty pounds. He resumed eating after forced feeding intervention was threatened and later that month at a second hearing, pleaded *not guilty*.

His path towards public accountability has followed a labyrinth following a November 2012 hearing to determine his competency to stand trial. He was diagnosed with paranoid schizophrenia, which made cooperation with his appointed public defender impossible based on his apparent incomprehension with the criminal justice system. During the trial, Goh was assigned a Korean translator. He briefly disrupted the proceedings once with an outburst when his defense attorney was discussing his mental competence.

During a third January 2013 hearing, a second psychiatrist's report re-confirmed the identical initial diagnosis. Goh reportedly has refused all medication while incarcerated and has been reportedly forcibly medicated. In a December 2015 hearing, an Alameda County Superior Court Judge ruled him incompetent to stand trial for murder.

The case remains in judicial limbo while Goh is confined to Napa State Hospital, a mental institution for treatment and subsequent competency reviews. During the interim, while his judgment is suspended, the three survivors and victim's families attempt to reattach their own disjointed puzzles.

Oikos University Campus

Oikos Nursing Classroom

Holzer Family Stabbing Spree: Unanswered Questions

It has become a depressingly too-familiar scenario.

On August 11, 2014, Nicolas Holzer snapped without apparent provocation. In the deceptively tranquil suburb of Goleta, Holzer, 45, stabbed his parents, William and Sheila Holzer, his sons Sebastian and Vincent and their family Australian shepherd. The six lived together in the parent's household.

Holzer dispassionately telephone police after the killings and made an immediate confession. He reportedly claimed that he had to fulfill his destiny, but did not elaborate.

Initially, there appeared no motive or premeditation.

Superficially, the family appeared genuinely harmonious. Former business colleagues described Holzer's performance as capable. He had however been unemployed for eight years since quitting steady work. His sons were observed as being well adjusted socially and in school.

He had no prior arrests and had obtained the full custody of his sons a decade previously from a divorce. Holzer and his sons had been living together for seven years.

Precedent motives emerged within in month following the initial reporting of the tragedy. Accusations of a continuous custody battle, sexual abuse and Holzer's intimidating and aggressive behavior surfaced. The previous marriage with his Mexican wife Juana came under suspicion as simply a sham by her to gain legal immigration status.

None of these claims against either Holzer have been substantiated. A public trial is anticipated for 2017.

The lack of conclusive answers lead to obvious questions regarding how such an individual could have obtained full custody rights. It appears unbelievable that no tangible warning signs were evident.

In February 2015, Holzer, despite his earlier confession, entered a not guilty plea by reason of insanity for the killings. Their severity and brutality may qualify him for a death penalty sentence if ultimately convicted. He remains currently in custody at the Santa Barbara County Sheriff's facility awaiting psychiatric evaluation and his impending trial.

In trying to fathom sense over a desperate act, speculations become baffling. One conclusion seems certain. Something was amiss in such a normal suburban household.

Holzer Residence

The Inevitable Slaughter of the Innocents

The slaughter of the innocents was preceded by an almost certain pattern of behavior exhibited by their shooter.

Patrick Edward Purdy's formative history made his massacre at the Cleveland Elementary School seemingly inevitable. The impending signs were blatant.

On the morning of January 17, 1989, an anonymous and vague death threat was telephoned to the elementary school. At noon, Purdy parked his van behind the school's playground area. He then set his firework-laden van on fire detonating an explosion. He strolled over to the playground filled with children during their lunch hour and crouched behind a portable building.

He scattered 106 rounds from a semi-automatic rifle into the assemblage within three minutes. His rampage killed five children and wounded thirty others including one teacher. The dead included Raphanar Or, Ram Chun, Thuy Tran, Sokhim An and Oeun Lim. Thuy Tran was from Vietnamese and the others from Cambodia.

As a defining gesture evading explanation, Purdy leveled a pistol to his head and discharged a single fatal cartridge. Investigators discovered that he had carved the words *freedom*, *victory*, *Earthman* and *Hezbollah* onto his rifle. On the flak jacket he wore, he'd scrawled *PLO*, *Libya* and *death to the Great Satin* (predictably misspelled).

His actions initially appeared incomprehensible. A closer analysis of his life confirmed otherwise.

How does a society prevent the chronically damaged from ultimately detonating?

Patrick Purdy had an early start on his sprint towards disintegration. His father was a professional soldier and fatally struck by a car when Purdy was fourteen. His parents had divorced when he was two with his mother citing a death threat by her husband as the cause. She relocated her son to South Lake Tahoe and then Stockton where he attended Cleveland Elementary between kindergarten and second grade.

His mother remarried when he was five and divorced four years later. Relations with her remained strained throughout his life. Child Protective Services were habitual visitors to their residence due to her suspected abuse. He was banned permanently from her household when he struck her in the face. A vagabond existence of foster care, homelessness in San Francisco and irregular high school attendance followed. He became an alcoholic and drug addict despite briefly relocating to Los Angeles in the custody of a foster mother.

Adolescence morphed into adulthood and his personality deterioration steadily heightened. He was arrested for numerous offenses including theft, underage drinking, weapons charges, drug dealing, armed robbery and vandalism. He attempted suicide twice and was described by associates as always miserable and self-loathing.

The shooting capsuled his sense of personal frustration about his accumulated failures. Innocent children became a convenient object for venting his sickness.

Why an individual with his background could purchase an automatic weapon became an obvious question in the aftermath. The answer was simply that none of his offenses were serious enough to prevent him from purchasing firearms.

The right to bear arms contingent will forever argue that guns as objects bear no malice. The flaw in their rationale is the proliferation and availability can and never will be adequately controlled.

The actions of human time bombs such as Patrick Purdy will remain the consequence of their professed *inalienable* right.

Site of Van Detonation

Cleveland Elementary Schoolyard

The Cult and Murder Consequence Traced to Family Abuse

Marcus Wesson occupies a unique niche in the history of revulsion and murder. His excessive abuse, manipulation and deviancy towards his own family seem unprecedented.

His legacy as Fresno's worst convicted mass murderer required decades to cultivate. It detonated with an abrupt police standoff on March 12, 2004. His victims were exclusively his own children. They were fathered with his wife and incestuous relationships with his daughters and nieces. In all, nine siblings were shot to death with a .22 caliber handgun as Wesson barricaded himself inside a back bedroom. The victim's ages ranged between infancy to 25-years-old.

In the early 1970s, Wesson began assembling an insulated cult of divinity worshipping him as a Messiah figure. After returning from a US Army European stint, he became sexually involved with the then married Rosemary Solorio. She separated and moved in with him accompanied by her children. With one daughter Elizabeth, he reportedly began pre-teenage sexual contact. Their tale turned increasingly sordid when he married her at fifteen. Together he impregnated her eleven times and fathered ten children. One of Elizabeth's younger sisters had seven children with him.

Wesson maintained his family's allegiance through strict discipline, frequent whippings and home schooling. His love was expressed to his sons in the form of stick and wire strand beatings. With his daughters, their fidelity was maintained via sexual relations and pregnancy. Obscured from public scrutiny, the family lived on the fringes of communities, often in wooded shacks, rundown boats and abandoned houses. Public records indicated that Wesson ultimately fathered up to 18 children with 7 different women. Five were his daughters.

He never held steady employment and lived off of the proceeds of welfare and his adult children's part-time incomes. In 1989, he was convicted of welfare fraud and perjury. Throughout this entire period of debauchery and manipulation, he eluded surveillance from neighbors and child protective service agencies. He sermonized daily and psychologically prepared his family for a pending Armageddon. On several occasions, he declared his intention to transport the family to Washington State where his parents lived.

The crumbling family unit was inevitable. As his children aged, it became simply a matter of time and circumstance until his stranglehold would disintegrate. Wesson was aware of his fragile hold and the impending mutiny.

The relocation to Washington would never materialize. On March 12th, a few disenchanted members of his extended family rebelled. They converged with Fresno police in front of his residential compound to demand a custody release of their children. He had fathered each of the children inside.

Wesson spoke with the officers that had knocked at his front door. He then retreated into a back bedroom and shut the door. The police waited his return. During an hour and twenty-minute interim, each of his nine children were shot deliberately through the eye and heaped in a room littered with antique coffins. He calmly returned to the front door with blood on his clothing and surrendered. Throughout the slaughter, the attending officers indicated they did not hear gunfire. Other witnesses contradicted this disclosure.

The carnage would have been worse if more of his children had been home.

At his 2005 trial, Wesson's attorneys blamed the shootings on his daughter Sebbrenah, also a victim. A lack of fingerprint and gun residue failed to prove who actually fired the murder weapon. The gun conveniently bore traces of her DNA. The actual triggerman mattered marginally to the jury. Wesson had repeatedly coached the children to kill each other if authorities had ever threatened to separate the clan. His training and teachings merely awaited an appropriate confrontation.

His *spectator only* defense did not spare the patriarch. Wesson was found guilty on nine-counts of first-degree murder, fourteen counts of forcible sexual assault and molestation imposed on seven of his daughters and nieces. He was sentenced to death and is currently jailed at San Quentin.

Members of his surviving family have demonstrated the monstrosity of his influence. Some continue to defend his unfair detainment. With time and distance other members have acknowledged him as *psychotic*, *delusional* and *narcissistic*.

The abuser will remain on death row until his demise. He cannot reverse his reprehensible damage. Abused survivors remain victims throughout their lifetimes. *Normal* becomes tragically subjective when tainted and perverted. Self-reflection and examination is nearly impossible under conditions of complete dependence.

One may only hope his legacy of abuse ceases with his own children.

The Wesson Fresno Compound

The Unfulfilled Crossover of Dorothy Stratten

Unrealized potential is a curse that has haunted emerging talents seemingly forever in disciplines as diverse as the performing arts, politics, sports and business. The space for the upper echelon of achievement is precariously limited. Timing, persistence and opportunity are often more crucial than raw talent.

Through no fault of her own, Dorothy Ruth Stratten (born Hoogstraten) was denied her aspirations to entertainment stardom following a promising beginning.

Emerging from suburban Coquitlam, adjacent to Vancouver, Stratten met Paul Snider, a local nightclub and promoter of diversely unsuccessful schemes at seventeen while working at a local Dairy Queen. Snider, nine years her senior, seduced the impressionable and physically stunning blond and blue-eyed Stratten. During the summer of 1978, with her mother's consent, he had professional nude photographs taken of her. He mailed the photographs to the editorial offices of *Playboy* magazine and interest was immediate.

Dorothy Stratten relocated to Los Angeles and ascended quickly within the Playboy hierarchy. She found employment as a bunny waitress at their Century City Nightclub and was selected as the August 1979 *Playmate of the Month*. 1980 *Playmate of the Year* honors soon followed. Her meteoric rise was gradually severing Snider's control despite his having coerced her into a marriage ceremony in June of 1979 in Las Vegas.

Snider had outgrown his usefulness and was universally perceived by her surrounding support team as a parasitic presence exhibiting erratic and overly possessive behavior. Stratten supported Snider financially throughout their marriage due to his inability to work legally with his Canadian nationality and his lack of a work visa. Her expanding prospects enabled no place for a limited capacity hustler. Snider had no intention of allowing his protégé to elude his stifling and desperate grasp.

Stratten was channeling her energies professionally and in her personal life elsewhere. Between 1979-80, she appeared in the light comedy films *Americathon*, *Skatetown USA*, *Autumn Born* and *Galaxina*, plus television episodes of *Buck Rogers in the 25th Century* and *Fantasy Island*. She was cast for a prominent role in Peter Bogdanovich's directed *They All Laughed*, a film that would be released in late 1980 following her death.

While none of these works remotely teased Oscar nominations, she had demonstrated crossover talent potential, unique within the Playmate selection universe. Her personal appeal, ambition and drive were encouraging signs. Her entertainment industry contact base was elevating. She had begun an affair with Bogdanovich during filming. He had similarly mentored actress Cybill Shepherd in the earliest stages of her career. Stratten moved in with him and officially separated from Snider.

Paul Snider coaxed her into one final visit at their former West Hollywood apartment during the daylight hours of August 14, 1980. Their discussion was intended towards arranging terms for a divorce agreement. Snider was sharing the residence with the building's owner. Other guests were present that day but allowed the couple their privacy.

Upon arrival, Snider escorted her into their former bedroom and closed the door. He immediately bound her without creating a disturbance or outburst and sexually assaulted her. He then blasted her with a shotgun he had recently acquired and turned the weapon on himself to complete the murder-suicide. Their strewn bodies were discovered without clothing several hours later. No one had overheard the commotion. Dorothy Stratten was 20 years and her potential and mainstream exposure was terminated.

Her brief life and tragic death prompted two exploitive films *Death of a Centerfold* and *Star80* (her personalized car license plate), several books and even musical recordings. Bogdanovich, in perhaps the oddest follow-up twist, financed her younger sister Louise's education and modeling classes following her death. He then married her at 20, the identical age he had lost Dorothy. The union lasted 13 years before a divorce in 2001. His gesture bore an ironical resemblance to Orpheus attempting to retrieve and reconstruct his beloved wife Eurydice from death and the underworld.

Dorothy Stratten was supplanted in 1981 as the annually honored Playmate by another striking beauty. Playboy Enterprises today lingers on the periphery of the cultural relevance it once commanded. The organization has lost the majority of its following and influence due to an aging readership and more explicit Internet viewing outlets. None of Stratten's successors have successfully bridged the transition from nude modeling into major entertainment success.

Murder Apartment of Dorothy Stratten

Laci Peterson: When Motive Convicts Beyond the Body of Evidence

On April 13, 2003, a couple walking their dog in Point Isabel State Park found a male fetus on the sands. The next day, the body of a pregnant woman washed ashore amidst the jagged stones nearby and was discovered by another dog-walker. The bodies were decomposed and hers was decapitated. DNA tests verified that they were the bodies of Laci Peterson and her yet born son, Conner.

The discovery ended a highly publicized hunt for the pair. Laci became the subject of a murder case after she went missing while seven and a half months pregnant with her only child. She was reportedly last seen alive on December 24, 2002. Law enforcement authorities already suspected her husband Scott of the being responsible for the murder. The finding of the bodies enabled prosecutors to formally press charges against him five days later.

Although the point at which both bodies washed up was approximately 90 miles from the couple's home, the site was a mere 5 miles from the Berkeley Marina where Scott had said he'd gone fishing the morning of Christmas Eve.

Scott Peterson was arrested on April 18, 2003 in La Jolla, California in the parking lot of a golf course. He claimed to be meeting his father and brother for a round of golf. At the time of his arrest, he was reportedly carrying $15,000 in cash, four cell phones, camping equipment, a gun, his brother's driver's license and 12 tablets of Viagra. His hair and goatee had been beached blond. Police speculated his intention might have been to flee to Mexico, where extradition procedures are complicated. As with all of his other schemes, the plan was poorly thought out and executed.

Scott and Laci Peterson resembled a happy young couple with good jobs, two nice cars, and a new house of their own in

Modesto. The relationships between their families and in-laws were warm and they were about to have a baby.

For Scott, his marriage was a façade masking deeper anxieties. He was worried about his job performance and about turning 30. Scott was reported to have told anyone who'd listen that he wasn't comfortable with his impending fatherhood. The couple was living beyond their financial means.

Assuming responsibility for his unhappiness, he could have left his wife and child. The consequences, however, would have probably saddled him with alimony and child support payments.

Instead of getting a divorce, court evidence indicted that he began to assemble a new identity and lifestyle persona. He took out a substantial life insurance policy on his wife. He planned her false kidnapping and murder while providing himself an alibi by taking a solo fishing trip on the day she would disappear.

His plan initially appeared solid, as his in-laws were very supportive of him in the beginning. Over time, the farce and flimsiness of his plot became evident. The disclosure of a mistress and his repeated deceptions and lying to all parties involved with the case, cracked any solidarity or empathy towards him and his plight. All that was lacking was a body and a murder weapon to put him on trial.

A massive citywide search effort and $500,000 reward for any information leading to Laci Peterson's safe return yielded nothing. Over 1,000 volunteers signed up to distribute information and to help search for her. Many observed that Scott Peterson's direct involvement seemed detached, remote and distant from the proceedings.

The bodies washed ashore, despite the killer's resolute efforts to keep them permanently submerged. Their discovery sealed his fate. His trial ran from June 2004 through March 2005 with enormous national press coverage. Peterson's defense team repeatedly tried to discredit any suggestion of motive and even formulated a fanciful theory about Laci's kidnapping being the work of a cult.

The jury rejected their arguments and reasoning. Motive and Peterson's pattern of suspicious behavior ultimately became the swaying factor towards their decision. Physical evidence was almost non-existent with the exception of traces of Laci's hair in his boat.

The jury deliberated for seven days before convicting Scott Peterson of murder in the first degree for Laci's death, and in the second degree for the death of their prenatal son, Conner. He was sentenced to death row at San Quentin State Prison where he is currently interned. The excessive exposure of the trial and legal grandstanding probably backfired for Peterson and contributed to his maximum sentence.

Laci Peterson suffered a cruel and callous death. As an innocent participant in Scott Peterson's fantasized love triangle, she paid exceedingly for her fidelity. The motive for her killing eventually emerged as obvious as the incompetence and deceit her husband played in the tragic drama.

Point Isabel

The Peterson Modesto Residence

Point Isabel Rocks: Where Laci's
Body Washed Up

John Morency: As the Adulation Ceased, the Poisoning was Administered

John Elbrect Morency was a professional football player, far removed in 1990 from an active career. The National Football League's historical player website has no record of him or his statistical participation. Like many notable athletes, he had once earned an affluent income, a *trophy* wife sixteen years his junior and a comfortable retirement residence in San Diego, close to the former Jack Murphy Stadium (now Qualcomm Stadium), the former home of the football Chargers.

Morency blundered one of the oddest acts of homicide against his wife Sue Morency, on July 21, 1990 when he poisoned her with strychnine, venom used to exterminate rodents. At the time, John was 46 and Sue was 30. Interviewed neighbors indicated he was a pleasant and engaging individual but the couple had suffered through a three-year stormy relationship. She was rumored to be in the process of leaving him. He had recently attempted to double the value of her life insurance policy. The act was a prelude to disaster.

In what must rank as one of the most idiotic killings in history, John Morency telephoned an emergency 911 call at approximately 10:38 p.m. on the day he had poisoned her. He indicated to the operator that his wife was not feeling well and required an ambulance. When the dispatcher attempted to transfer the call to the appropriate service, he hung up without giving his name or address.

The dispatcher called him back immediately. Morency indicated that his wife, who could be heard screaming in the background, *might* be suffering from food poisoning. The intellectually challenged Morency was possibly unaware that *all* 911 calls are traced and perhaps had placed his initial call for appearance sake to console his ailing wife.

An emergency team arrived. Morency tried to downplay the

seriousness asserting their services were unnecessary. He implored them not to transport her to an emergency room as they were leaving on a vacation the following day. The paramedics ignored him upon hearing her pronounced screams.

They found Sue Morency nude and convulsing on a bed. Her limbs were violently twitching and muscles constricting. In between episodes of agony, she remained lucid and was capable of answering questions from the medical team. After Sue Morency concurred with her husband against a trip to the emergency room, she suddenly lost consciousness, ceased breathing and exhibited no pulse. En route to the hospital, she went into cardiac arrest.

Strychnine is an odorless crystalline powder; bitter tasting that can be dissolved in liquids and food. At the trial, it was revealed that he had laced her tequila drinks. The consequences of strychnine poisoning suffocate the victim by creating rigidity in their muscles so that their lungs cannot expand. Sue Morency had absorbed four times the lethal dose within her body. She lingered on life support for five days before painfully expiring.

A 2001 television episode entitled *Tequila Sunrise* appeared on a now forgotten documentary series *Arrest and Trial*, narrated by actor Brian Dennehy. Actor Charles Allen, whose own career has eluded permanent visibility, portrayed John Morency.

The inspiration for his portrayal was spared the death penalty but convicted of life imprisonment without the prospects for parole. He is currently incarcerated at the California State Prison in Lancaster. Unlike his forgotten former football tenure, his prison status is permanently etched and documented remotely from any future adulation.

Entrance to Morency Condo

Artie and Jim Mitchell: Contemporary Cain and Abel

The ancient biblical Genesis account of Cain slaying his younger brother Abel appears remote and removed from contemporary culture. A morality tale, it often remains shelved and dust encrusted next to Shakespeare's historical tragedies. Most ancient and modern commentators assumed that Cain's motives were jealousy and anger triggered by his insufficient sacrifice to God, in comparison with his brother's.

Cain's often-repeated defense when asked the location of his dead brother was, *Am I My Brother's Keeper?* The expression simulates comparisons amidst the interweaving fate of brothers Jim and Artie Mitchell. Theirs is a classical murder story lacking heroes and conclusive explanations. Their narrative answers vanished with the victim's immediate death and the protagonist's demise a decade later. Yet the evil root was not fully severed by a single tragic act. Murder would resurface twenty years later by the actions of the perpetrator's male offspring.

The crime location city of Corte Madera is an intimate Marin Country suburb of 9,000+ where little of significance purposely occurs. Residents gravitate towards upscale conclaves like Corte Madera to escape the unpleasant realities of urban crime. Promoting minimal novelty except an occasional restaurant opening is sufficient. Stability and a sense of security are larger priorities and appreciating real estate values.

Within the San Francisco Bay area, suburban fortresses of protection are diminishing. Criminal activity has encroached beyond traditional civic boundaries. Random chaos sometimes infiltrates from the outside but more increasingly from within.

The street of Artie Mitchell's homicide resembles innumerable American neighborhoods. The houses lack extravagance despite their equity value and indistinguishable facades appear absent of menace. Early morning weekday commutes vacate the neighborhood. Weeknight and weekend foot and vehicle traffic are negligible.

On one arbitrary evening during the winter of 1991, the veil of invincibility was lifted.

Artie Mitchell lived in a community like Corte Madera to escape his own contentious workplace, located on the periphery of the outer Tenderloin district of San Francisco. The Tenderloin has been forever seemingly a refuge of the homeless, mentally ill and marginalized outcasts of society. Artie Mitchell was the co-proprietor of the O'Farrell Theatre, then one of the most influential pornography film production and sex club companies nationally.

The O'Farrell Theatre was founded in 1969 by Artie's older brother Jim and became the epicenter of San Francisco debate over public obscenity enforcement regulations. Jim, the elder by three years, mentored Artie into the enterprise assuming the role of his Brother's Keeper. The brother's were raised in Antioch and considered close. Their father made his livelihood as a professional gambler. Their mother was a homemaker. There were never published disclosures indicating any form of abnormal dysfunction within their family unit.

Jim inherited his father's speculative intuition. He attended San Francisco State University focusing on film courses. His supplementary work in pornography cinema convinced him this medium offered significant unrealized financial potential. His instinct proved correct. The brothers collectively pioneered profitable, efficiently budgeted films even if an actual plotline proved as absent as the clothing on participating actors and actresses.

The enterprise sprouted into eleven operating theatres by 1974 and a prominent rostrum of public supporters and clientele. Their biggest mainstream audience success became the 1971 production of Behind the Green Door grossing reportedly in excess of $25 million based on a modest $60,000 production budget.

The brothers remained cohesive publicly but personality differences, Artie's reported drug abuse and rumors of financial mismanagement created extreme dissension internally. Jim assumed responsibility for cleaning up the mess and determined a direct confrontation with Artie was the best way.

The tragedy following his approach created speculation towards his genuine motivations. Were they based on concern towards his brother's erratic behavior or premeditated murder designed to end hemorrhaging cashflow? Only Jim Mitchell could account for his actions. Disclosure was not forthcoming at his public murder trial.

Jim Mitchell drove to Artie's tranquil Corte Madera residence on the evening of February 27, 1991. He arrived unannounced, hushed and armed at the front entrance parking lot. The sole potential witness was Artie's live-in girlfriend Julie Bajo.

Hearing outside rustlings while lounging in bed, Artie approached his front door cautiously armed with a pistol. Bajo barricaded herself in a bedroom closet mute and terrified. She claimed to have heard neither conversation nor warning before the shooting. Did Artie Mitchell cautiously walk into an impending ambush?

Jim pumped eight rounds from a .22 rifle into his brother killing him instantly in the driveway. Artie's pistol was not discharged. Mitchell was apprehended 100 yards down the block from Artie's home presumably returning to his car. He had stuffed the fired rifle into a pants leg and also carried an unfired pistol in a holster. In a community where little of significant happens, the police response was immediate.

At Jim Mitchell's trial, prosecutors presented a computer-generated video recreation of the killing. It was the first time this technology was employed in a murder trial. Mitchell testified his actions were prompted by an earlier conversation with Artie, whose tone was angry and threatening when confronted about his substance abuse. Mitchell further claimed he used the rifle as a bluff tactic for intimidation purposes, but as Artie elevated his pistol towards him, he felt compelled to retaliate in self-defense. His testimony included a memory loss of events transpiring after firing the first round and being apprehended.

The jury found Mitchell not guilty of murder but guilty of voluntary manslaughter. He was also convicted of unlawfully discharging a firearm and brandishing a firearm to a police officer. Several notable San Francisco political luminaries and law enforcement officials spoke on his behalf-requesting leniency during the sentencing phase.

In 1992, Jim was sentenced to three years for manslaughter and an additional three for the use of the firearm. Five and a half years later, he was released from San Quentin Prison followed up by three years on parole. He controversially founded an *Artie Fund* to support a local drug treatment center. Artie's children denounced his effort finding it outrageous that their father's killer would have the audacity to honor him after the act. Ten years later Jim died of a heart attack and was buried in his native Antioch adjacent to Artie.

This apparent closure did not cease the family curse. In 2009, Jim's son James savagely murdered Danielle Keller, the mother of his two-year-old daughter, in spite of an outstanding restraining order against him. The site of the killing was in suburban Novato, located fifteen miles from Corte Madera. In 2011, James was convicted and sentenced from thirty-five years to life for first-degree murder, kidnapping and assorted domestic violence charges.

The enduring legacy of Cain's act to his brother Abel reminds us our innate nature and actions have not altered profoundly throughout the centuries. Our protective suburban citadels prove inadequate against the fatal occurrences of primal behavior.

San Francisco's O'Farrell Theatre

Former Artie Mitchell Residence

Murder Site

The Nicole Brown-Simpson and Ronald Goldman Murders: A Publicized American Travesty

Blind justice and dispassionate judgment became just another spectator during the 1996 murder trial for the arraigned killer of Nicole Brown-Simpson and Ronald Goldman.

Lost amidst the circus performance and innuendo factory that constituted the publicly televised trial, judgment regarding two homicides was determined. Suspected murderer, ex-husband O.J. Simpson, was acquitted by a criminal jury. The following year, he was found liable for the two deaths in a less publicized civil suit brought by the victims' families. The compensation award of over $33 million dollars will never be fully paid by Simpson.

The amount of the award raised the perpetual question as to what is the appropriate financial measure for a stolen life. Money, revenge and hyperbole characterized the tragedy behind the killings and an attempt to bring a responsible party to accountability.

The twin verdicts proved far from straightforward decisions. Public opinion had predominately convicted Simpson, a once popular former professional football player and television personality. The perception of the publicly charismatic Simpson changed with revelations about his private life. The polished glean of the idyllic, approachable hero became forever tarnished by disclosures of previous spousal abuse, drug use and marital infidelities.

The criminal jury's decision revealed a chronically gaping racial divide within America. Suspect O.J. Simpson was of African-American origin. Nicole Brown-Simpson and Ronald Goldman were Caucasian. Their racial orientations should have been irrelevant in determining guilt or innocence. However, Simpson's defense lawyers accentuated this significance. The tactic influenced the outcome.

O.J. Simpson and Nicole Brown-Simpson had married in 1985 following an eight-year relationship commencing when he was still married. The couple had two children together and contentiously divorced in 1992.

On the evening of June 12, 1994, Brown was killed at her condominium in Brentwood, approximately three blocks away from the neighborhood's most famous former resident, actress Marilyn Monroe. Slain with her was acquaintance Ronald Goldman, present after returning eyeglasses she'd inadvertently left earlier at the restaurant he worked at nearby.

The ferocious stabbings were ghastly. Blood splattered indiscriminately. Footprints, a glove and other incriminating evidence were strewn everywhere. Simpson's alibi proved dubious. Considered immediately a suspect of interest, Simpson impulsively attempted a surreal escape in a white Ford Bronco cruising leisurely south along interstate Highway 405. The captivating moment became pure theatrics as Simpson held a pistol to his temple and threatened to pull the trigger. He didn't.

He eventually instructed his friend who was driving, to return to his residence where he voluntarily surrendered for questioning. The act, interpreted as an admission of guilt, proved not only premature, but a foreshadowing of the absurdity to follow.

Considered arguably the most sensational murder trial of the 20th century, the legal proceedings were broadcast daily over an excruciating eight-month television run. A mesmerized international audience followed every banal element including evidence introduction procedures and live courtroom witness cross-examinations. Excessive expert analysis and commentary over every minute detail of the trial dominated the media headlines. Reputations were inflated, withered and courtroom performances graded. The anticipation for a verdict announcement created more tension than any comparable Academy Award ceremony.

When a verdict of *not guilty* was announced, a secondary wave of emotion gripped global spectators. Many felt betrayed by a judicial process that had failed two innocent murder victims. Others felt vindicated that an individual of color could be acquitted against insurmountable odds. The polarity of interpretation was usually determined by an individual's own racial orientation.

The prosecution team was generally panned for their failure to secure an apparent straightforward conviction. The trial affirmed that clear-cut convictions are nonexistent against a well-prepared and financed legal defense team of specialists. Their failure to convict Simpson was attributed to their substandard jury selection and inability to clearly demonstrate conclusive guilt. Defense lawyers were able to create suspicion amongst the jurors that the investigative team of the Los Angeles police force planted and mishandled evidence. The fact that there was a substantial amount of evidence *not* introduced made the jury's decision even more complicated.

At the non-televised civil trail, the jury expediently and unanimously convicted Simpson based on that suppressed evidence which *was* introduced. Both trials exhibited the best and worst extremes of the American judicial process. Several participants emerged as temporary celebrities. Most ultimately receded back into anonymity. By the conclusion, the overexposure of the case and travesty of the proceedings inflicted a public viewing hangover.

O.J. Simpson would escape criminal punishment but not adverse karma.

His life following the adverse civil suit decision became a series of misdemeanor infractions coupled by his attempted financial evasions from the Internal Revenue Service, representative lawyers and two families awarded damage revenues.

In 2007, he was arrested for leading an armed group of men into a Las Vegas hotel/casino to reclaim signed sports memorabilia by force. A year later, he was convicted of multiple felony counts including criminal conspiracy, kidnapping, assault, robbery and using a deadly weapon. He was sentenced to a 33-year prison term with the possibility of parole following nine years. The sentence appeared excessive based on the severity of the crime. Few observers were astonished by the ironical twist. Most of the arrested participants testified against him. He is currently incarcerated at the Lovelock Correction Center in Nevada.

Amidst the whirlwind of the initial O.J. Simpson's arrest and trial, *Time Magazine* flagrantly darkened his facial image on their front cover and titled the issue *An American Tragedy*.

O.J. Simpson will never stand trial again for the murders. The American constitution protects individuals against *double jeopardy* or being criminally tried multiple times for the identical crime. Announcements regarding a continuing investigation into the double murders have become nonexistent. The entrance gate to Nicole Brown-Simpson's condominium is currently shrouded in vegetation and the address number absent from public view. O. J. Simpson's former residence has been demolished and since rebuilt due to the notoriety.

The Los Angeles Police Departure was convinced that they arrested the correct culprit. The American judicial circus set him free...briefly.

Entrance to Nicole Brown-Simpson's Courtyard

Lyle and Erik Menendez: The Sins of the Son's Bury Their Father

For many, it is inconceivable that the avarice and greed of two brothers could callously destroy the lives of two parents who'd lavished on both an unimaginable life of prosperity and wealth.

Yet these very gifts became the motive for murder.

It may be understandable that two siblings, Lyle and Erick Menendez, then aged 21 and 18 years old respectively, might seek an accelerated inheritance. Their impatience might even seem more urgent if they lacked the determination to earn their own wealth. Such ambitions have adequate precedent.

The most striking element behind the savagery of shooting their parents on August 20, 1989 was the ferocity behind their aim. Jose Menendez, their father, was shot point blank in the back of the head with a 12-gauge shotgun. Kitty, their mother, was shot in the leg, causing it to fracture. She was then finished off with shots in the arm, chest and face, leaving her unrecognizable. Both parents were strategically shot in the kneecaps to simulate a professional hit.

Professional hitmen have little need to fire at kneecaps once a victim has been effectively immobilized and dispatched. The multiple firings and placements were more indicative of intense hatred towards their objects.

It becomes difficult to dissect the relationships within an American family, particularly one with prevalent ease and comfort.

Jose Menendez was an accomplished entertainment industry business executive. He arrived in the United States at the age of 16 following the upheaval of the Cuban Revolution. He attended college in Illinois, met his wife and earned an accounting degree in New York. He elevated his professional success through executive positions at Hertz and RCA. He was being elected as CEO of LIVE Entertainment, most notable for Carolco Pictures, known primarily for violent action films.

The boys enjoyed a privileged upscale childhood. Both exhibited average grades during their academic years. Lyle was suspended from Princeton University based on allegations of plagiarism. There is no accurate gauge precisely how happy or dysfunctional the family operated. During the murder trial, numerous observers offered conflicting opinions. Four individuals know the truth. Two are dead.

The Menendez Brothers planned the killings loosely based on their simplistic arrogance they would never be caught. They arbitrarily tossed the murder weapons. The pair attempted to construct an alibi following the killings. They had intended to view a feature film. It was sold out. They ended up at an alternative film creating time gaps. They met with friends at a local restaurant following the showing and *officially* returned home around midnight.

They telephoned police to report the murder and play-acted their devastation and grief. Investigators immediately considered them prime suspects but had little evidence to base their suspicions. Neither was tested for shotgun residue on their hands. The home security system had not been tampered with.

The cloud of suspicion hung over the brothers as they spent lavishly, foolishly and traveled internationally. Neither remained in the family's Beverly Hills residence, preferring separate penthouse apartments in Marina del Rey.

Their united front dissolved when younger brother Erik related the murders to his psychologist. His indiscreet confession was accompanied by a death threat. The therapist informed police of both.

Each was arrested and remanded without bail. They were

segregated from each other.

Their initial trial was broadcast nationally on Court TV during 1993. The television production stimulated more theatrical drama than justice. Erik's defense team defamed both parents in the vilest of degenerate terminology citing a lifetime of sexual abuse, cruelty and pedophilia provoking the killings. The dead cannot respond. The tactic temporality succeeded with the jury deadlocked on conviction.

The brothers were immediately retried and the judge forbade cameras in the courtroom. The jury rejected the abuse defense and concluded that the murders were committed with the intent of gaining immediate control over their parents' considerable wealth.

Both brothers were convicted on two counts of first-degree murder and conspiracy to commit murder. The jury discounted the death penalty due to their lack of a felony background. Both were sentenced to life in prison without the possibility of parole. Each is currently isolated from other prisoners.

The brothers have unsuccessfully appealed their conviction on the state and federal levels. Both have married while incarcerated.

Neither spouse will ever enjoy the wealth that marriage might once enabled. The brothers reportedly have had no contact with each other for over a decade. Lyle is currently incarcerated at the Mule Creek State Prison and Erik at the R. J. Donovan Correctional Facility.

The poverty accompanying their present and future circumstances is bitter compensation for the wealth of their father they could not secure prematurely.

The Menendez Family Mansion

Living Room Murder Site

A Convincing Performance Behind the Killing of Bonnie Lee Bakley

The trail of circumstance and motive led investigators to a single suspect in the 2001 killing of Bonnie Lee Bakley.

The victim had a history of marital exploitations having wedded reportedly eleven times. During her 1999 courtship with actor Robert Blake, she simultaneously dated Christian Brando, son of actor Marlin Brando. Bakley became pregnant and informed each suitor that the baby was his. The infant was named after Brando but a DNA paternity test proved that Blake was the biological father.

Robert Blake married Bakley in late 2000 and the couple commenced their union under conditions he soon found intolerable and manipulative.

On the evening of May 4, 2001, Blake took his wife to one of his favorite Italian restaurants in Studio City. After the meal, the couple returned to his car parked around the corner from the restaurant. Blake excused himself to return to the restaurant where he had allegedly left his handgun. Bakley waited in the vehicle for an unexpected surprise.

In the brief interim between his return (or possibly upon), Bakley was killed by two gunshot blasts to the head while sitting in wait. Her passenger side window was rolled down indicating that she was likely familiar with her killer. The murder weapon was found in a dumpster a few yards away from the shooting.

Nearly one year later, Blake and his longtime bodyguard Earle Caldwell were arrested and charged with conspiracy in connection with the murder. At trial, two former stuntmen and associates of Blake testified against him. They each claimed that he'd attempted to hire them to kill Bakley.

The trial began in December 2004 following Blake's

imprisonment and house arrest. Neither forensic evidence nor direct ties to the murder weapon were able to implicate Blake. Tests to determine whether Blake's hands had contained gunpowder residue had not been performed by the responding investigative police officers. The defense lawyers destroyed the credibility of both witnesses by citing their prior history of drug use and conflictive points in their testimony.

Three months later, a jury found Blake *not guilty*. All criminal charges were dropped and he was not retried. Three of Bakley's children filed a civil suit against Blake the following year based on the assertion he was responsible for her wrongful death. The civil trial jury found him liable and he was ordered to pay a judgment of $30 million. In 2008, the verdict was upheld, but the assessment cut in half. In 2010, Blake declared bankruptcy due to debts resulting from his legal fees and tax liens imposed by the state of California and Los Angeles County.

Throughout Blake's extended professional acting career, he was considered very capable and inspiriting. The murder of Bonnie Lee Bakley became either a terrible coincidence of circumstance or one of his finest performances.

Bonnie Lee Bakley's Last Supper

Street Parking Around the Corner and Murder Site

Vincent Brothers: The Convicting Insects on the Radiator

The state of California's educational system has been derided for decades regarding the declining standards of school administration and administrators.

If Vincent Brothers were the standard bearer for intelligence amongst his peerage, the source of the deterioration would be obvious. Brothers was a Vice Principal at the John C. Fremont Elementary School in Bakersfield.

Little is known about his management competency. Much has been written about his extra-curricular activities.

He was reputed to be having marital problems due to his extramarital affairs. He had been married four times and briefly incarcerated for spousal abuse. His 2003 marriage to wife Joanie Harper was his second to her. They had divorced three years previously. The experiment teetered precariously and Brothers moved out of their shared home three months after the ceremony.

The pressure of financially supporting his wife and their three children became a tiresome burden to the educator. In July during summer vacation, he hatched a plan that defied intelligence and ultimately evasion.

On July 2, 2003, Brothers flew to Columbus, Ohio from the West Coast under the pretext of visiting his brother. Upon arrival, he rented a car and immediately drove 2,000 miles back to Bakersfield.

His wife Joanie (39), his two sons Marques (4), Marshall (6 weeks), and daughter Lyndsey (2) were living with his mother-in-law Earnestine Harper. The five were last seen together at their church on July 6. Returning to their residence afterwards, Brothers planned a homecoming surprise.

He staged a fake break-in and violently killed the entire family including his mother-in-law. He used a .22 caliber gun and sharp stabbing weapon that were never recovered.

He immediately returned back to Ohio and turned in the rental car. He then drove with his brother to North Carolina to visit their mother. The bodies of the five victims were discovered on July 8 while Brothers was heading towards the East Coast.

His alibi might have been successful with the exception of two major stupidities. The odometer on his rental car exceeded 4,500 miles, unusual for a five-day rental. The second and most incriminating discrepancy introduced at his trial were the several hundred dead insects found on the rental car's radiator and inside the air filter. The flattened bugs bred exclusively from states west of the Rocky Mountains.

He was considered the sole suspect from the outset, but not officially arrested until April 2004. During the interim stretch, he played the role of grieving husband and parent at the funeral service. His acting, as with his preparation, proved ineffective. The evidence against him was irrefutable.

A jury convicted him in May 2007 of first-degree murder with special circumstances. He was sentenced to death and is currently interned at San Quentin. His lone surviving daughter from an earlier university liaison disinherited him and changed her surname.

To add to his idiocy during the hearings, Brothers planned an escape by hiding handmade handcuff keys in his hair and placing leg restraints solely on one leg, rendering them ineffective. As with his earlier meticulous planning, his ruse was discovered and never allowed to germinate.

Vincent Brother overestimated his capacity to outsmart law enforcement. Unobservable and incidental insects proved his undoing. The California education systems lumbers forward today with one less obstacle amongst its administrative roster.

The Murder Site

Front Entrance

The Marin County Barbeque Murders

This twisted narrative appears on the surface like a classic film noir story of deception and manipulated murder. A femme fatale teenager convinces her obsessed older boyfriend to murder her abusive parents. The plot deepens when a ferociously struck hammer blow to the head kills the mother. Who is the responsible party?

The girl's father is consequently shot to death upon returning home unexpectedly following the killing. Was his death the result of falsely assuming the boyfriend's guilt for his wife's death?

Nothing appears entirely clear in evaluating this story decades later.

What is known is that on June 21, 1975, Naomi and Jim Olive were murdered inside their Terra Linda residence. Their bodies were then transported by the killers to a barbeque pit at the nearby China Camp recreational park. They were doused with gasoline and burned. The perpetrators abandoned the park briefly while the bodies were smoldering. During their absence, the reduced corpses were discovered by a fireman and mistaken for a deer carcass. The responsible parties returned later to dispose of the remains.

The victims, Jim and Naomi Olive had settled in Marin County during the early 1970s after he lost his marketing job with an oil company in Guayaquil, Ecuador. Upon his return, he began a small business consultancy. During the couple's residence overseas, they adopted Marlene. She had spent her childhood and early teen years in Ecuador.

The return transition into a Northern California way of life proved challenging. The family was splintering. Marlene fought constantly with her mother. Her father's priorities were devoted towards establishing his business enterprise and their relationship became distant.

Marlene felt alienated amidst the more permissive local teenage culture. Her sheltered existence in Ecuador had not prepared her for such an extreme clash of values. She gravitated towards other outsiders, immersed in drugs, alternative music, witchcraft and even reportedly prostitution.

One of her drug suppliers, 19-years-old Charles *Chuck* Riley found Marlene an ideal solution for his own demons and ingrained sense of inadequacy. Riley weighed in excess of 300 pounds. His childhood obesity kept him socially solitary and lonely. He was anxious to reward any attention that Marlene paid him. He supplied her with free drugs, transportation and gifts. She was his first girlfriend. Eventually, despite her revulsion regarding his weight, they became lovers.

Marlene controlled their fragile relationship, breaking up with him on multiple occasions to reaffirm her dominance. One of her ongoing confided obsessions included murdering her adoptive parents. She sensed that she had recruited the proper foil based on his desire to please her and fascination with guns.

Months prior to the murder, the pair went on an extended shoplifting spree. They were caught in the act and arrested for grand larceny. Their arraignment provoked Marlene's parents to permanently forbid her from spending time with Riley.

Riley was arrested a second time in May 1975 for possession of marijuana and a sawed-off shotgun. His life was unraveling and the sole intact strand appeared to be the volatile Marlene. Now he was losing her.

Her parent's prohibition prompted more disagreements. Riley blamed Marlene on instigating the murder. She protested her innocence claiming the killing was carried out by Riley exclusively. Two versions of the unfolding drama were introduced during their trial.

Most of the facts were drawn from Riley's original confession. According to his version, Marlene summoned him by phone following a heated argument with her mother. The dispute likely concerned their relationship.

Realizing he might permanently lose access to her, he agreed to finally carry out Marlene's ongoing request to kill her parents. Marlene left a door unlocked while her mother slept. She had arranged to meet with her father away from the house for an undisclosed reason. Riley confessed to having ingested LSD before his arrival. He entered the Olive residence with a loaded . 22 caliber revolver. Upon viewing the sleeping Naomi Olive, he confessed to having struck her *many times* with a hammer, stabbed her and finally suffocated her. Such a killing frenzy seemed odd directed towards someone he was scarcely acquainted with.

Before Riley had vacated the house, James Olive returned. Viewing the carnage, he grabbed a knife and approached Riley with the intention to kill him. Riley instinctively responded by shooting him fatally four times with his revolver.

This account seemed plausible to a jury. His detachment from the events seemed explainable based on Riley and Olive's behavior afterwards.

The doomed couple, with help from friends, attempted to sanitize the killing location. The pair remained in the house for several days. They attended a rock concert, shopped and ate out, covering their expenses with her parent's cash, checks and credit cards. Remorse for their act was nonexistent.

As inquiries about Jim Olive's whereabouts started, Marlene began fabricating excuses for her parent's disappearance. A police visit to the house confirmed something was amiss and inconsistent with her story. The murder room was the sole orderly area in a household of complete disarray.

Acting on a tip, the police discovered the disposal barbeque pit. They determined that it had contained fragments of burnt human remains. Although DNA evidence had not yet been fully developed, they felt confident enough over the couple's guilt to arrest and charge both with the murders.

A seemingly straightforward killing with motive took multiple swerves during the trial. Finally cognizant regarding the severity of the charges against him and freed from the burden of protecting Marlene, Chuck Riley began to alter his portrayal of events.

Under hypnosis, Riley recanted parts of his initial confession. He indicated that upon entering the Olive household, he had found Naomi Olive bleeding profusely from head wounds and near death. He speculated that Marlene had struck her mother in the skull earlier with a hammer. The employed tool had been initially used to repair one of Marlene's loosened platform soles. He claimed that he suffocated Naomi simply to end her misery and shot James out of fear and self-defense before being lethally attacked. He stressed that his original confession was given solely to protect Marlene from guilt.

The ferocity of the hammer blows seemed to corroborate his revised version, but was viewed with suspicion. Marlene did appear a more credible suspect in her mother's death.

The jury concluded Riley's amended confession lacked credibility and pronounced him solely guilty of the double murder and sentenced to the death penalty. In 1976, when capital punishment was temporarily rescinded in California, his term was changed to life imprisonment with the possibility of parole.

Based on her juvenile status, Marlene Olive was convicted of a Section 602 charge. This nebulous violation covered crimes committed by a minor ranging from petty theft up to murder. She served four years at the California Youth Authority Center in

Ventura and was released.

The futures of Chuck Riley and Marlene Olive veered into distinctly diverse directions upon his incarceration. She would visit him only a single time in prison during 1981.

While at San Quentin, Riley lost his girth and earned the equivalent of a college degree. He applied for parole a dozen times and was routinely denied. Finally in 2015, the California parole board ruled him fit for release. Governor Jerry Brown overturned their ruling. In an odd twist of fate, Riley appealed Brown's decision and won. He was released from prison in December 2015.

Marlene Olive's reformation took an immediate nosedive during her initial correctional stay. Weeks before her parole date, she escaped and moved to New York City where she worked as a prostitute. She was apprehended and returned to complete her California term.

Upon her official release, she relocated to Los Angeles and began a forgery, identity theft and drug ring. She was arrested and changed her name on multiple occasions before relocating to Bakersfield to resume her illegal activities. She was once again caught passing fictitious checks and sentenced to seven years in prison. She has since been paroled but the question persists, under which alias?

Chuck Riley and Marlene Olive's cautionary example exemplifies two aimless lives that lacked direction. Riley may one day contribute something positive to society. Olive has made her intention abundantly clear that she has no desire to.

The Former Olive Family Residence

China Camp Recreational Park

Delayed Gratification Thwarts A Perfect Killing

Dale Ewell had successfully constructed an airplane sales dealership from a formerly failed enterprise. His earned fortune enabled his family a comfortable Fresno area existence in the Sunnyside district.

Dale's son Dana enjoyed the fruits of his father's accomplishment and attended Santa Clara University studying finance. During his first three academic years, he boasted incessantly to friends about his stock market investment prowess. A 1990 *San Jose Mercury News* front-page article depicted Dana as an academic tycoon dressing in elegant suits, selling mutual funds and building a formerly bankrupt airplane dealership into a $4-million windfall. His fabricated narrative caught the attention of his unappreciative father. Dana was still financially dependent on his parents and had no role in the family business.

Both males had premonitions regarding their futures. Dana assumed that he might accelerate his ascendancy into wealth without actually doing anything. Dale developed an extreme distrust towards his son. He immediately raised Dana's age requirement for his inheritance. He would receive only half of his share at the age of thirty and remainder at thirty-five. Dale's secret maneuver with this modification assisted in the later resolution of his own tragic fate. After the *Mercury News* article appeared, he informed Dana that his financial support would cease upon his graduation.

On April 19, 1992, Dale, his wife Glee and their daughter Tiffany were returning home from a visit to the family beach house near Watsonville. Glee and Tiffany drove together while Dale piloted his private plane. Dana, then 21, remained in nearby Morgan Hill to dine with his girlfriend's family. Her father was ironically an FBI agent.

Upon Glee and Tiffany's arrival, a concealed intruder was

waiting for them. He shot Tiffany first in the kitchen as she passed by. He then silently approached, straddled and shot Glee four times in the den. The killer had sufficient time to change magazines in his gun, put on fresh gloves and relocate his position. Dale entered the house thirty minutes later clutching a newspaper. He was executed in the back of the head unaware of the preceding murders. The house was then ransacked to appear like a botched burglary.

The family execution seemed quick and flawless. The killer had shaven from head to foot leaving no DNA traces. All that was left for police was a qualifying motive and grieving son with a seemingly flawless alibi.

The case languished for three years without resolution. Two possible directions were explored.

Glee had formerly worked for the CIA during the later 1950s. She had been stationed in Argentina as a Spanish-language translator for a few years before she met and married Dale. This option led nowhere.

Dale's former airplane business associate had been arrested in 1971 for organizing a substantial Mexico-to-Fresno drug smuggling venture. After his associate's imprisonment, Dale assumed the dealership. Suspicion insinuated that continuing bad blood between the partners or renewed drug smuggling activities might be cause for murder. These suspicions were investigated and then discounted.

Ewell's fortune was attributed to hard work and shrewd farming investments. Some of his business ventures had been tinged by lawsuits, but none appeared serious enough to warrant an entire family contract killing.

The investigation's prime suspect focused on Dana Ewell. His inheritance was sufficient motive but the reported $8 million estate would not be within his control until many years later. His apparent lack of initial grief over the slayings and furious reaction when informed about the will modification steepened doubts about his innocence. His uncles began to question if Dana was behind the murders to police.

Circumstantial evidence weighed against him. The killer needed to know the Ewell's home alarm security code to enter undetected. He also needed to be aware of the family's arrival time.

Investigators sought a smoking gun as the key to their case. Ultimately the murder weapon became the source for conviction of the perpetrators.

The original procurer of the 9-mm pistol was an acquaintance named Ernest Ponce. He acknowledged buying the murder weapon for Ewell's college roommate Joel Radovcich who had told him that he intended to resell it for profit. What prompted Ponce to come forward three years after the killing was the 1995 arrest of Ewell and Radovcich on first-degree murder charges.

Similar charges were filed against Ponce and Radovcich's brother for their presumed involvement in the killings. Ponce accepted an offer of immunity in exchange for his testimony. His acceptance enabled him to evade further scrutiny although he admitted to burying the gun after the murder. He repeatedly denied any knowledge of the gun's intent and successfully passed a lie detector test.

His testimony proved critical to the prosecution and confirmed their suspicions about Dana Ewell's scheme and direct involvement.

According to Ponce, Ewell convinced Radovcich to execute his family in return for a percentage of his anticipated inheritance. Even though Ewell had yet to control the majority of the estate, he had immediate access to approximately $800,000. Nearly $124,000 in cash since the murders was unaccounted for. Police traced activity in 47 of his bank accounts to confirm that he had funneled money to Radovcich. Evidence confirmed that Radovcich had spent in excess of $30,000 on flight lessons without the benefit of employment. As history has often confirmed, sudden illicit affluence is rarely accompanied by restraint or prudence.

Both men were tried together in 1998. While the jury typified Ewell as *evil*, some expressed empathy towards the actual killer. They viewed him as a used pawn. The Santa Clara University students forced to testify that knew both men expressed similar reactions.

Both were convicted on three counts of first-degree murder and sentenced to life imprisonment without the possibility of parole. Ewell is currently imprisoned at the Corcoran State Prison and Radovcich is interned at the Mule Creek State Prison in Ione.

In the end, Ewell lost his sole claim towards a blood money inheritance as the assets were split between relatives. The unworthy and impatient son would not enjoy the fruits from his own enterprise.

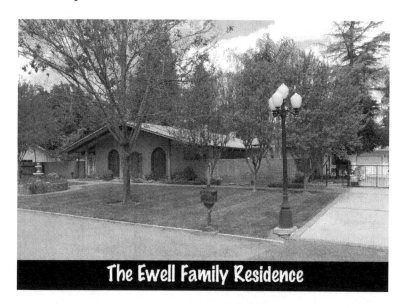

The Ewell Family Residence

The Slaying of Captain Walter Auble and Impressive Public Response

The respect and reverence that law enforcement once generated was profoundly evident with the public slaying of Los Angeles Police Captain Walter Auble during the daylight hours of September 9, 1908.

A beloved member of the Los Angeles police force for 23 years including a term as police-chief, Auble and his partner, Detective Paul Flammer were investigating a tip from a suspicious landlord about two potential burglary suspects, Carl Sutherland and Fred Horning. The policemen were admitted into an adjoining room where they overheard the suspect's casual conversation over their intent to commit a serious robbery within 48 hours. When the two suspects left their apartment, the police detectives discreetly searched their premises to confirm their suspicions.

A *Los Angeles Herald* newspaper article reported that they had found braces, jimmies, chisels, saws, electric flash lamps and keys of multiple varieties. In the bottom of a dressing case, under a pile of dirty clothes, two black masks, a blackjack, slingshot and two large sized revolvers were discovered. In the drawer of a table was a signed letter by Sutherland addressed to Horning advising him of their two major targeted addresses.

Attempting to thwart the imminent robbery, both officers dressed in plain-clothes and were escorted around the city. Auble sighted Sutherland and Horning strolling towards downtown from their eastbound passing car on Ninth Street. Their driver stopped the vehicle mid-block and let the two detectives out. They began following the men and but the pair suspected that they were being tailed. The two suspects diverted their routing towards Grand Avenue.

Both bolted into a sprint but were overtaken by the two unarmed officers at the northeastern corner of North Grand and West Ninth Streets. Horning was seized and thrown headlong into a corner storefront carpet-beating establishment. He was arrested without further incident.

Sutherland responded to Captain Auble's demand to surrender by pulling out a long revolver from his coat pocket and firing point blank into Auble's neck. As Auble crumpled to the ground he continued in an attempt to wrestle the gun away from the slightly built Sutherland. The suspect eventually fired three more shots amidst their struggle before Auble collapsed and released his grip on the weapon. He was taken to a nearby police receiving hospital where he died, despite emergency surgery from his wounds. It was reported that he shook hands with each of his surgeons personally and was surrounded by his family members when he expired.

Sutherland escaped immediate capture but the intensity and variety of his subsequent pursuit would be unimaginable today. An estimated 2,000 citizens participated in the manhunt via automobiles, on foot and on horseback following his trail of blood and random sightings. Officers from every department in the city and county donated their services.

Sutherland, who reportedly was habitually high on opiates, had the presence of mind to reload his gun at the intersection of Ninth and Hope Street. He sat down on the edge of the curbside, bound his bleeding left hand and then rolled and smoked a cigarette. He then penned a note, which he left lying on the spot swearing he would not be captured alive. He returned to his rooming house on Georgia Street and exited with a single item before continuing his escape towards the Pacific Ocean via streetcar.

He had few options for escape. He was married but his wife was purportedly ignorant of his activities and true character. She was gainfully employed as an operator by the Home Telephone Company of Long Beach and well regarded.

Sutherland was sighted definitively near Redondo Street. Several bloodhounds were borrowed to resume the chase. Police were advised that he would likely seek sanctuary at an acquaintance's house that evening on South Broadway Street near the present day intersection of 77th Street, then an isolated and lonely country road. The acquaintance worked with Sutherland as a waiter at both the California and University Clubs.

Sutherland walked into the stakeout twelve hours after the shooting and was arrested without resistance. He appeared anemic and casually tossed his revolver to the ground. He raised his right hand above his head. With his left hand, he deftly inserted a small bottle into his lips and swallowed the contents.

The liquid cyanide he had retrieved from his rooming house almost immediately contracted his muscles once the handcuffs were attached. Despite frenzied respiration techniques by the arresting officers, he slipped silently into death inside a patrol car that was rushing him to the same hospital as Auble.

Captain Auble was considered a model and universally popular officer, particularly within ethnic communities. A bizarre request for his killer Sutherland's cadaver was made by members of a Chinatown merchants committee and later published. The delegation wished to boil Sutherland's body in a preparation of acids, then heap abuse upon it and throw it out on a refuse heap where it could rot in the sun with none of the sacred Chinese emblems employed to drive away evil spirits.

The request was denied as his grieving wife was allowed to make burial arrangements. The outrage and sorrow felt by the community and press was genuine. Only a half-century earlier, Los Angeles was a disbursed settlement of intolerance, intemperance and lawlessness defined by enormous sprawling rancheros and a small concentrated city base. Vigilantes loosely supplanted established law enforcement and governed the unmanageable anarchy.

The frontier era had passed and Los Angeles had evolved into an expanding urban center of 300,000 by 1910. Within the following ten years, the population would double following a post-World War I boom.

Fred Horning was originally charged with murder. Those charges were dropped but he was still sentenced to fourteen years at Folsom Prison where he had recently been imprisoned. Following his subsequent release, his name would disappear from public archives.

Today, the corner of West Ninth and South Grand Streets is undergoing yet another transformation. The storefront and sidewalk where Auble was shot are a vacant lot under excavation. A church adjacent north of the site on Grand Avenue at the time of the killing was razed to be replaced in the 1920s by a 9-story office building. This structure is currently in the stages of further renovation or demolition.

Reminders of Los Angeles' architectural past today are often given historical protection status. With the steady evolution of downtown vertical development, planning boards have attempted to maintain equilibrium between legacy and progress. This philosophy is in direct contrast with mid-20th century haste that leveled first and built indiscriminately afterwards.

Captain Walter Auble's death has become a casualty consigned to obscure memorial plaques and records. The cooperative and enthusiastic public involvement involved with his killer's capture proved an insightful contrast to contemporary attitudes and apathy towards law enforcement. The tragedy behind his death is only equaled by the tragedy of the public and media's eroded faith and trust.

The Fatal Intersection of South Ninth
Street and West Grand Avenue

Oscar Grant III: When The Facts Behind a Killing Become Secondary

Oscar Grant III was a 22 year-old father when he was fatally shot by BART (Bay Area Rapid Transit District) police officer Johannes Mehserle at approximately 2:00 a.m. on New Year's Day 2009. The altercation was precipitated by six officers responding to reports of a fight on a crowded BART train returning from San Francisco. Police officers detained Grant and approximately a dozen other passengers on the platform at the Oakland Fruitvale Station based on the complaint.

The ensuing New Years Eve chaos created a hostile and explosive environment for the officers once they removed the offending passengers from the train. Insults and aggressive behavior were traded. The removed passengers were seated against a station wall. Mehserle and another officer were restraining Grant, who was lying face down and refusing to submit to handcuffing. According to Mehserle during testimony, Grant was reaching for his waistband where he sensed perhaps a handgun might be hidden.

In response, Mehserle drew his gun, a SIG Sauer P226 and shot Grant once in the back. Grant was unarmed. He was pronounced dead the next morning at Highland Hospital in Oakland. Mehserle insisted that he was reaching for his Taser and pulled out the heavier gun in error. The events were captured on multiple digital video and cell phone cameras. The footage was distributed to media outlets and websites worldwide, where millions watched it.

The killing was magnified because Grant was African-American and Mehserle, Caucasian. The following days witnessed protests in downtown Oakland. Initial daytime protests against the ruling were peacefully organized. Looting, arson, destruction of property and small riots broke out after dark. Nearly 80 people were eventually arrested.

The shooting has been variously labeled as accidental or an impulsive execution depending upon ones perspective.

American society has yet to fully resolve and bury its persisting racial divide. Tragedies as these become divisive issues to stir old wounds and provide forums for self-serving interests and causes. The continuing financial gulf and perceived inequity between social classes habitually raises the thorny issues of racial inequality. Grant's death served as a pretext to rekindle the debate between the haves and have-nots.

No direct evidence or public admission by Mehserle's suggested that his action was racially motivated. Yet in the eyes of many professional activists and protestors, the skin difference between the two men was sufficient.

On January 30, 2010, Alameda County prosecutors charged Mehserle with murder for the shooting. He resigned his law enforcement position and pleaded not guilty. Slightly over six months later, a jury found Mehserle guilty of involuntary manslaughter and not guilty of second-degree murder and voluntary manslaughter. He was sentenced to two years, minus time served. He served his time in the Los Angeles County Jail, occupying a private cell away from other prisoners. He was released on May 3, 2011.

Several wrongful death claims were filed against the publicly funded transit district. BART settled with Grant's daughter and mother for a total of $2.8 million in 2011.

A killing under these extreme circumstances provokes the eternal question as to true motive.

Was Mehserle simply incompetent and emotionally overwhelmed by firing his handgun amidst the chaos of events? Or was his act a simple execution because he had been pushed over the edge by taunting? We cannot truly know his intention but the act ruined his livelihood and reputation. It will remain his lifelong epitaph and trail him the rest of his life.

The act itself cost Oscar Grant III his life.

Sometimes in society's search for clarity, reason prevails. Too often this search is drowned out by conflicting voices. The actual details behind the tragedy became secondary in many people's eyes. The racial implications attached to the case clearly tinted the facts and the perception of each party's responsibility.

We must continually ask who is ultimately responsible for dispensing justice in our society? At what point must individuals assume responsibility for their actions and direct challenge to authority? In Grant's case, his actions clearly contributed to the tragic and lethal consequences.

We ask many things of our law enforcement community. We demand their instantaneous discernment in manners of conflict and crisis. We insist that they shield and protect the victimized while bringing accountability to their perpetrators. We assume their actions will reflect fair judgment despite harassment, antagonism and often indifference.

What happens to these expectations when their actions become deflected by circumstance or their own flawed decision-making? Are they allowed to be human and make errors?

The consequences of Mehserle's instantaneous act became a lifelong stain for all involved parties. The condemnation and blame unfortunately will never be commuted nor resolved.

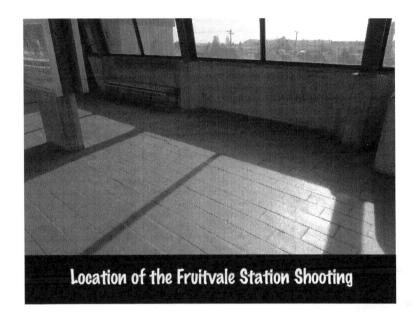

Location of the Fruitvale Station Shooting

Peace Mural at the Fruitvale BART Station

The Deadliest Firefight in California Highway Patrol History

Every time a law enforcement officer pulls a vehicle over for a traffic infraction, the potential for danger becomes the scariest part of their job. There are never *routine* stops absent of this fear.

The worst-case scenario for the California Highway Patrol (CHP) occurred on April 5, 1970, when two heavily armed criminals engaged officers in a deadly shootout at a Newhall restaurant parking lot.

Bobby Davis, 27, and Jack Twinning, 35, were career criminals with extended histories of violent felonies. Twinning had the dubious distinction of having spent five years in Alcatraz, during which he killed another prisoner in self-defense. The pair had met in jail. Both had been recently released from prison and Davis was on parole status in Houston.

Unsuccessful in finding legitimate jobs, they drove together from Houston to Sacramento, returning to more comfortable employment, robbing banks. They were unsuccessful. They headed to southern California and rented an apartment together in Long Beach.

En route, they observed construction in the mountainous Grapevine section near Gorman on US Interstate 5. They anticipated stealing explosives from the site for use in future bank robberies and particular armored cars.

On the evening of April 5th, the two initiated their plan to return to the construction site armed with handguns, rifles and shotguns. Davis dropped Twinning off near the site with the intention of stealing the explosives. Davis inexplicably made a U-turn across the highway median, barely avoiding another vehicle heading southbound.

The driver of the near miss yelled at Davis and both vehicles pulled off to the side of the road. In the course of their heated exchange, Davis pulled out a firearm. The other driver, a military serviceman convinced the dull-witted Davis that CHP officers were nearby. Davis drove off and picked up Twinning. The driver telephoned the incident to the nearby highway patrol station complete with a description of Davis and his vehicle.

Several minutes later, CHP squad car partners Walt Frago and Roger Gore spotted the distinctive red Pontiac near Castaic and followed it. Another patrol car with Officers James Pence and George Alleyn awaited the two vehicles in nearby Valencia as back up.

The tailing officers instructed Davis to pull over at a freeway exit that today leads to the Six Flags Magic Mountain theme park and into a restaurant parking lot. The lot remains in operation today under a different eating establishment. The officers ordered the pair to exit their vehicle. Complying, Davis left his driver's seat and walked to the front hood of his car where Gore began to search him.

Frago approached the passenger side armed with a shotgun, but tilted airborne. Twinning exited the passenger seat and immediately fired upon Frago with two shots from his .28 revolver killing him instantly. Gore drew his service revolver and attempted to return fire. He had lost track of Davis adjacent to him. Davis yanked a .38 Special from his waistband and fired two lethal shots into Gore at close range.

Shortly after the initial exchange, Officers Alleyn and Pence arrived and initiated a subsequent firefight. The ensuing gun battle between the two sides resulted in the deaths of Pence and Alleyn who were badly outgunned. Twinning was superficially wounded. Gary Kness, a former U.S. Marine driving to work, entered the fray using one of the fallen officer's pistols against the perpetrators. A fragment from one of his bullets lodged in Davis's chest. Out of ammunition and realizing the hopelessness of battling unarmed, Kness escaped to cover in a nearby ditch.

The gun battle continued as a third CHP cruiser arrived at the scene. More shots were exchanged and both criminals fled in the darkness armed in separate directions. Davis carjacked a parked camper near a dirt road three hours later after a shooting exchange with the owner. He was spotted within hours, pulled over and lacking loaded guns, surrendered.

Three miles away from the parking lot, Twinning broke into a rural house and took the owner hostage. His wife and son escaped and telephoned police who immediately surrounded the house. After hours of negotiation, Twinning released the hostage the next morning. He bragged extensively to his hostage about the previous evenings exploits. As police pumped tear gas into the house and stormed in, Twinning committed suicide with Frago's shotgun.

Davis was sentenced to death for the murders of the four CHP officers. The sentence was commuted to life in prison with the abolishment of the death penalty. He committed suicide while incarcerated at the age of 67 in 2009.

The four slain officers were all between 23-24 years old, married and with a combined total of seven children. Each of them had been with the CHP for less than two years. Post-investigation scrutiny towards the chain of events resulted in approach and training procedural changes as well as upgraded armaments. None of the officers wore bulletproof vests, which might have prevented three of the fatalities.

Today, the stretch of Interstate 5 near the shootings is named after the deceased officers. Signage acknowledging their sacrifice is passed routinely by vacationers visiting the theme park or locals commuting through the now congested Santa Clarita Valley.

As maddeningly stressful and often expensive being pulled over remains to a driver, the inherent risk for each patrolman is significantly steeper.

Site of the Restaurant Parking Lot Shootout

Officer Thomas Guerry: A Legacy Award For An Abruptly Ended Life

Long before the introduction of advanced electronic communication devices and fingerprint and background databases, police patrols were hampered by an absence of detailed information when responding to dispatch calls. Much of their daily response was based on observation, intuition and experience.

Eight-year police detective Thomas Guerry was a stellar patrolman instinctively suspicious about the walking pattern of two men. His concern proved founded. On January 12, 1970, three felons had entered into Santa Barbara following an extensive cross-country robbery spree. One of the three immediately turned himself into a California Highway Patrol bureau and confessed to an impending robbery planned locally.

The information was transmitted to the Santa Barbara Police Department where Guerry and his partner opted to scour the streets for the remaining criminals, brothers Frank and Bruce Bowersox.

While patrolling in their squad car during the early evening of January 13, the Bowersox brothers were spotted walking together and then splintering off. The squad car briefly trailed them. The brothers became aware they were under surveillance and backtracked to each side of the police vehicle. As the detectives stepped from their vehicle, the brothers opened fire with their handguns.

Thomas Guerry was slain on the spot and Bruce Bowersox wounded in the shoulder by his partner. Guerry was 28-years-old with a wife and two children. Frank Bowersox was immediately arrested and his brother shortly afterwards. Bruce was sentenced to death, which was then commuted in 1972 to life imprisonment. Frank was sentenced to life imprisonment. Both died while incarcerated never being paroled.

Guerry's death was mourned throughout the region. The Santa Barbara City Council established a prestigious award in Guerry's honor given to deserving law enforcement officers in agencies throughout the county. The annual commendation has survived longer than the unfortunate officer lived.

Intersection of the Shootout

Lovelle Mixon: A Desperate Final and Fatal Gamble Towards Escape

Commuters daily pass a highway sign on Interstate 580 daily with minimal regard. The memorial eulogizes Oakland Motorcycle Sergeant Mark Dunakin (40), Motorcycle Officer John Hege (41), SWAT Sergeant Ervin Romans (43) and SWAT Sergeant Daniel Sakai (35) killed by a convicted felon.

Their murders equaled the single deadliest attack on California police offers since the Newhall massacre in 1970 when four California Highway Patrol officers were shot and killed by two men in Newhall.

On Saturday, March 21, 2009 at 1:00 p.m. Lovelle Mixon's 1995 Buick Sedan was pulled over by officers Dunakin and Hege for a routine traffic violation on the 7400 block of MacArthur Boulevard.

Mixon had multiple reasons for concern besides a simple citation. The driver's license he produced for Dunakin was fake and he was wanted on a no-bail warrant for a parole violation. Seven hours before, he had raped two women at gunpoint in another sector of East Oakland.

Dunakin suspected the license was fraudulent and signaled for his partner to arrest Mixon. Whether or not Mixon noticed the gesture couldn't be determined. He leaned out of the vehicle's passenger side window and opened fire on both with a 9mm semiautomatic pistol. He methodically wounded both officers twice, exited his vehicle and approached each. He finished them off execution style in the back. After admiring his handiwork, he fled southbound on foot.

Both officers had died before the ambulances arrived. The manhunt to apprehend Mixon was immediate and involved over 200 officers from various law enforcement agencies throughout the county.

Mixon didn't have time to escape far and chose the most predictable destination, his sister's apartment one-block down the street. He was spotted entering the two-bedroom ground level apartment. A SWAT team was immediately ordered to surround the building.

Unknown to them, Mixon had secured an SKS carbine presumably stored within his sister's apartment. The lead officers present concluded that other building residents were at severe risk should they be forced to evacuate through a single front building entry door. The same officers were also suspicious over the credibility of the eyewitnesses.

Rather than wait for a full SWAT team to assemble or simply surround the apartment and delay, a decision was made to storm the unit. The decision proved premature and fatally flawed.

Mixon had barricaded himself in his sister's bedroom, which was poorly illuminated. Shock flashbang grenades that were tossed in by the approaching police team created more confusion. As the initial SWAT team members broke down the front door and entered, Mixon ambushed them. Sergeant Pat Gonzales, the first assault member was wounded in the shoulder and Sergeant Romans following him was mortally wounded.

In the ensuing firefight, SWAT member Sakai was killed and Mixon ultimately felled by a barrage of gunfire. The raid lasted less than fifteen minutes.

The history of Lovelle Mixon's brief life makes gloomy reading. At the age of 13, his antisocial behavior had manifested itself through multiple assault and battery occurrences. At 20, he was convicted for felony assault with a deadly weapon stemming from an armed robbery in San Francisco. He served six years at Corcoran State Prison. Upon his release, he violated the terms of his parole and was returned for another nine months.

No one could accuse him of ignorance towards the consequences of parole violation.

Yet even Satan has his advocates. Mixon's family vehemently protested that he was not a *monster*. One member indicated his latest parole violation stemmed from a feud he was having with his parole agent. Mixon was angered that his agent had missed earlier appointments. Mixon chose to miss subsequent mandatory sessions in protest.

The future for Lovelle Mixon was not encouraging based on his precedent behavior. Redemption and reform did not appear to be his personal priority. Two months following his death, DNA evidence positively linked him to another rape of a 12-year-old.

Understanding the actions of a desperate man driven to extremes is not difficult. Recognizing that our criminal justice system cannot contain violent felons such as Mixon keeps everyone at risk. For Mixon, there will be no public trial, condemnation by jury, contrition or apologies by him to the widow and grieving families.

The trade of four vital law enforcement officers for one utterly insignificant felon proved a poor exchange for society.

7400 Block of MacArthur Boulevard

Demetrius DuBose: A Shooting Death of the Nearly Famous

The life and tragic death of Demetrius DuBose provides an insight into the temporal, capricious and disposal nature of American sports fame. It is the antithesis tale to the traditional Horatio Alger theme that concentrated hard work ultimately enables success and accompanying financial rewards.

This dream of recognition and compensation motivates athletes globally to sacrifice all of their physical, emotional and intellectual gifts for the ultimate glamour and financial prosperity associated with superstardom. The dream is realized by only a small percentage. Those ranks that come precariously close are more plentiful. The stories of the nearly famous are typically more beguiling and compelling than the minority who ultimately achieve success.

Demetrius DuBose achieved a recognized level of success in his chosen specialty, football, but not to his or others elevated level of expectation. As with many former athletes, once they are removed from active participation, obscurity becomes an unwelcome substitute.

DuBose's ascent within the ranks of football was meteoric and well documented. He was rated one of the premier high school athletes in the state of Washington. He continued as a team captain and Second Team All-American at prestigious Notre Dame University and the 34th overall pick out of 224 players in the 1993 professional football draft by the Tampa Bay Buccaneers.

His upward trajectory towards stardom had been uninterrupted with only a single blemish. He was suspended for two games as the result of an improper recruitment gift from two Notre Dame boosters. The citation was a relatively minor infraction in comparison with the school's multi-billion dollar football institution. The infraction did not significantly affect his professional football prospects.

What ultimately derailed his prospects was the competitive environment of the National Football League and a superior player on his team at the identical position, Hardy Nickerson.

Nickerson completed a distinguished fifteen-year professional career and essentially accomplished what DuBose aspired towards. He was signed by the Buccaneers with five years of existing professional experience and relegated DuBose's promising status to that of reserve player. For three years, DuBose struggled to breakthrough to starter status, but found his professional advancement stymied.

In the business world, vertical promotion and advancement are expected for an individual to be elevated to top management. Professional football is no different. Each year, another 200-400+ fresh and elite prospects enter the workforce with the intention and design to supplant existing players. Sentimentality, loyalty and comradeship mean little in a universe where immediate success and results are the sole measure that insures job security.

DuBose was a competent reserve player, but this level merely kept him on a team's roster. Professional sports are a grim and brutal business that accommodates less than 1% of athletes at all playing levels who are convinced that they have the necessary skills. DuBose took a gamble by leaving the security of a Buccaneer's contract to play for another team, the New York Jets in 1997. His tenure was terminated during training camp and he was released by the Jets to find employment with another team.

No additional teams opted to contract his services. At the age of 26, he was unemployed and likely undesirable for the sole profession he had prepared his life and future prospects for.

By all published accounts, Demetrius DuBose was considered a very intelligent, gifted and vibrant individual. He was multi-dimensional in his interests, pursuits and well-traveled. Like many former athletes without grounded business experience, much of his football income had been reportedly squandered on failed business enterprises including a clothing line and professional beach volleyball league.

At the time of his death, he was grooming his future ambitions to become a professional beach volleyball player. F. Scott Fitzgerald wrote *there are no second acts in American lives* and predictably DuBose's secondary passion promised miniscule odds of success.

In professional sports, crossover is rare. Despite DuBose's acknowledged gifts and imposing physical stature, he lacked the volleyball experience and training a dedicated athlete accumulates from years of playing. The circuitous road to excellence demands single-minded focus. Exceptional athleticism is rarely enough to compensate for the strategy cultivated skill set the highest level of play requires from a single specialty.

DuBose realistically understood the mirage of reinvention he was pursuing.

Unlike many of his gladiator peers, he was injury free and arguably in the best physical condition of his life at the time of his demise. Doubtlessly this worked towards his disadvantage during his fatal confrontation with law enforcement officers. Professional sports, most notably football, has an extended precedent of leaving its former players in varying states of disability due to the repeated punishment absorbed from collisions and concussions. Elevated levels of brain and physical trauma have drained some of America's finest athletes of their elite capacities by their mid-twenties.

It is a wishful thinking mirage to imagine the conduct and rules of football can be modified to prevent these inevitabilities. The sport has achieved an unprecedented popularity and financial funding base. Fans, television broadcasts and all related endorsement entities expect and demand extreme violent player collisions to sustain this level of popularity.

The allure of fame and compensation will continue to attract future generations of prospective players like Demetrius DuBose. Innovations such a structurally redesigned helmet will not ultimately prevent a player's predictable disabilities following extended participation. Players understand and accept this risk. DuBose was in excellent physical condition but had drifted from the lifestyle that had defined his life. His new lack of structure and identity as a *former* player proved disorienting.

Numerous published accounts indicated that he'd severed most of his friendships and professional acquaintances. Few of these individual's seemed to know where he was residing and with what means of sustenance. One report suggested he was destitute and habitually sleeping in his car, not out of preference.

In the interim between his release from football and death at 28, he was arrested at a nightclub in South Bend, Indiana, the site of Notre Dame University. While being escorted out of a bar for disorderly conduct by an off-duty police officer, he pulled down a ceiling pipe flooding the club with 1,600 gallons of water. He was arrested for the act, spitting on the officer and for possession of marijuana.

At the time of his death, he was temporarily living with an acquaintance in the Mission Beach area of San Diego. Reports indicated he opened a sliding door to a neighbor's apartment and had fallen asleep in an upstairs bedroom. When the neighbor returned home in the evening, he demanded that DuBose leave immediately and telephoned the police suspecting a potential burglary.

Two officers arrived and began questioning DuBose, who was apparently compliant in the beginning. The accounts vary distinctly from that point. Most accounts agree that DuBose resisted being handcuffed, appeared intoxicated and responded incoherently.

Several accounts had DuBose knocking down each officer when they tried to subdue him. He attempted to flee from the scene despite being sprayed with mace. When the officers pursued and caught up with him, they attempted to immobilize him with a then popular martial-arts weapon, nunchukas.

Both officers apparently struck him repeatedly with full force. DuBose was unfazed by the beatings and wrestled both sets from the officers. The officers claimed he was prepared to use the weapons against them and began a charge in their direction despite their repeated warnings to cease. This observation was both confirmed and contradicted by eyewitnesses.

Mission Bay Boulevard is a heavily traveled thoroughfare and any early evening violent confrontation would attract attention. Seventeen confirmed witnesses viewed the altercation. Two small markets face the site of the clash between Queenstreet and Redondo Courts. Behind the structures are a walkway, beach sand and the Pacific Ocean.

In the confusion that followed, DuBose was fatally shot twelve times by both officers with 9mm handguns. Did the officers overreact? DuBose's purported erratic behavior would have certainly made his actions difficult to interpret. Toxicology reports during the autopsy indicated that DuBose had tracings of alcohol, cocaine and the drug ecstasy in his system.

Law enforcement shootings are rarely typified by distinct black and white enactments. The sequence of events accelerates out of control. Amidst moments of chaos, actions are often interpreted subjectively. DuBose was African-American. The two police officers were Caucasian. Was his killing racially influenced? Both officers vehemently denied this accusation. DuBose's imposing physical stature and strength however would certainly have been intimidating factors.

A follow-up review of police reports and witness transcript accounts by the FBI and U.S. attorney for the Southern District of California decided there was no evidence that the officers violated DuBose's civil rights. The killing was judged a justified *use of force* based on the circumstances.

Protestors of American racial policies did not accept this official opinion and a brief period of public demonstration followed the death and review.

In hindsight, the circumstances behind DuBose's death were unfortunate and preventable. Calm cooperation with the investigating officers could have diffused the explosive consequences. Perhaps DuBose assumed that his version of the actual events would be discounted and compliance, an admission of guilt. We will never know his exact mental state. The dead cannot assume accountability for their irresponsibility and impulsive acts. The results become fatally conclusive.

The ascent to professional sports stardom is a desirable stratum for any young man or woman who has ever seriously and competitively participated. Athletes are revered for their exploits and their successes and failures become their epitaph.

Most professionals exit this exalted stage at young stages of their productive existence. The average career of a professional football player is 3.3 years and even amongst the players receiving minimal contact such as kickers and punters, 4.87 years. Injury and intense competition create abbreviated professional lifespans.

Demetrious DuBose's career matched the average length, but the evaluation by most observers was that it was both *disappointing* and an example of *unfulfilled potential*.

Fans and spectators frequently confuse elite athletic skills and performances as heroic character tendencies. Just as actor's personalities are often defined by their character portrayals, their actual personality may not assume such an easily definable and simplification. Remove the individual from their profession and they often become flagrantly mortal. Dim the attentive spotlight from their activities and most resemble banal and ordinary personalities.

A significant percentage of contemporary athletes, despite their initial promise and financial compensation have lapsed into severe and dire circumstances following their exit from sports. This scenario is not surprising considering their previously extravagant spending habits and abrupt absence of financial resources once they cease playing. Many drift into coaching. Others simply flounder minus the glare of exposure.

The deity status assigned to professional athletes for most are supported on foundations of fragile clay and illusion. Inappropriate and exhibitionist behavior is tolerated and often encouraged until the individual is no longer a contributing cog to a winning organization. Amputate the athlete from the protective cocoon of their profession and such behavior is viewed as narcissistic and boorish.

Demetrious DuBose's death was a tragedy on many levels, based both on the swiftness of his demise and his transference from adulation to insignificance. Our society places too much significance and relevance on entertainment and events that ultimately marginalize the participants. Similarly it seems few citizens bemoaned the fate of acclaimed Roman gladiators in their era despite the ultimate sacrifice their profession demanded, death.

Most top athletes do not anticipate nor are simply ready for their professional mortality. They do not prepare adequately for the required adjustment afterwards. Within three abbreviated years, DuBose lost both his vocation and life. Very little coherence or moral has been gleaned from the calamity.

First Contact Point w/ Officers

Sidewalk Where DuBose Was Slain

Policeman Matthew Pavelka: Officer Down From Following A Fateful Back Up

Burbank Police Officer Greg Campbell's narcotics division training and instincts sensed that something was amiss with the parked Cadillac in the rear hotel parking lot.

On the early evening of Saturday, November 15, 2003, 20-year veteran Campbell cruised past the vehicle without license plates. The hotel property had suffered from a poor reputation for decades based on repeated drug dealing and prostitution despite a mid-1980s facelift and renovation. Its location straddled the boundaries between suburban Burbank and gang infested Sun Valley, a suburb of Los Angeles.

Following departmental procedure, Campbell radioed into his dispatch for back up. Rookie officer Matthew Pavelka responded and stationed himself at a rear passenger side position. Campbell approached the driver. On the surface, it appeared a routine infraction.

There are *never* routine traffics approaches.

Neither Campbell nor Pavelka knew the occupants of the car, Ramon Arranda and David Garcia were members of the violent Vineland Boys gang. The gang's operations focused on drug and weapons trafficking and their vehicle was laden with both. The gang had direct ties to the Mexican Mafia. Arranda, who had been previously incarcerated, was fixated on never returning to jail. He would get his wish.

Arranda handed Campbell a false drivers license and could not produce a current vehicle registration. He was asked to exit the car. In the interim between the arriving back-up officer and Campbell's approach, Arranda had armed himself with a concealed handgun. He initially appeared to comply with the instructions, but instead raised his gun and fired point blank into Campbell. He fired twice hitting Campbell in the stomach and right side of the head. Campbell was seriously wounded and fired in retaliation missing twice.

Pavelka engaged Arranda in a fierce short-range exchange wounding each severely. Arranda collapsed mortally wounded. Pavelka was seriously injured and began crawling back to his cruiser for cover. Passenger David Garcia, who'd yet to participate in the firefight, exited the car and began firing at the wounded Pavelka, ultimately, incapacitating him. As Pavelka lay vulnerably in the rain with thirteen bullet wounds, Garcia dispassionately walked over and fired a lethal shot into him.

Garcia escaped and with assistance from his two brothers, was transported to Tijuana, Mexico. In a rare example of Mexican law enforcement cooperation, Garcia was apprehended two weeks later on Thanksgiving Day. Mexico extradited him back because he was considered an *undesirable* American citizen.

Garcia may have faced the death penalty, but opted to plead guilty in a plea bargain deal in 2012. He was sentenced to life imprisonment without the possibility of parole. He is currently incarcerated at the California State Prison in Lancaster. Campbell suffered damage to his spinal cord leaving him partially paralyzed and deaf in his right ear.

In 2006, nine members of the Vineland Boys gang were prosecuted and convicted of federal drug, racketeering and money laundering charges in a trial that lasted 45 days. The two leaders were sentenced to life imprisonment and the other seven were given prison terms of between 10-20 years.

Pavelka became the first Burbank police officer killed in the line of duty.

Parking Lot Shoot-Out Location

Another Shoot-Out Site Perspective

The North Hollywood Doomed Heist and Subsequent War Exchange

On the morning of February 28, 1997, Larry Phillips, Jr. and Emil Matasareanu were prepared for combat. Phillips had fitted himself with over 40 pounds of protective equipment including a bulletproof vest and various plate guards for shielding his extremities and organs. Matasareanu was similarly armored. The pair was armed with an arsenal sufficient for a military brigade.

Eight months of planning preceded by two successful armed bank robberies in Littleton, Colorado and Winnetka, California had prepared them for another high-risk operation. The North Hollywood Bank of America branch appeared an ideal target to further their idealized goal of incalculable wealth.

The two had initially met at a prominent Venice gym and shared a passion for weightlifting and firearms. Both had been unsuccessful with a conventional lifestyle. Phillips had been a habitual criminal offender, responsible for multiple unsuccessful real estate scams and shoplifting offenses.

They anticipated the entire Bank of America operation would require eight minutes. As with their previous robberies, they would paralyze and take control of the bank operations by firing their automatic rifles airborne before emptying the safe deposit vaults.

Phillips and Matasareanu ingested tablets of the barbiturate Phenobarbital to calm their nerves before entering the branch at 9:17 a.m. Their protocol was well rehearsed. They immediately seized control by opening fire into the ceiling, discouraging resistance. Matasareanu shot open a bulletproof door (resistant only to small-caliber rounds) and gained direct access to the tellers and vaults. The assistant bank manager assisted in filling the robbers' money sacks. From that point, their carefully orchestrated plan evaporated.

Unknown to them, a passing police patrol spotted their entrance into the bank. A request for back-up assistance was radioed in. Police units began to surround the branch in strategic firing positions. A modification in the bank's delivery schedule left the vault with less than half of the currency that Matasareanu had anticipated. He berated the manager and fired 75 rounds into the bank safe to no avail. His shooting destroyed most of the remaining money. The pair would attempt to flee the bank with slightly over $300,000.

The robbers required twelve minutes to complete their heist. They exited the building surrounded and with police demanding their surrender. The pair surveyed their hopeless predicament and opted to exchange fire.

The robbers' higher caliber armaments initially outgunned the police officers. Police were unable to pinpoint headshots with their limited range pistols due to the heavy spray of return gunfire. Within the first seven to eight minutes of the exchange, numerous officers and civilians were wounded. Matasareanu slipped into their white sedan to attempt a getaway. Phillips opted to remain crouched behind other parked vehicles and considered an escape on foot.

Their tactics were pointless. The sedan had the tires shot out. Matasareanu attempted to carjack another vehicle, but it would not operate as the driver fled with the keys. SWAT teams and television news helicopters were arriving simultaneously on the scene.

The gunfire raged and echoed with the intensity of a war zone. The robber's body armor reportedly absorbed ten direct bullets, but did not deter them from continued shooting. At the conclusion of the gun battle, 1,100 rounds were fired by the two and approximately 650 by police.

Phillips and Matasareanu were hemmed in and vulnerable. They separated. Remaining behind their sedan, Phillips, under constant fire, discharged a round into his chin killing himself instantly. Uncertain why he had dropped his gun, police riddled him with shots once he had fallen.

Three blocks away having relocated, Matasareanu was shot 20 times in the legs, apprehended and cuffed by arresting police. They called for an ambulance, but uncertain if there were additional suspects, delayed the arrival for over an hour. Matasareanu expired from excessive blood loss in agony, swearing profusely and attempting to goad the officers into shooting him in the head.

In the aftermath, his family had the audacity to file a lawsuit against the Los Angeles Police Department for violating his civil rights in allowing him to bleed to death. The suit was dismissed without settlement.

Eleven police officers and seven civilians were injured and numerous vehicles and property were destroyed. No one miraculously, except for Phillips and Matasareanu was killed. Police officers have since been armed with heavier firepower and semi-automatic guns. Today, the shooting sites have resumed their former nondescript neighborhood appearance.

Emil Mastasareanu's Death Site

Larry Phillips Shootout Position

The Zodiac Killer: A Stain That May Never Be Eradicated

The most notorious serial killer in Northern California operated in the late 1960s and early 1970s. His legacy began violently in my hometown of Vallejo, California.

On December 20, 1968 along an isolated stretch of Lake Herman Road, two high school acquaintances of my older sister, Betty Lou Jensen and David Faraday were viciously murdered shortly after 11 p.m. The couple was on their first date together. Lake Herman Road was a diversion from their original plans of a high school Christmas concert.

They wanted time alone. Instead, they became the victims of a cowardly execution.

For approximately 45 minutes prior to the shooting, Faraday parked his mother's Rambler in a gravel turnout, a well-known spot of intimacy. Another vehicle pulled up beside. The killer exited and ordered the couple out of the car. Jensen exited first and when Faraday was halfway out, the killer shot him point blank in the head.

Fleeing from the killer amidst the open gravel turnout instead of heading towards protective shrubbery, Jensen was gunned down twenty-eight feet from the car with five shots through her back. The killer had taped a flashlight atop his gun for sighting purposes in the pitch dark. After convinced that both of his victims were dead, he drove off. The execution was completed within a ten-minute gap between passing vehicle traffic.

Thus began the first in a series of attacks and fortuitous escapes by the Zodiac killer.

What followed the first killings within the community was stunned silence and disbelief. The viciousness and arbitrary nature of the murders forever destroyed a local sense of security, however illusionary, residents shared. Speculation initially focused on individuals who might have a motive for killing either of the two victims. Soon it became apparent there was neither motive nor probable suspect within their circle of acquaintances.

Then the Zodiac struck again less than four miles away.

Around midnight on July 4, 1969, Darlene Ferrin and Michael Mageau drove into the Blue Rock Springs Parking lot, a popular local recreational facility. As in the previous murder, a second car drove up beside them but didn't linger, immediately driving off. Returning 10 minutes later, the driver parked directly behind them and exited his vehicle.

Mageau claimed on numerous occasions that Ferrin was familiar with the driver. He approached the passenger side door of Ferrin' car carrying a flashlight and 9 mm Lugar. He blinded both with the flashlight beam before firing five times. Ferrin was killed and Mageau miraculously survived despite sustaining wounds in the face, neck and chest. He would become one of two living survivors.

Forty-five minutes later, the killer telephoned the Vallejo Police Department to claim responsibility for the attack and the killings six and a half months earlier. The call had been placed only a few blocks from the police station. This signature taunting would ultimately become an important component of the killer's terror tactic.

For then residents of Vallejo, the mention of Lake Herman Road and Blue Rock Springs Park would perpetually intervene into our nightmares. To this day, I subconsciously accelerate my vehicle past each location.

What separated these homicides from other multiple murderers was that the killer chose his own name, Zodiac in a series of letters sent to Bay Area news outlets. These letters included four cryptograms. Of the four cryptograms sent, only one was definitively solved. What made him globally recognized and ignited significant law enforcement and amateur investigation was that he was never apprehended. Over the years many suspects have been named and researched, but conclusive evidence has never resulted in an indictment.

On August 1, 1969, the Zodiac killer began his correspondence with the print media by mailing out identical letters establishing him as the source of the homicidal mayhem. Certain letters promised he would reveal his identity. All guaranteed subsequent killings would follow. The newspapers obediently printed his letters and a predictable media circus ensued.

His pattern of boasting and taunting rhetoric would continue over the next five years resulting in innumerable false leads, inflated and false boasts by the killer and massive speculation about his identity. His writings became a dialogue with evil. In his letters, the Zodiac often included details about the murders, which had not yet been released to the public to establish the credibility of his identity. In future letters, he would even include fragments from a shooting victim's bloodstained shirt.

On the afternoon of September 27, 1969, the Zodiac varied his method with a knife attack at Lake Berryessa in Napa County. Two college students Bryan Hartwell and Cecelia Shepard were picnicking when a man approached them wearing a black executioner's style hood and clip-on sunglasses over the eyeholes. The bizarre outfit included a bib-like device on his chest with a white 3x3" cross-circle symbol (resembling a target sight) embroidered on.

The man concocted a strange narrative about being an escaped convict in need of immediate cash and transportation. He was armed and convinced the pair to tie each other up. What they assumed to be a simple robbery turned grisly as he pulled out a knife and began stabbing both savagely and repeatedly. Thinking both were dead, the killer hiked 500 yards back to their vehicle. He drew the cross-circle symbol on Hartwell's car door with a black felt-tip pen and wrote beneath it the dates and locations of his previous killings.

At 7:40 p.m. the killer telephoned the Napa County Sheriff's office from a pay telephone to report his latest double homicide. The phone was found, still off the hook only minutes later a few blocks from the sheriff's office. A damp palm print was lifted from the receiver but never successfully matched with any later suspects.

What the Zodiac didn't realize when he placed the call 27 miles from the crime scene was that neither of his victims had died from the stabbings.

Cecelia Shepard was conscious when two Sheriff's deputies arrived, providing them with a detailed description of the attacker. Hartnell and Shepard were taken to a hospital in Napa by ambulance. Shepard lapsed into a coma during the transport and never regained consciousness. She died two days later, but Hartnell survived to recount his tale and become the second survivor of the Zodiac.

The final documented killing occurred two weeks later on October 11, 1969. A lone passenger entered a taxi driven by Paul Stine at the intersection of Mason and Geary Streets in San Francisco. He requested to be taken to the corner of Washington and Maple Streets in the Presidio Heights district.

Stine drove one block past Maple to Cherry Street for reasons that were never determined. The passenger then unexpectedly shot Stine once in the head with a 9mm pistol. He then methodically removed Stine's wallet and car keys and tore away a section of Stine's bloodstained shirt. He then wiped the cab down before exiting towards the Presidio, one block to the north.

Three teenagers observed the sequence of events across the street at 9:55 p.m. They telephoned the police while the crime was in progress. Two blocks from the crime scene while responding to the call, a San Francisco policeman observed a white male strolling nonchalantly before stepping into a nearby neighborhood stairwell. The encounter lasted only five to ten seconds.

The man was not questioned because the police radio dispatcher had erroneously identified the sought after suspect as an African-American male. The white male was passed over. Was it the Zodiac? In later correspondence, the killer claimed it was. The three teenage eyewitnesses collaborated with a police artist to render a composite sketch that has become the sustaining image of the killer's portrait.

Further patrols that evening produced no additional suspects and once again the Zodiac vanished into the night eluding the grasp of law enforcement.

The San Francisco, Napa County and Vallejo police departments assigned special investigators to the case. Each department kept the investigative files closeted as each successive lead failed to conclusively produce a confirmed identity, arrest and closure. Many reasons have been cited for the failure of law enforcement officials to ultimately arrest a suspect who had left a preponderance of incriminating evidence. The San Francisco department alone claimed to have investigated over 2,500 suspect leads. The case remains open.

The most frequent excuses for law enforcement failure were the poor cooperative efforts between police departments, tainted and lost evidence and simple professional jealousies. The most glaring reason however is that scientific forensic techniques and DNA comparative testing were non-existent or in their infancy stages during the late 1960s and 70s. The Zodiac was fortunate to have escaped both arrest and the advancement of technology.

Several letters, cards and cryptograms would follow during the subsequent years abruptly ending in 1974. The Zodiac killer made numerous outrageous claims and threats boasting future massacres, terrorist activities and to have killed in excess of thirty individuals. He liberally and pathetically assumed credit for crimes that received substantial media exposure. No substantive proof ever linked or confirmed his participation in any subsequent homicides.

Most researchers and observers of this unsolved mystery have concluded that the Zodiac killer is probably dead. There have been many explanations as to the reasons why he ultimately ceased his public communications. We may never know his identity. Websites, films and books continue to be released suggesting fresh speculations and overlooked data.

What we do know is that his vicious unsolved killings and self-delusional correspondence traumatized many innocent citizens and irretrievably stained the topography of the San Francisco Bay area. Whatever renown or romantic allure the global media has attached to this iconic killer, the facts behind his acts ultimately proved far less glamorous.

Lake Herman Road Killing Ground

Site Where Betty Lou Jensen Was Gunned Down

Blue Rock Spring Parking Lot

Paul Stine Murder Site

Charles Manson: De-Mythdefying an Iconic Serial Killer

More publications, websites and editorial space have been devoted towards Charles Manson, his cult followers and their subsequent atrocities than any comparative serial killer. Yet comparisons become scarce since Manson did not empty a single cartridge or physically kill any of his victims.

Instead, Manson manipulated a raggedy band of followers into murdering at least ten victims and potentially more. In particular, seven gruesome killings within a two-day spree in August 1969 introduced his public notoriety.

Manson's techniques were neither novel nor inventive. An avowed racist, he embraced a self-perceived mantra of apocryphal killer ushering in a prophetic American racial Apocalypse. He erroneously envisioned that his planned killings would initiate class warfare motivated by race that would forever sever the American class and social hierarchy. His band of mesmerized puppets rarely exceeded two-dozen members. Yet his admiration base has curiously grown substantially during his absence and incarceration if solely by distant and abstract adoration.

Amidst his own philosophical rants, he plagiarized lyrics from the Beatle's macabre *Helter Skelter* song, spouted revolutionary rhetoric common for the era and enforced subservience with tactical brainwashing techniques. These tactics included isolation, starvation, sexual and excessive drug dependence.

Over a progression of nearly three intense years, he assembled a young, disenchanted and predominantly female follower base that bent obediently to his will. They viewed him as a magnetic messiah figure. His self-assured propaganda played well to impressionable minds seeking direction amidst an age of turmoil and dissension. His charade has been thoroughly documented by cult members, commentators and countless portrayals. Yet as with many of the icons of the 1960s protest era, he continues to fascinate fresh generations of spectators.

A candid appraisal of Charles Manson's activities would confirm that in a leadership role, a complete role reversal of his earlier past, he was able to assert dominance and submissive consent to weaker minds and temperaments. Without boundaries of morality or restraint, evil consequences typically take root.

But who is and was Charles Manson? Cloistered from the scrutiny of public expression, social and traditional media exposure, his true identify and character has been misrepresented into a toxic mythology. Why does there exist a continued fascination towards a lifelong habitual criminal and failure?

Manson was born in November 1932 and his itinerant father never identified. His mother and uncle were convicted of robbing a service station in 1939. He lived with another aunt and uncle in West Virginia during their internment. Upon her 1942 release and parole, he accompanied her as they drifted together throughout Midwest boarding houses. Soon they separated as his mother proved no more capable of raising a son than he adhering to a traditional upbringing.

He bounced around residences throughout Indiana, Utah, Ohio, Washington State and D.C, Virginia, and Texas. His random existence was accompanied solely by the certainty that he would always find legal entanglements.

A sequence of petty and minor felonies followed including burglaries, armed robberies, sodomy, pimping and car theft throughout his next twenty-five years. His perpetual criminality was consistent with his mundane anti-social fueled conduct. The miniscule accomplishments he had accumulated and squandered had scarcely prepared him for the infamous attention he would later acquire.

Charles Manson was briefly married twice, divorced and the father of four documented children. Each has eluded public exposure. He likely played a nonexistent role in their upbringing with his transience and incarcerations.

When he was arraigned in 1969 for murder conspiracy, he was identified as an unemployed former convict who had spent the majority of his life in correctional institutions. He had been an unsuccessful singer and songwriter on the external fringe of the Los Angeles music industry chiefly due to chance encounters with insiders by women in his cult.

His twisted charisma, which ultimately influenced murder without remorse or hesitation made him unique. More likely, the timing, location, eminence of certain victims and savagery of the killings set him further apart. In context, the timing of his most known seven slayings was committed during a zenith of social turmoil.

Between 1968-69, the Vietnam War raged uncontrollably and university campus became protest vortexes. Violent racial clashes were erupting. Unresolved serial killings were rampant. The Soviet Union had crushed a nationalist uprising in Prague. Two of the most calming influences, Martin Luther King and Robert Kennedy had been assassinated. A perception and belief confirming society's imminent implosion was not unfounded.

Manson offered no solutions. His certainty, paranoia and tirades appealed to submissive individuals seeking sanctuary from reality.

It is imperative to separate man from myth to understand a homicidal motivator. Charles Manson, over time and distance, merits no more introspection and insight than any other manipulative mass murderer.

The homicides that Manson was considered legally accountable for included:

His assistance with Bobby Beausoleil regarding the July 1969 knifing and slaying of Gary Hinman over a money dispute. Manson reportedly sliced off Hinman's left earlobe with a sword two days before the killing. Cult members Mary Brunner and Susan Atkins accompanied Beausoleil and reportedly took turns smothering Hinman after his initial stabbing. Beausoleil was convicted of murder and condemned to life imprisonment. He is currently serving his sentence at the Oregon State Penitentiary. Brunner served 6 1/2 years at the California Institute for Women before her release. Atkins served 38 years of her sentence at the California Institute for Women before dying in 2009 of brain cancer.

On the evening of August 8, 1969. cult members Charles *Tex* Watson, Susan Atkins, Linda Kasabian and Patricicia Krenwinkel were instructed to *destroy* the residents of an elevated property located on Cielo Drive in Beverly Hills. A prior tenant to the property was record producer Terry Melcher, the son of actress Doris Day who had briefly shown interest in Manson's music. Manson felt slighted when Melcher evaded offering him a contract and had lost interest in his talents.

It has been reported that Manson knew Melcher was no longer living on the premises, so the reason behind his selection remains unclear. Some cult members suggested that the dwelling represented to him an *establishment* that would neither accept him as a person or his genius. Motion picture director Roman Polanski and his wife, actress Sharon Tate were leasing the residence.

The four cult members parked their vehicle at the lower base of Cielo Drive and walked up the access road to the house's entrance gate. The upper stretch of Cielo resembles an extended driveway to one of the lower households when passing streetside. It is easy to overlook for someone unfamiliar with the street and remains absent of signage. Manson had visited the property previously seeking Melcher, so he was intimately familiar with the layout.

The house featured an extended rancho styling with a phenomenal view of the Hollywood basin. A modest wood shingled gate and fence were the sole barriers to access. The group simply scaled the five-foot fence shortly around midnight without detection. To their surprise and chagrin, 17-year old Steven Parent, a friend of the live-in groundskeeper, William Garretson was exiting the property simultaneously in his father's car via the electronic gate. Watson emerged from the shadows and confronted Parent. Despite his pleas for mercy, Watson callously slashed the watch off of Parent's wrist and shot him four times in rapid succession.

The group entered the house where the Sharon Tate and her guests were retiring for the evening in separate quarters. The subsequent mayhem and executions by excessive stabbings and shootings created a horrific carnage. The excess was due to their inexperience and incompetence. None were hardened convicts. Instead, each was simply acting on blind compliance to Manson's instructions.

Polanski was overseas filming during the calamity but his wife Sharon Tate, eight and a half months pregnant, became the most prominent victim. Others fatalities included Jay Sebring, a noted hairstylist, Abigail Folger, heiress to the Folger coffee fortune and a writer, Wojciech Frykowski. The killings were graphically detailed in print. With the premises presumably insulated by security devices, the public terror was heightened. The groundskeeper Garretson claimed that he heard nothing from his detached residence. Any personal curiosity exhibited by him or one of the neighbors over the noise would have added to the casualty list.

The former Cielo Drive structure has since been razed and reconstructed into a sprawling multi-level Mediterranean style mansion. The present colossus mirrors reconstruction trends prevalent amongst affluent Beverly Hills real estate. Security protection has been enhanced and any vestige of the former structure is left to the imagination of the viewer.

Manson was displeased by the group's careless handiwork and accompanied the same four along with Leslie Van Houten and Steve Grogan to orchestrate another execution the following evening. Manson selected the home of supermarket executive Leno LaBianca and his wife Rosemary, a dress shop co-owner living in the Los Feliz sector to rectify the previous evenings debacle. He apparently decided on their residence because he had attended a party next door the previous year. Once again the house was located atop an elevated driveway. The group surprised the couple sleeping in separate rooms.

Both were bound and then repeatedly stabbed. Once again, the slaughter was brutal and planning equally inept even with their leader present. No evidence directly linked Manson with physically stabbing either victim.

Manson proved no more proficient at planning murder than evading capture. Initially, despite the amateurish sanitizing of the crime scene, serious leads or motives did not materialize for each apparent senseless killing. The police had not yet linked the two murders as directly related. Manson's cult lived isolated and significantly below suspicion inhabiting a former San Fernando Valley movie production complex called Spahn Ranch in the hills above Chatsworth.

The group's anonymity would soon be exposed....but not as murder suspects. On August 16, the Los Angeles Police Department raided their compound and arrested all 26 residents as suspects in an auto theft ring. Weapons were seized during the raid, but because the text of the warrant was misdated, the group was released from custody.

Manson suspected that Donald *Shorty* Shea, a ranch hand had assisted in setting up the raid hoping to evict the cult off of the property. Revenge was immediate. Three group members Bruce Davis, Tex Watson and Steve Grogan murdered Shea. His body was rumored to be dismembered, but in 1977, Grogan drew authorities a map of the cadaver's location where it was discovered intact. He was released from prison in 1985 and remains the sole cult member convicted of murder to be paroled. Bruce Davis is currently interned at the California Men's Colony Prison in San Luis Obispo. He has been approved for parole on four occasions, but denied multiple times by successive California governors.

Following Shea's murder, the cult relocated to Barker Ranch in even more remote Death Valley. Short on credible suspects, investigators began recognizing the similarities between each execution pointing towards the identical culprits. Informants detailed linkages directly to Manson's collective.

In October of 1969, the majority of the group members were arrested at the Barker Ranch. Persistent rumors of additional killings and desert burials abounded during that stretch. Bodies have never been unearthed.

Tex Watson had taken flight back to Texas after assisting with Shea's murder. Like Manson had repeatedly attempted during his deranged life, he sought to reinvent his personality with a respectable haircut and more conventional lifestyle. He was arrested in late November 1970 and fought extradition for nine months. He would be tried separately from the other suspects for this reason.

Arriving back in California several months after the group's conviction, Watson pathetically feigned mental illness by attempting to regress into a fetal state, refusing to talk or eat and shedding 55 pounds. His performance proved unsuccessful, as he was declared sane and fit for trial after a 90-day observation period at Atascadero State Hospital.

Patricia Krenwinkel had also relocated back to her native Alabama after her father had bailed her out of jail following the second arrest. She was extradited back to California to stand trial with the other principals.

The nine-month trial began in July 1970 with extensive global media coverage. Manson, coveting the performance spotlight, shaved off his hair completely and carving an X prominently on his forehead for theatrical effect claiming he was Satan's reincarnation. Years later, he would modify the simple cross into a swastika which still remains embedded.

A few of his female admirers would replicate his appearance. Some of the female defendants appeared blissfully absent and smiled sheepishly on camera. They appeared unconcerned towards the gravity or consequences of their actions. Viewers were appalled by their indifference. Despite their collective theatre, the magnitude of their monstrous acts sobered the jury. The seven-month trial resulted in Manson, Atkins, Krenwinkel and Van Houten being condemned to death. When Tex Watson was finally able to stand trial in October 1971, he was convicted in two weeks on seven counts of first-degree murder and condemned to death.

A curious aside to the proceedings was the abrupt disappearance of defense attorney Ronald Hughes representing Leslie Van Houten. He vanished while on a camping trip during a ten-day recess from the Tate-LaBianca murder trial in November 1970. His body was found four months later but the cause of death was undeterminable. Many suspected that cult members murdered Hughes as an act of retaliation for his verbal disagreements with Charles Manson over defense strategies.

When the death penalty was briefly abolished in California in 1972, each of the prisoner's sentences was commuted to life in prison.

Initially incarcerated at San Quentin on death row with Watson, Manson was transferred to Folsom Prison and then the California Medical Facility at Vacaville. Manson has been returned twice to each location and spent time in Pelican Bay State Prison and Corcoran State Penitentiary (twice) where he resides today. He has been attacked twice, once by a member of the Aryan Brotherhood, a white supremacy gang and on another occasion by a Hare Krishna resulting in severe burns. Even the celebrity incarcerated face risks from peers seeking reputations. He has been disciplined while imprisoned on multiple occasions.

He granted four national television interviews during the 1980s. Each appearance merely reinforced his profound psychosis, paranoia and need to be permanently separated from society. Since those public exposures, Manson has remained isolated, stoic and resigned to his damnation. He has allowed his supporters, detractors and biographers to construct his personal mythology absent of personal contribution. His psychotically penetrating stares, public posturing acts and absolute lack of contrition have distanced him from any possibility of society's forgiveness. He will never be admitted back. Death will become his sole release.

Despite or because of his association with evil, numerous disenfranchised fringe individuals and groups have adopted his personage as their symbolic patron. The atrocities he is responsible for are distantly removed from the headlines. He has been erroneously linked as a folk hero outlaw and example of independent alternative living outside of the constraints of society.

In truth, he is marginally more than a bombastic, barbaric criminal with a self-absorbed personality. His proponents lionize him from afar because intimate inspection would prove disillusioning.

His apocalyptic visions were as vacant as his hypnotically drugged follower's eyes and the grandiose legacy he envisioned. Despite a post-incarceration pleura of often flattering music, books, television and motion picture portrayals, he has consistently proven himself mediocre. He will perish delusional and unrepentant in a solitary Corcoran Prison cell, shriveled and outcast. Only the weak-willed and similarly deluded will mourn his death.

Charles Tex Watson is currently imprisoned at the Mule Creek State Prison in Ione. Patricia Krenwinkel and Leslie Van Houten are interned at the California Institution for Women in Corona. Each has been denied parole on multiple occasions.

Linda Kasabian served no jail time as she received immunity in exchange for her damaging testimony against the cult. She evaded public scrutiny by returning to the east coast but was arrested in a Washington State drug raid in 1996. She publicly resurfaced in a 2009 interview with *The Guardian* newspaper. The article repeated known facts regarding the killings and reinforced her diminutive role in their commission. Her whereabouts are currently unknown.

In examining the wreckage and catastrophe of so many wasted young lives, it becomes difficult to illuminate even a penlight of brightness amidst the darkness. The convicted murderers, with the exception of Manson, became generally model and compliant prisoners as one might assume of subservient personalities.

Each has uniquely channeled their personal misfortune into guidance and positive counseling towards their fellow inmates. Some have earned college degrees online and have become promoters of prison literary, drug and alcoholic rehabilitation programs. A few publicly espoused religious conversions in their lives and established ministries. Each has repeatedly expressed remorse and begged forgiveness for their actions.

Their positive prison activities have doubtlessly exceeded any contribution they may have ultimately offered had they been released to society. They may or may not be granted liberty one day, but without exception, it will be at an advanced age.

An aging but recollecting society, the victim's families and acquaintances will probably never fully forgive them. Perhaps God ultimately will.

The Incline Up Cielo Drive

Modified Front Entrance Gate

Site of the Former Scalable Fence

Pathway Leading to House

The Reconstructed Cielo Drive Palatial Mansion

LaBianca Residence in Los Felix District

Dorothea Puente: Arsenic and Old Lace and Killing for Profit

Dorothea Puente clearly understood the predicament faced by the elderly, destitute and addicted margins of society. She comprehended the vulnerability of societies invisibly forgotten. She knew further that each was compensated monthly with social security benefit payments that barely covered their living expenses.

Puente preyed upon this population by offering illusionary security, boarding and care. She evolved into one of the most unassuming convicted American serial killers.

During the 1980s, Puente ran a boarding house in downtown Sacramento on F Street and cashed the Social Security checks of her elderly, alcoholic and mentally disabled boarders.

Her own turbulent childhood, four marriages with accompanying abuse steeled her resolve to escape poverty at whatever cost. The children she bore were given up immediately for adoption. She was arrested on multiple occasions for fraud and forging signatures on checks.

In 1960, she was arrested for owning and managing a brothel. After her release, she was arrested again, this time for vagrancy and sentenced to another 90 days in jail. Following that, she began a criminal career that over time became more serious. She found work as a nurse's aide, caring for disabled and elderly people in private homes. In a short time, she started to manage boarding houses.

Puente began to spend time in local bars trawling for older men who were receiving benefits. They became a primary source for lodgers. She forged their signatures to steal their money, but eventually was caught and charged with 34 counts of treasury fraud. While on probation, she continued to commit the identical fraud. In 1981 Puente began renting out her infamous boarding house. The nine murders with which she was charged in 1988 were associated with this building.

Puente's motives for killing tenants were financial. Police estimates speculated her income exceeding $5,000 per month. Puente accepted primarily elderly tenants and was popular with local social workers because she accepted hard to place clients including drug addicts and abusive tenants.

Puente never told social workers about her five felony convictions for drugging and robbing the elderly and they never did their homework. It seemed inconceivable that federal parole agents, who visited Puente 15 times during the two years leading up to her arrest, never realized she was running a boarding house for the elderly-in direct violation of her parole. She collected tenants' monthly mail before they saw it and paid them stipends, pocketing the rest for expenses.

A repellant stench hovered over her Sacramento neighborhood like a putrid fog. Her neighbors were familiar with the source of the odor, but not why. Puente blamed backed-up sewers, rats rotting under the floorboards and even the fish emulsion she'd used to fertilize the garden.

She tried to eradicate the odor by dumping bags of lime and gallons of bleach into the yard. She sprayed air freshener regularly but the odor refused to fade. Her boardinghouse was cursed but the source remained unknown.

The gruesome discovery of seven buried bodies in her backyard garden following a tip from a social worker resolved the cause.

During the initial investigation, Puente was not immediately a suspect, and was allowed to leave the property, ostensibly to buy a cup of coffee at a nearby hotel. Instead, after buying the coffee, she fled immediately to Los Angeles, where she befriended an elderly pensioner she met in a bar. The pensioner, however, recognized her from police reports on television and called the authorities. She was arrested shortly after.

Her trial was moved to Monterey County and began during October of 1992. The prosecutor called over 130 witnesses. He argued to the jury she had used sleeping pills to put her tenants to sleep, and then suffocated them. She would then hire convicts to dig the holes in her yard.

The prosecution case's main weakness was that there were no living eyewitnesses to the alleged murders. The prosecution could only prove the cause of death in the case of one tenant, Ruth Munroe. The other bodies were too decayed. Toxicology tests did reveal that there were traces of Dalmane (flurazepam), a prescription-strength sleeping pill in all of the remains.

A handwriting expert confirmed that Puente had signed the names of seven dead tenants on 60 federal and state checks that were mailed to her house.

After a year of weighing the testimony, the jury found Puente guilty of murdering Dorothy Miller, Benjamin Fink and Leona Carpenter. The jury couldn't reach a verdict on the six other murder charges, and Superior Court Judge Michael Virga declared a mistrial on those counts.

After several days of deliberations, the jury was deadlocked 7–5 for life imprisonment. Virga, declared a mistrial when the jury said further deliberations would not change their minds. Under the law, Puente received life without the possibility of parole.

She was incarcerated at California Women's Facility (CCWF) in Chowchilla. For the rest of her life, she maintained her innocence, insisting that all her tenants had died of natural causes. Puente exhibited no emotion when the verdict was read.

She died on March 27, 2011 in prison in at the age of 82 from natural causes without outside assistance.

The F Street Boarding House

The Current Boneyard Covering

Efren Saldivar's Definition of Assisted Medical Homicide

The curious and bizarre example of Efren Saldivar may serve one day as a preliminary case study in the debate over sanctioned medically assisted suicide and mercy killings.

Saldivar was once a respiratory therapist employed by the Glendale Adventist Medical Center. Working the night shift with minimal staff, he injected terminally ill patients with a paralytic drug inducing either respiratory or cardiac arrest.

What separated his actions from traditional homicides is that each of his victims were unconscious and close to death. His selection process made detection nearly impossible.

Following his employment termination in March 1998, he underwent a crisis of conscience and voluntarily confessed to 50 murders. He later retracted his confession. An internal investigation by Adventist Health, the hospital's corporate entity suggested that the actual number potentially exceeded 120 fatalities.

Proving homicides to the soon dead in court proved difficult. Many families had already cremated the victim's bodies. In search of evidence to obtain a conviction, police exhumed twenty buried cadavers that had died during Saldivar's rounds. Six bodies were discovered to have an excessive concentration of Pavulon, Saldivar's preferential drug.

He pleaded guilty to the six counts of murder on the discoveries in his 2002 trial. He received six consecutive life sentences without the possibility of parole and is currently incarcerated at Corcoran State Prison.

What blurs the ethics behind his actions is that one day they may become standard operating procedures with appropriate consent. The ethical debate continues as some states have legalized assisted homicides and others are contemplating equivalent legislation.

Efren Saldivar may not survive to witness society's evolutionary position change. Within his lifetime, his sentence may one day appear excessive. His actions however in their context created a fresh interpretation to the term *Angel of Mercy*.

The Final Corridor For
Terminally Ill Patients

Ted Kaczynski: To Arms Against A Faceless Society and Enemy

It is difficult to isolate the juncture where genius and madness intersect within a troubled personality. Once these paths have diverged, conventional understanding behind an individual's homicidal behavior becomes incomprehensible.

In theory, it is understandable that genius may not recuperate using traditional mental illness therapies and medications. A highly developed thinker rarely views the world through a mainstream perspective. The complexity and elevated rational capacity that ultimately separates genius may potentially alienate it from society.

Ted Kaczynski was a recognized mathematical genius but his legacy will remain as the Unabomber Killer. His mania was responsible for the death of three people and injury of 23 more before his arrest in 1996.

A high school academic prodigy, he was accepted to Harvard University in 1958 at the impressionable age of 16. While at Harvard, Kaczynski was taught by famed logician Willard Van Orman Quine, scoring at the top of his class. Dr. Henry Murray selected him amongst 22 other undergraduates as guinea pigs for a series of ethically questionable experiments. Murray subjected each of the participants to extreme stress levels including verbal abuse, personality attacks and complete disregard for their own their cherished belief system.

The focus of these aggressive studies was purportedly to measure participant's abilities to adapt to acute pressure. In one instance, it may have triggered a latent mania buried beneath a simply shy and undeveloped personality.

Over thirty-five years later during his murder trial, Kaczynski's lawyers attributed some of his emotional instability and dislike of mind control techniques to his participation in this study. His legal team attempted to enter an insanity defense to save Kaczynski's life, but Kaczynski rejected this plea. A court-appointed psychiatrist diagnosed him as suffering from paranoid schizophrenia but declared him competent to stand trial.

After graduating from Harvard at the age of 20 in 1962, Kaczynski continued his studies at the University of Michigan. At Michigan, he taught classes and worked on his widely lauded dissertation. Five years later he earned his doctoral degree.

Kaczynski was hired as an assistant professor of mathematics at the University of California at Berkeley for the 1967-68 and 1968-69 school years. The general catalog for the 1968-69 academic year shows Kaczynski was scheduled to teach four courses: Number Systems, Introduction to the Theory of Sets, General Topology and Function Spaces. He lived in a compact Regent Street apartment, remote from nearby campus vehicular and pedestrian traffic. Typified by colleagues as being pathologically shy, Kaczynski struggled at Berkeley. His abilities as a lecturer and his poor communications with students made his tenure impossible. His loner persona doubtlessly conflicted with the student protest mentality and activism of the era.

At Berkeley it was theorized that he developed a disdain for technology and many of the trappings of modern life. During his tenure, he was the author of six professional papers published between 1965 and 1969. He voluntarily and abruptly resigned from the university following the 1969 academic year and spent the next few years drifting from city to city. Was this defiant act the genesis of his degenerative personality?

In 1971 Kaczynski and his brother David purchased a plot of land near Lincoln, Montana and it was there that he would spend most of the ensuing 24 years. In a remote 10x12' cabin without electricity or running water, he lived as a recluse while learning survival skills in an attempt to become self-sufficient.

The intensity of his estrangement from society resulted in fatal consequences. From 1978 to 1995, Kaczynski sent 16 bombs to targets including universities and airlines, killing three people and injuring 23. How and why he selected his victims was never adequately publicly explained during his trial. Several of the injuries were unfortunate individuals who were responsible for opening incoming mail.

It is problematical to understand ideological homicide. How does one empathize with an individual who would randomly wound or kill without certainty of their intended victim? Surely he understood that each unique killing spawned numerous subsequent victims? Kaczynski's rational appeared the most pathological and senseless of motives; understood only by himself.

Kaczynski's unveiling and capture began when he anonymously mailed a letter to *The New York Times* on April 24, 1995. He promised to cease his killing spree if *The Times* or *Washington Post* published his now infamous Unabomber Manifesto (Industrial Society and Its Future). Apparently even recluses can succumb to the seduction of public exposure of their ideas.

The Times published his 35,000-word text that stressed the erosion of human freedom necessitated by modern technology. His brother David recognized many elements of the writing and forwarded his name to federal investigators. The tip led investigators to the Montana cabin where Ted Kaczynski was arrested on April 3, 1996.

The cabin featured a compacted trove of incriminating evidence linking Kaczynski to the attacks including journal entries, bomb diagrams and parts and handwritten drafts of his manifesto. Would his assaults realistically have ended with the publication of his Manifesto? No evidence was ever discovered to indicate either way except Kaczynski's promise.

Kaczynski was arraigned in California and New Jersey, the locations of his three fatal bombings. On January 22, 1998, he pleaded guilty to the charges against him in exchange for a sentence of life in prison without the possibility of parole. The sentence isolated Kaczynski even further from society and an explanation towards his precise motives.

Did he truly envision his Manifesto would alter the direction of civilization? It is not difficult to concur with his premise that society has restricted personal privacy and freedom with today's technology. It is a disturbing phenomenon that individuals may so freely discard rights, which required generations and centuries to earn.

Yet isolated homicides such as Kaczynski's have not impacted change in the slightest. His Unabomber Manifesto has not cracked the mandated reading lists of any recognized academic institution including his own. Were his observations, due to his mathematical genius more relevant than anyone else's?

Contemporary society has the capacity to estrange all social classes. Individuals are required to assimilate to the frenetic pace or risk being marginalized and alienated from the future. At some juncture, each individual may ultimately have to determine their jumping off point from the pace.

But at least for now, that option is freely given by choice.

Ted Kaczynski's Berkeley Apartment

The Two Night Stalkers: Terror Amidst the Twilight Hours

The *Original Night Stalker* has successfully eluded capture, while maintaining an absence of public recognition.

Underexposed by the significant number of serial killers prowling California during the 1970s and overshadowed by the apprehension of his successor Richards Ramirez in 1985, he terrorized both ends of the state with unprecedented horror. The extent of his butchery has never been fully documented.

During his estimated reign of fear between 1976-86, he was suspected to have committed at least fifty sexual assaults within Sacramento and Contra Costa counties. During his northern California rampage, he was labeled the *East Area Rapist*. As his audacity worsened, he was credited with ten confirmed and possibly three additional murders in Southern California. DNA matching linked him to the murders.

His confirmed murder victims included Dr. Robert Offerman, Debra Manning, Charlene and Lyman Smith, Keith and Patrice Harrington, Manuela Witthuhn, Cheri Domingo, Gregory Sanchez and Janelle Cruz.

The psychopath began as a common house burglar. He intensified his activities into rape and finally murder. He would stalk middle class neighborhoods during the evening hours sizing up his potential prey. He initially targeted women who were alone in single story residences and then escalated his pattern to couples. He entered the premises during the late night or early morning, awakening his victims. He bound or forced them to bind each other before ruthlessly attacking.

On numerous occasions, he was spotted during his neighborhood scouting. Once a law enforcement officer chased him immediately after a murder. Once an individual chased him and was shot in the head during his pursuit. Despite eluding capture, a composite drawing and speculative character profile was

412

formulated.

The scariest attribute from his published psychological profile was his ability to blend unnoticeably into mainstream society. His non-threatening appearance, masquerade personality and cunning made him inconspicuous and dangerous.

Amidst the shadows from which he emerged as a mist, the stalker's identity ultimately proved untraceable. He left abandoned weaponry, bicycles and even footprints at murder scenes. His heightened evasion intuition enabled his escapes.

His discernable pattern of killings ceased shortly after the mid 1980s. He may have left California, committed suicide or even been confined in a mental institution. Several potential suspects have been cleared by DNA testing, alibi or following detailed investigations.

He simply evolved into the one that got away.

Unlike the invisible *Original Night Stalker*, his successor neither eluded capture nor recognition.

Richard Ramirez terrorized Californians via highly publicized home invasions between June 1984 and August 1985. The serial killer, rapist and burglar became the more recognized *Night Stalker* by a morbidly fascinated media. Ramirez spouted Satanically motivated oaths while committing his callous attacks. He employed diverse weapons including handguns, knives, machetes, tire irons and hammers. The attention that his exploits generated diverted investigative and public attention away from the original killer.

Ramirez's confirmed fatalities included Mei Leung, Jennie Vincow, Maria Hernandez, Christina and Mary Caldwell, Dayle Okazaki, Tsai-Lian Yu, Vincent and Maxine Zazzra, Harold Wu, Edward Wildgans, Peter Pan, Elyas Abowath, Bill Doi, Mary Louis Cannon, Joyce Nelson, Lela and Maxon Kneiding and

Chainarong Khovananth. He seriously wounded, violated and traumatized numerous other surviving victims.

Ramirez epitomized the extremes of evil, but not intelligence.

His ruthless but careless attacks left innumerable clues, eyewitnesses and finally a license plate sighting of his vehicle. His law enforcement traced mug shot from numerous prior arrests was broadcast nationally via multiple medias. He had casually followed the public scrutiny of his crimes, but did little to conceal his identity. His sole attempt at evasion was once tossing out an identified size 11 1/2 pair of tennis shoes into the ocean.

Ramirez impulsively chose victims randomly. Despite the intensive public manhunt, he simply continued his aimless and drifting lifestyle. His capture was precipitated when he casually strolled into his own arrest.

Ramirez was naively unaware of his public notoriety. He boarded a roundtrip bus in an unsuccessful attempt to visit his brother in Tucson. Upon his return, he casually exited the terminal located in East Los Angeles. Miraculously he eluded police surveillance that was concentrating on outbound buses.

A group of elderly Hispanic women identified him when he slithered into a nearby convenience store. He fled immediately. A chase ensued by neighborhood residents. Ramirez unsuccessfully attempted to carjack multiple vehicles. He was subdued, severely beaten and held by the assemblage until police finally booked him into custody.

Courting the media for maximum exposure, Ramirez achieved a macabre celebrity status. He fed mesmerized reporters with quotable quips, a blood scrawled pentagram on his forehand and exhibited a complete absence of remorse. His trial and sentencing required over a year. He was convicted on 13 counts of murder, 5 attempted murders, 11 sexual assaults and 14 burglaries. A jury convicted him and he was sentenced to death. He died in 2013 of complications from B-cell lymphoma, while awaiting an execution at San Quentin that potentially may have extended his life decades.

Foolish supporters cultivated a morbid fascination via correspondence with this brazen unrepentant criminal. Ramirez married while incarcerated.

The two Night Stalkers could not have been more divergent in either personality or technique. They shared in common savagery and a vile disregard for human life. The saddest commentary of their narratives was that their victims were relegated to mere statistics desecrated by their maniacal urges.

Charlene and Lyman Smith's Residence

Cheri Domingo and Gregory Sanchez Murder Site

Housesitting Mayhem

Janelle Cruz's Residence

Dr. Robert Offerman and Debra Manning's Residence

The Zebra Killings: A Racially Intended Genocide?

After over forty years following their commission, certain murders haunt and still remain scalding to the touch. Their secrets and searing hot implications remain immune to in-depth public and media excavation. Feature films will not be financed. Memorials and reenactments for public consumption are nonexistent. The killings are simply too lethal to the touch and remain only superficially reported and archived. A desire to forget this story has buried it for over four decades. But did the murders ever truly conclude?

The most disturbing series of San Francisco homicides in the 1970s were unquestionably the Zebra murders. Two principle reasons still provoke outrage over the serial killings amongst those who choose to remember. The killings were exclusively racially motivated and a cover-up by law enforcement agencies masked the territorial extent and number of actual killings.

Between August 1973 and April 1974 within San Francisco alone, fifteen execution-style murders and eight serious assaults with survivors were publicly documented. Amongst the surviving victims was future San Francisco Mayor Art Agnos, then a member of the California Commission on Aging, who was attending a meeting in Potrero Hill. Agnos was shot twice in the back and miraculously survived the attack.

Police identified the case as Zebra after the special police radio "Z" band they assigned for the investigation. The designation seemed equally appropriate given the racially motivated nature of the attacks. Twenty-two individual crimes within a six-month spree were attributed exclusively to at least four convicted African-American suspects. Evidence suggests however, that their capture and conviction was merely the extreme tip of a much larger targeted genocide.

The term racial genocide conjures up comparatives with recent and 20th century holocausts and mass exterminations. The intent behind the acts were no different and ultimately become a question of comparison and semantics. At what victim quantifying level do admittedly racially motivated killings qualify as genocide?

During the 179 days of terror, the murders caused widespread panic in San Francisco. People gathered in groups as a safety precaution or simply remained indoors. The city suffered economically as tourists stayed away. In reaction, a significantly increased police presence was ordered throughout the city.

The killings continued. Police remained baffled by an apparent lack of motive, the brutality and lack of remorse by the perpetrators.

Certain consistencies were known about the killings. All of the shootings involved two different .32 caliber pistols. The murders were excessively swift, brutal and savagely executed. All of the victims were Caucasian and most either elderly, slightly built or defenseless. All of the killers were identified as African-Americans. Most of the victims were shot multiply and generally to the body (enabling unintentional survival for some). One victim was raped and two were hacked to death by machetes and knives.

A special task force was formed to try to solve and stop the murders. On the evening of December 28, 1973, five shootings alone were recorded with four fatalities.

After the final killing, out of desperation and a lack of concrete leads, local law enforcement authorities initiated a program of controversial racial profiling that today would be inconceivable. African-American males resembling the composite sketches of two suspected killers were systematically stopped, searched and questioned. Once they'd completed an examination process, they were given a specially imprinted Zebra interrogation card, which they could display to police officers if stopped again.

419

This action by the police provoked vocal and widespread criticism from the African-American community. A US District Judge within a week ruled the program unconstitutional and the operation was suspended. Although the program did not result in any arrests, it was suggested that it prompted an informer within the murder ring who resembled one of the drawings to come forward. Aside from his fear of capture, a $30,000 reward he claimed ultimately pierced the veil of secrecy behind the killings.

Anthony Harris, an estranged employee from the Black Self-Help Moving and Storage on Market Street met with Zebra case detectives in Oakland. He provided an avalanche of incriminating evidence and to solidify his credibility, detailed precise facts about a homicide that had not been reported by local news sources.

Harris was present at many of the killings but denied actually killing anyone.

Harris provided the police with names, dates, addresses and details-enough information to issue arrest warrants against multiple suspects. Harris subsequently sought, and received, immunity for his help in breaking the Zebra case. He, his girlfriend and her child were relocated and given new identities. Under extreme pressure to end the bloodshed and apprehend the responsible perpetrators, many observers questioned whether police granted immunity to an individual equally responsible. Harris narrowly escaped his own execution before testifying by organizers of the massacres.

On May 1, 1974 simultaneous raids during the pre-dawn hours were made, resulting in the arrests of Larry Craig Green and J.C.X. Simon in an apartment building on Grove Street. More suspects were arrested fearing their flight at the Black Self-Help Moving and Storage's facility. Of the seven arrested that day, four were released for lack of conclusive evidence including the manager and his assistant at the moving facility. Manuel Moore was the only additional detainee along with Green and Simon.

What surfaced publicly following the arrests was the existence of a sordid murder cult, called the Death Angels, aimed exclusively towards the extermination of the Caucasian race. The Nation of Islam Mosque #26 based in San Francisco, then located at the Fillmore Auditorium (or a splinter sect within) was prominently fingered as the conspiratorial organization behind the attacks. Charges against the organization were never pursued in court.

The Nation of Islam group, headquartered in Chicago, paid the attorney fees for Green, Simon and Moore. They did not pay purposely for Jessie Lee Cooks as he had earlier pled guilty for a spree-related murder and was incarcerated. Pleading guilty for any crime was considered an affront to the group's separatist philosophy. He was charged simultaneously along with the other three members for his participation in the murder spree.

The trial of the accused started on March 3, 1975. Exhaustive efforts were employed by defense attorneys to discredit Harris. Their tactics proved to no avail as he methodically and exhaustively spilled all of the grisly details over 12 days of testimony.

One of the two .32 caliber Beretta automatic pistols used in many of the later killings had been recovered and traced methodically and directly to the manager and his assistant of the Black Self-Help Moving and Storage facility. The two were never indicted.

The trial featured the testimony of 108 witnesses, 8,000 pages totaling 3.5 million words worth of transcripts, and culminating in what was then the longest criminal trial in California history. Larry Green, J. C. X. Simon, Manuel Moore and Jessie Lee Cooks were convicted of first-degree murder and conspiracy to commit first-degree murder in 1976. Despite the length of the trial and mountainous testimony and evidence, the jury unanimously arrived at their verdict within 18 hours of deliberation.

Larry Green is currently serving his sentence at the California State Prison in Vacaville, Manuel Moore at the California Heath Care Facility in Stockton and Jessie Lee Cooks at RJ Donovan Correctional Facility in San Diego. J. C. X. Simon expired in his prison cell near midnight on March 12, 2015 in San Quentin. There is no public record of his personal remorse towards any of his victims.

The most troubling element of the Zebra serial killings was the extent and geographical magnitude of the murderous spree. There was significant evidence introduced to indicate the San Francisco killings were only a smaller component of a more aggressive statewide and potentially national program of extermination. None of the responsible organizers of the mass killing program were apprehended, publicly identified or punished.

In 1979, writer Clark Howard's book *Zebra* was published. Howard's work has been acknowledged by numerous credible sources as the most definitive, thorough and authoritative book on the murders. Using court records, police reports, witnesses and interviews with the killers themselves, Howard was able to piece together the horrid details behind the murders and the unrelenting hatred that inspired the killers.

Howard's book detailed the sobering criteria employed by the responsible cell group within the Nation of Islam that were designed solely towards the objective of murder. Howard described the vicious, sometimes impulsive and universally cowardly nature of the attacks.

According to his book, the minimum criteria for becoming a Death Angel required the confirmed killing of 9 white males, 5 white women and 4 white children. The book cited that by October 20, 1973, at least 15 accredited death assassins were operating within California. Based on their requirement criteria, this would result in a minimum of 270 fatalities.

Other published sources have speculated that as many as 50 qualified operatives were at work within the state. Their blood counts were employed as recruiting devices by massacre organizers to swell the prospective killing base of fresh inductees.

The book introduced chilling confirmation that the California attorney general's office had compiled a list of 71 execution-style murders committed around the state. The murders were facilitated with either a machete or pistol, in which, the killer or killers was always a well dressed and groomed youngish black man, and the victim always white.

In addition to San Francisco, the murders were carried out in Oakland, San Jose, Emeryville, Berkeley, Long Beach, Signal Hill, Santa Barbara, Palo Alto, Pacifica, San Diego, Los Angeles, and in the counties of San Mateo, Santa Clara, Los Angeles, Contra Costa, Ventura and Alameda. This intended racial genocide program was estimated by some sources to have begun approximately three years before the San Francisco killings.

Regardless of the exact toll, the heartlessness behind synchronized murder becomes sickening reading. What sort of monster(s) or organization could condone such depravity? It remains unimaginable to assume that only four individuals should bear the sole responsibility for such heinous behavior. Yet only four insignificant foot soldiers ultimately did.

None of the remaining three convicts have ever publicly asked forgiveness or expressed shame for their actions despite forty years of incarceration. Were compassion and humanity possible emotions to accompany their blind obedience? Do they share any resentment towards bearing the punishment for the acts alone?

Their superiors eluded public disclosure, capture and accountability.

The most widely circulating rationalization then by authorities for downplaying the fatalities was to avoid widespread public panic and alarm. In truth, this underexposure potentially created more victims unknowingly vulnerable.

The fatalities in the San Francisco spree included Quita Hague, Frances Rose, Saleem Erakat, Paul Dancik, Marietta DiGirolamo, Ilario Bertuccio, Neal Moynihan, Mildred Hosler, Tana Smith, Vincent Wollin, John Bambic, Jane Holly, Thomas Rainwater, Nelson Shields IV and one anonymous victim labeled John Doe #169.

The seriously wounded included Richard Hague, Ellen Linder, Art Agnos, Angela Roselli, Roxanne McMillian, Linda Story, Ward Anderson and Terry White.

It has been over four decades since the Zebra Killings. With the exception of Clark Howard's book, little has been written since that has profoundly re-evaluated the murders. San Francisco civic victim memorial ceremonies or remembrances have never been held. The 23 victims remain essentially published footnotes and forgotten. The primary buildings involved in the drama have been remodeled, renumbered and facades freshened. Layers of applied paint can never completely cover the stainage.

Not everyone has conveniently forgotten the terror and carnage.

A trail of human extermination leaves many witnesses and survivors within its wake. Their eyewitness stories have the capacity to preserve the indignity for generations. This criminal narrative may have temporarily disappeared from the mainstream media and public consciousness but for many it will never remained buried.

The callousness and evil behind the attacks remain a permanent scandal. The violence symbolized an unjustified affront against both humanity and public disclosure. For the present time, there appears little interest to penetrate deeper.

Former Black Self-Help Moving & Storage Building

The Former Railroad Tracks Where Quita Hague was Hacked to Death and Richard Hague Mutilated

Site Where Frances Rose Was Slain In Her Car

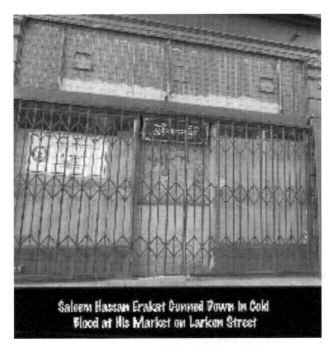

Saleem Hassan Erakat Gunned Down In Cold
Blood at His Market on Larkon Street

Former Site of Telephone Box
Where Paul Dancik Was Shot

Potrero Hill Location Where
Art Agnos Was Shot

Murder Site of Marlena DiGirolamo

Intersection Where Ilario Bertuccio Was Gunned Down

Location Where Angela Roselli Was Gunned Down

Neal Moynihan Killed Taking a
Teddybear to his Little Sister

Mildred Hosler Gunned Down
on Opposite Sidewalk

Upstairs at the Black Self-Help Moving Building Where Killing Meetings Were Staged and Victim John Doe Slain

Location Where Tana Smith Was Shot Dead

Vincent Wollin's Shooting Site

Launderette Where Jane Holly Was Gunned Down

House Where Roxanne
McMillian Was Shot

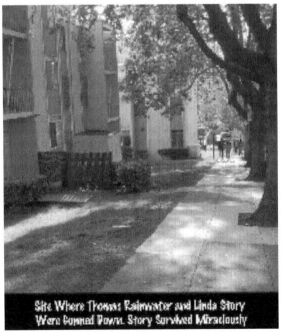

Site Where Thomas Rainwater and Linda Story
Were Gunned Down. Story Survived Miraculously

Bus Stop Where Ward Anderson
and Terry White were Slain

Residence of at Least Two of the Aspiring Death Angels

The Heaven's Gate Cult Shutters Operations Abruptly and Permanently

The discipleship in one of California's oddest cults was typified as intelligent, truth seeking and ultimately fatally misled. The Heaven's Gate group based in San Diego professed one of the most unorthodox and embellished doctrines lifted straight out of a science fiction screenplay.

Two charlatans, Marshall Applewhite and Bonnie Nettles founded the movement in the mid 1970s blending a twisted mix of reincarnation, supernatural and interpretive Christianity. The organizer's intellectual arrogance elevated Applewhite into the status of prophet and quasi-Messiah. The Heaven's Gate theology revealed that a savior would arrive from Texas. Applewhite coincidentally was born in the humble Texas community of Spur, not to be confused with Bethlehem.

His early formation was strongly religiously influenced, as his father was a Presbyterian Minister. Applewhite's vocation initially mirrored his father as he earned his bachelor's degree in philosophy and enrolled in theology studies with the intention of becoming a minister.

He shifted his direction by opting to pursue a music career and was retained as a music director for a Presbyterian church in North Carolina. He married and fathered two children. He was drafted into the Army in 1954 and served as a member of the Army Signal Corps while being stationed in Austria.

He left the military in 1956, earned a master's degree in music and concentrated on musical theatre. He taught briefly at the University of Alabama.

His sexual orientation sabotaged his teaching position and marriage. He divorced in 1965 and migrated to Texas and a variety of teaching positions. His emotional state fluctuated between polar extremities and during his years in academia, he openly courted both genders as sexual partners.

His frequent spells of depression ultimately unraveled his teaching career and by 1971, he was operating a delicatessen in New Mexico. He returned to Texas later that year following the death of his father. He was in debt, emotionally deflated and severely depressed. He was arrested in August 1974 for failing to return a car that he had rented in another state and served six months in prison.

It appears incredulous and even comical to examine such a flawed messianic biography. Tragically, the manipulated death of over forty followers deflates the irony.

His partner, Bonnie Nettles led a conventional existence as a wife, mother of four and registered nurse. Her unconventional beliefs ultimately alienated her family. Her philosophies and studies were rooted in a fascination based on spiritualism and the afterlife. She dredged up an obscure 19th century monk for guidance and employed séances, fortunetellers and mediums to contact deceased spirits.

In mid-1972, she met Applewhite at a drama class he was teaching. They became enamored with each other but maintained a platonic relationship. Based on her astrological interpretation of their intertwined destinies, she left her family to establish with him the Heaven's Gate movement.

The initial reception towards their united theology was marginal. They flexibly modified their teachings in alignment with many of the prevailing spiritual teaching tactics, while inserting their own extraterrestrials linguistics. At the apex of their collaboration, the cult peaked at approximately 80 members. They concentrated their recruiting on college campuses towards students fascinated by a countercultural lifestyle with occult leanings.

For thirteen years, Nettles actively worked in partnership with Applewhite formulating a certainty that they would ascend to the next level of consciousness together. They renamed themselves multiple times until settling on the designations of *Do* and *Ti*. In 1985, liver cancer interfered with their destiny. Despite their denials and protestations regarding the accuracy of the medical prognosis, she had an eye removed and eventually succumbed that year,

During the next dozen years, the group's cohesion and momentum began to dissipate. Applewhite's lunacy honed towards an extreme fixation that the end of civilization was nearing. Extraterrestrials foretold him the future and persuaded him to lead a divine assignment. His apocalyptical visions reinforced the couple's dominant role in the reincarnation movement.

As practiced by leadership in most cults, devotion, secrecy and fidelity become paramount and reinforced by collective pressure. Applewhite differed in tactics from many cult leaders. He would express his *opinion* rather than issue direct commands. This manipulative tactic enabled his flock to be subtlety but still forcefully fleeced. Member's desperate desire to cultivate favor with their leader made any outward form of dissention an *unappreciated* response.

Isolation became the most powerful and necessary tool for manipulation. In a cloistered environment, reality becomes distorted and idealistic conformity the accepted standard. Group members were often arbitrarily tested to prove their devotion.

Mind control began incrementally until repeated obeisance blurred any divide between critical thinking and subservience. As part of their eligibility for membership in a second evolving level, participants were obliged to relinquish all human-like characteristics including family, friends, jobs, money, possessions, sexuality and individuality. Effective brainwashing always leaves the affected with the impression that their behavioral choices are uniquely their own.

Applewhite reinforced adherence once with an extreme suggestion that several male members willingly consented to. Sexual relations between members were discouraged and considered an affront to their pure aesthetic lifestyle. He required members to adopt similar clothing and haircuts stressing their asexual appearance.

Upon Applewhite's urging, several men from the group underwent castration procedures in Mexico to proclaim their separation from base sexual urges. Noting the enthusiastic reception and bonding generated, Applewhite himself underwent the procedure.

His theology was not particularly original despite his vernacular, which appeared at odds with contemporary society. The Cathar movement during 12th century Southern France embraced similar sexual and lifestyle purification mannerisms, while awaiting their next level of existence. The Catholic Church shortened their wait significantly by literally exterminating the movement and its practitioners. The reigning Pope disapproved of heretical competition.

The Heaven's Gate group ultimately imploded instead of gradually dissolved. Group membership stagnated following Nettles *inconvenient* death. Their numbers had plummeted to only twenty by 1990. A membership resurgence was generated by a 1993 full-page advertisement in *USA Today* warning of a catastrophic judgment destined to befall the Earth.

Applewhite's complicated theology and his morbid fascination with death, would never have sustained a large following.

The group oscillated between rural New Mexico and residential San Diego during the 1990s. In October 1996, the group leased an upscale mansion in Rancho Santa Fe for their headquarters and living compound. The fenced-in and elevated property would become a temporary launching site for Applewhite's mass evacuation into an accelerated reincarnation. Rumors suggested that the urgency of this next stage was prompted by Applewhite's own declining health and his fear towards a cancer diagnosis. On March 19-20, 1997, Applewhite videotaped a series of lectures explaining the doctrine behind the impending group suicide.

His mass suicide of 39 members was premeditated and efficiently organized. The voluntary killings were done in three stages during successive days. Each member wore identical black shirts, sweat pants, designer athletic shoes and armband patches.

Stealing a cue from the ancient ferryman's legend about paying a tariff to enter paradise, each member carried a five-dollar bill and three quarters in their pockets. Intergalactic travel had inflated the price over the centuries.

The participating member's ultimate destination was a trailing spacecraft following a tailing comet. Their souls were pre-booked for passage once they had exited their earthly confinement. A symbolic square, purple cloth covered each face and torso.

The voluntary adherents, between the ages of 26 and 72, died over a three-day span beginning on March 24, 1997. A contingent of fifteen perished on the first day, another fifteen on the second and the remaining nine including Applewhite on the final day. It was presumed that each succeeding group cleaned up after the previous.

The macabre ceremony was methodical and diabolically choreographed. Each victim swallowed a concoction of the barbiturate Phenobarbital mixed with applesauce. The lethal combination was washed down with vodka. Plastic bags were secured around each head following ingestion to insure asphyxiation. Each body was neatly laid on top of their own bunk bed as they slipped into nearly immediate unconsciousness.

It has been speculated that Applewhite was the third from the final member to die. Two women remained after him and were the sole members without the obligatory plastic bags slipped over their heads. The corpses were discovered two days later. Many of the bodies had already begun to decompose due to the heat from the spring weather. The deceased were cremated. Two additional former members would later commit suicide within the next two years bringing the casualty rate to 41.

The membership ranks were decimated, with a sole apparent exception.

Member Rio DiAngelo (formerly named Richard Ford) claimed to be the lone non-participant of the mass killing. His apparent exit from the compound a month before the procedure was based on his own opposition to suicide. He implied in published interviews that he had unfinished projects left on earth.

These contributions since the suicides have amounted to a single book detailing his experiences and multiple defenses of the movement within media circles. Demand for his first person accounts has dwindled along with the public fascination towards the movement.

The Heaven's Gate organization ceased their physical but not their Internet presence. Their website is renewed annually and Applewhite's doctrinal reference guidelines for living (or dying) remain despite their dated references.

The remaining families of the dead victims likely share disgust towards the website's continued existence. Cults may sever relationships, but love is ultimately a prevailing force. Allowing Heaven's Gate to actively proselytize is the equivalent of enabling similar homicidal monsters such as Jim Jones and David Koresh to exert influence over a fresh contingent of impressionable minds.

The Heaven's Gate cult escaped law enforcement scrutiny primarily due to their modest size, harmless appearance and discreet confines. They may have continued inoffensively had Applewhite's vision not turned lethal.

Did his own failing health influence his timely and extreme call to obedience? Assuming oneself as deity is the ultimate narcissism. Gods do not habitually respond or assume responsibility to the inquiries and laws of mere mortals.

No one may ever truly comprehend Applewhite's accelerated descent into madness. Two facts are certain. Manipulating over forty separate individuals into choosing a voluntary death is the strongest grip an individual may exact upon another. The willingness and weakness of the participants to accept such terms reflect the vacancy and desperation certain individuals share about their existence.

The Gate to the Headquarter Compound

Heaven's Gate Compound

Location of Mass Suicide

Edmund Kemper III: Constructing the Perfect Frankenstein

Edmund Kemper III shared many distinguishing characteristics with Mary Shelley's literature creation of Frankenstein. His hefty and hulking physical stature classified him into an outsider's role from an early age. Like the vile monster, he ultimately turned on his creator, killing his mother and both of his grandparents.

This twisted wreckage of a human creation exhibited an early fascination with morbidity and death. He cut off the heads of his two sister's dolls and stabbed the family cat to death at 13. Following his parent's divorce in 1957, he shuttled between residences before ultimately ending up with his mother, Clarnell and his sisters in Helena, Montana.

Kemper blamed his mother's alcoholism and persistent criticism for aggravating his personal demons. He claimed while living in her household, she had forced him to live in a locked basement away from his sisters fearing he might rape both. Her foreshadowing of his dark pathological tendencies would later prove prophetic.

After the cat killing, he was sent to live with his paternal grandparents on a 17-acre mountain ranch in North Fork, California. He detested the rural environment and their strictness, accentuated by their confiscating his rifle after he'd killed several birds and other small animals. At fifteen, he ultimately shot both of them to death.

As punishment, he was sentenced to the California Youth Authority where his imposing size, elevated intelligence and diagnosed paranoid schizophrenia separated him from traditional juvenile delinquents. He was transferred to the Atascadero State Hospital for the Criminally Insane.

He acclimated well at Atascadero, befriending and assisting his assigned psychologist who gave Kemper access to other prisoners' test results. Reportedly his own I.Q. results measured

136 and as an adult 145. These evaluations would classify him into genius status.

At the age of majority, 21, he was discharged from Atascadero after serving less than five years. He was released to his mother's care in the Santa Cruz area where she had relocated. The monster measured 6'9" and weighed nearly 280 pounds. His juvenile arrest records were expunged.

He attended community college classes and worked a series of menial jobs before finding employment with the State Department of Public Works (Caltrans). He was rejected from his dream job as a state trooper due to his excessive size. He did however befriend several Santa Cruz police officers at a popular law enforcement frequented bar. The regulars took him into their confidence regarding various cases and periodically lent him their equipment. His personal car resembled a police cruiser.

The same year Kemper began working with Caltrans, he was hit by a car while riding his motorcycle. His arm was badly damaged and he received a civil suit settlement of $15,000. Unable to work, he began another pursuit with lethal consequences.

During the 1970s, hitchhiking was considered normal alternative transportation and particularly along the coastal regions. Kemper began picking up female hitchhikers. Always experimenting with fresh deviations, initially he drove them to their intended destinations. His darkest fantasies intervened at some point and they ceased arriving. Frankenstein had discovered a stimulating diversion and perversion.

For approximately one year beginning in May 1972, he embarked on a murderous spree amidst the isolated thoroughfares of the Santa Cruz Mountains. He varied his attack techniques between stabbing, shooting and smothering. His six discovered victims included Mary Ann Pesce, Anita Luchessa, Aiko Koo, Cindy Schall, Rosalind Thorpe and Alice Liu.

He had disturbing company in his killing pursuits. John Lindley Frazier and Herbert Mullin were simultaneously terrorizing the region, designating Santa Cruz with the dubious distinction of *Serial Killer Capital.*

Kemper's murderous impulses and sickness exceeded all boundaries of depravation. He decapitated and dismembered his victims and engaged in sexual activity with their corpses. He viewed each killing as an experimental test case and randomly tossing their remains into forests, ocean waters or even an open field when they'd exceeded their usefulness to him.

The climax of his binge culminated on Good Friday, April 1973. Following yet another unpleasant exchange with his mother, he savagely killed her as she dosed off to sleep. The monster had viciously revenged one of his principle creators. He then invited over one of her friends, Sally Hallett for dinner and a movie and murdered her immediately upon arrival.

He fled the area by car after hiding the bodies. Upon arriving in Pueblo, Colorado, he telephoned the Santa Cruz police department who regarded the call as a hoax. Upon detailing the crimes explicitly to one of his drinking associates at the station, his confession was accepted.

He was arrested without resistance in Pueblo. His trial began in October 1973 and ended one month later with a jury convicting him on eight counts of first-degree murder. A telling remark by Kemper illustrated his mindset when the judge questioned him as to the punishment he deserved. He responded that he should be tortured to death.

The State of California had removed this option with the abolishment of capital punishment in 1972. The *Coed Killer* as the media christened him was given eight concurrent life sentences. He has been denied parole twice. He remains incarcerated at the California Medical Facility in Vacaville.

As with most serial killers, an accurate body count will probably follow him to the grave unless one day his conscience feels obliged towards revelation. A conscience unfortunately appears to be the primary element lacking within him.

Kemper's Residence After Grandparent's Murder

Lawrence Bittaker and Roy Norris: Pitch Darkened Hearts

The habitual smirks photographed on convicted mass murder Lawrence Bittaker's face during his 1981 trial summarized the depth of his human depravity. Seemingly during each photo opportunity, a smile of self-satisfaction greeted the camera lens.

For over thirty-five years, he has remained the poster boy for the fractured California Death penalty. He is an individual absent of conscience, incapable of remorse for his victims and proud of his responsible misery.

He has evaded his execution by the popular tactic of stalling by filing frivolous lawsuits as employed by many of his peers. In 1993, he was declared a *vexatious litigant* and only allowed to sue with the express permission of an attorney or judge. Fortunately for his obsession, there remains an extensive roster of attorneys anxious to litigate for prisoners, particularly when reimbursed by the State of California.

His companion in crime, Roy Lewis Norris is equally pitiful. He has become even more so by his protestations of minimal responsibility towards his actual participation in the murders. The blame according to Norris, hinged on Bittaker's fascination with torture and controlling the fate of his victims. Norris claims, he simply wanted to have sexual intercourse with young women.

The serial killing duo was referred to as the *Tool Box Killers* due to their employment of instruments commonly stored inside a household toolbox.

The killings were so vile and impacting that the chief investigator of the murders, Paul Bynum committed suicide at 39, citing the case prominently in his ten-page suicide note. The FBI Academy reportedly still uses the audio tape that Bittaker and Norris created of themselves raping and torturing one of their victims to train and desensitize new agents to the raw realities of torture. Several aired documentaries and books following the trial attempted to make sense of the magnitude of their degeneracy.

Evil acts are usually only comprehendible to the perpetrator. Tracing the biography of two confirmed psychopaths becomes a direct expressway into understanding how obvious their outcomes were determined.

The question still lingers. Are individuals born evil or created by their formation, environment and circumstances?

Bittaker was raised on the East Coast, abandoned by his birth mother and adopted as an infant. His legal defiance with authority began at twelve. He never finished high school despite a supposedly elevated IQ. His adopted parents disowned him by the age of 18 and relocated to another state. No attempts were made to later contact him.

Norris was conceived out of wedlock in Colorado and his parents married to avoid the stigma of an illegitimate birth. He was repeatedly placed in the care of foster families. He began his criminal activities at sixteen and during a brief stint in the Navy, cultivated a habitual use of marijuana and periodically heroin.

Bittaker and Norris' lives became a revolving compilation of anti-social and criminal behavior coupled by periodic incarcerations. Their offenses included theft, leaving the scene of an accident, burglary, armed robbery, assault, battery, attempted murder, rape and stalking. Each time, their arrogance, impulsiveness and predictable stupidity enabled their expedient capture.

Their partnership bond from hell was cemented while both were incarcerated at the California Men's Colony in San Luis Obispo. They shared fascinations about the bondage, violation and murder of teenage girls. Upon their release, they initiated their sordid fantasies into action.

They were initially meticulous in preparation. They secured a silver cargo van that was windowless on the sides and featured a substantial passenger-side sliding door. They fitted the inside with contraptions that would enable immobility of their captors. These features streamlined abductions. Between February and June 1979, the pair claimed to have picked up approximately 20 female hitchhikers on trial runs. None were assaulted. They were practicing ruses to successfully to lure girls into the van. They scouted out secluded locations.

On one fire road in the San Gabriel Mountains, Bittaker brazenly destroyed a lock with a crowbar and replaced it with one he owned

During the summer of 1979, their terror would commence. The abductions followed a familiar pattern. The creepy pair would initiate a conversational with their victim from the van offering cannabis or alcohol. If the girl complied, she entered a vehicle sealing her doom. Most refused. As passenger, Norris would exit the van, forcibly overpower the girl and toss her into the interior rear area. She was often incapacitated with mace, bound and gagged. Excessively blaring music would muffle any protesting screams.

The killings were meticulous, brutal and beyond human comprehension. The killers photographed their helpless quarry. The bodies were usually tossed over steep embankments with the hope that animals would devour the remains and incriminating evidence. Two of the cadavers were never recovered. The five victims positively confirmed included Lucinda Schaefer, Andrea Hall, Jackie Gilliam, Jacqueline Lamp and Shirley Ledford. Most were abducted while hitchhiking and not immediately reported missing. There were likely more undocumented victims based on photographs later recovered from the murderer's premises.

Their process of their capture began when Norris encountered a friend and fellow ex-convict from his incarceration at the

California Men's Colony. Norris bragged about Bittaker and his exploits and elaborated in graphic detail.

His friend being a *noble* ex-con and intent on leveraging the details for his own benefit for future sentencing was advised by his attorney to inform law enforcement authorities. Detectives began comparing his stories with filed cases and noticed the consistencies.

Bittaker and Norris had become sloppy in completing their killings. A careless rape of a woman enabled her escape and a living witness. Their victim identified both men as her captors and each was detained. An evidence trail accumulated in the search of Bittaker and Norris's apartments including incriminating weaponry, photographs and mementos from their victims.

Norris was becoming increasing edgy about the tightening noose of evidence surrounding them and confessed first. He implicated Bittaker and agreed to testify against him in exchange for the eventual opportunity to earn parole after serving a minimum 30-year sentence.

In his confession, he attempted to divert the sadistic level of brutality and barbaric behavior exclusively towards Bittaker. He pleaded guilty to four counts of first-degree murder, one count of second-degree murder, two counts of rape and one of robbery. His testimony enabled him to avoid the death penalty and a life sentence without the possibility of parole. He was sentenced to 45 years to life imprisonment and is presently interned at the R. J. Donovan Correctional Facility. He didn't bother to attend his initial parole eligibility hearing in 2009 and it was automatically denied. In the opinion of most observers, he shouldn't bother in the future either.

Bittaker was charged with a total of 29 counts of kidnapping, rape, sodomy and murder in addition to multiple firearms charges, He remained silent when the judge requested his plea.

During the trial, he grinned habitually during testimony regarding his activities. He smirked. He sat stoically impressed by his own inventiveness and cleverness.

He also witnessed Roy Norris utterly expose him as a human degenerate on the witness stand and deny him any possibility of freedom within his lifetime. The jury found Bittaker guilty on five counts of first-degree murder, one charge of conspiracy to commit first-degree murder, five charges of kidnapping, nine charges of rape, two charges of oral copulation, one charge of sodomy and three charges of unlawful possession of a firearm.

The jury required merely 90 minutes to concur on the death penalty. He remains putrefying on San Quentin's death row confident his own day of execution will never be forcibly administered. In articles published immediately following his conviction, his lone expressed regret was that he was captured before he could commit more murders.

No media outlet has since expressed an interest for an interview or investigation into his twisted pathology.

Lawrence Bittaker's Motel Residence

Juan Corona: The Macabre Massacre of the Invisible

One of the strangest, most prolific and careless serial killers within California was Juan Vallejo Corona.

During a six-week period in mid 1971, he was accused of murdering 25 itinerant farm laborers. His gruesome crimes represent some of the worst brutality conceivable and the nastiest aspect was his death toll was likely significantly larger.

Corona's life, absent of his mania, might have represented an immigrant's success story.

He was born and raised from the humblest of origins in the state of Jalisco, Mexico, crossed the American border illegally at 16 and picked carrots and melons in the Imperial Valley. He migrated north to the Sacramento Valley in May 1953, found work at a local ranch while settled briefly with his half-brother Natividad already residing in Marysville. He married five months later.

In 1956, he was diagnosed with schizophrenia and committed to the DeWitt State Hospital in Auburn. He received 23 electro shock treatments, was pronounced recovered and released after a three-month stay. He was deported to Mexico upon his release, but returned legally with a green card and newfound sobriety. He would remarry again in 1959 and have four daughters.

Corona developed a reputation as a reliable and hard worker. By 1962, he had elevated his vocational status to licensed labor contractor. He became in charge of hiring workers to harvest the local fruit ranches. During that era, the nomadic lives of migrant workers were ignored and for Corona conveniently unscrutinized.

In March 1970, Corona's schizophrenia incapacitated him once again and he was re-committed to DeWitt State Hospital. His contracting business suffered during his absence. He experienced intense economic pressure to sustain his family and the two houses he had accumulated. His legacy of violence has been attributed to start following his release. Isolating an exact starting point for murder becomes as complicated as it was to recover the entirety of his buried cadavers.

Sadistic violence seemed deep rooted. His half-brother Natividad was accused and convicted of a brutal slashing attack on a young gay man. He fled to Mexico rather than pay a $250,000 dollar court judgment against him.

Juan Corona was reputed to detest any exhibitions of a gay lifestyle and flaunted his virulent machismo. Curiously, all of his male victims would endure the same macabre pattern of killing. Each were sodomized and slashed to death with a machete and then buried in holes dug a few days previously in the orchards owned by his client ranchers.

Corona, despite his own humble beginnings was tough and verbally abusive to his employees. He was also one of the few contractors offering opportunity to homeless alcoholics. He housed the majority on his property, Sullivan Ranch, providing their basic food and shelter. They were considered functional necessities by employers and scarcely human. Totally dependant on his resources, these forgotten and inaudible voices became pawns to his sexual addiction. Their sudden absence or disappearance alarmed no one, caused no concern and remained unreported.

Their invisibility made him careless. Several of his victims were buried with employment receipts signed by Corona in their pockets. These oversights made him instantly traceable upon their discovery.

In May of 1971, his casual pattern of murder became uncovered. One of his employers found a freshly dug seven-foot deep hole on his property. The following day when he returned, the hole was filled. Notifying the authorities, the mutilated corpse of

Kenneth Whitacre was found when the hole was unearthed. Whitacre had been sexually assaulted and stabbed repeatedly.

On May 26, 1971 Corona was arrested in his Yuba City home by investigators. Two bloodstained knives, a machete, a pistol and blood soaked clothing were confiscated. The most chilling find was a work ledger containing 34 names and dates. At Corona's trial, the prosecution would refer to this document as a death list recording the dates the men were murdered. Only 7 of the 34 names were confirmed murder victims. The other 27 were unaccounted for.

Over the next ten days 25 additional graves were discovered scattered throughout the fruit ranches of Sutter County, Corona's Sullivan Ranch and along the Feather River north of Yuba City. All of the males were entombed in shallow graves. All were sexually assaulted and hacked. Many led an evidence and paper trail directly to Juan Corona. Several of his victims had been seen last riding in Corona's pick-up truck.

It is a wishful assumption that all of his casualties were ultimately recovered. Who knows how many of their silenced voices remained muted? The vulnerable have no advocates. Juan Corona denied guilt.

Corona's legal defense consisted initially of a public defender who immediately ordered a psychological evaluation for his client. Their agreed upon strategy was to plead not guilty by reason of insanity. Given his two precedent mental health internments and extreme treatments, the logic was sound.

Twelve days following his arraignment in early June 1971, Corona switched his representation to privately retained council. Their arrangement was atypical. The attorney offered his legal representation in return for exclusive literary and dramatic property rights to the defendant's life story and the proceedings against him.

His new counsel immediately discarded the insanity plea and fired the psychiatrists. He opted for a more risky tact by pleading innocence. The trial loitered another year before starting, California abolished the death penalty and the venue was changed to Solano County.

His gamble failed. The trial lasted four months and on January 18, 1973, Corona was convicted on 25 counts of first-degree murder and sentenced to 25 terms of life imprisonment. His first incarceration was at the nearby California Medical Facility in Vacaville. Later during the year a fellow inmate stabbed him 32 times in his cell. He survived the attack. He was transferred afterwards to the Correctional Training Facility in Soledad.

In May of 1978, the California Court of Appeals overturned Juan Corona's conviction. Their ruling was based on a claim that his original legal team had been incompetent in their representation by not pleading insanity. A new trial based on old evidence was ordered.

The re-trial began in February 1982 and extended over seven months. His defense team claimed the actual murderer of the ranch workers was Corona's half-brother Natividad, who'd conveniently died eight years earlier in Guadalajara. He became a convenient foil based on his earlier slashing conviction and known homosexuality.

The jury dismissed the defense's creative theory based on the volume of conclusive evidence, the work ledger discovery and the fact that Natividad hadn't been in the Marysville area often enough to commit the bulk of the killings.

Juan Corona was transferred to Corcoran State Prison in 1992 where he remains rotting away in a wheelchair and forgotten as his faceless victims. He has been eligible for parole on multiple occasions and denied each time. A film project depicting his life history and accompanying first trial generated absolutely no interest.

How many bodies remain buried in the
Orchards of Yuba County?

The Orchards Yield Profaned Fruit

Richard Trenton Chase: The Consummation of Darkness

Darkness pervaded the life and soul of Richard Trenton Chase. There exists criminal behavior so heinous; it defies human compassion and comprehension. If one believes in hell, Chase's existence provided a case study in depravity. His ultimate mania and homicidal spree were predictable extensions of deviant precedent.

Born in 1950, Chase was raised in a household where paternal beatings were common. From this childrearing debris, he evolved into a teenage alcoholic, fire starter and animal mutilator.

His pattern of behavioral degeneration continued until 1975 when he was involuntarily committed to a mental institution. He was institutionalized after being taken to a hospital for blood poisoning. He contracted the toxins after injecting rabbit's blood into his veins. Chase escaped from the hospital and fled home to his mother.

Throughout his life, she was an imposing influence, facilitating his abnormal behavior and weaning him prematurely off of his anti-schizophrenic medication. She financed his isolated living expenses as he descended profoundly into an inescapable deterioration. There is no penalty in our culture for depraved parenting. Society bears the cost in multiple facets.

While living within the mental institution, the staff, among themselves, began referring to Chase as *Dracula* after he had captured two birds through the bars on his bedroom windows, snapped their necks, and sucked their blood out. After undergoing a battery of treatments involving psychotropic drugs, Chase was deemed no longer a danger to society. In 1976, he was released into the recognizance of his parents, a spring-loaded bomb waiting to detonate.

His parents financed the rent for an apartment where his deviant behavior towards animals continued. He reportedly developed obsessions towards serial killers, Nazi and UFO conspiracies and firearms. He was allowed to legally purchase several handguns.

Chase began to lose interest in caring for himself. He neglected personal hygiene and ceased regular eating habits, eventually becoming extremely gaunt. His errant behavior and pre-warning signs continued. On August 3, 1977, Nevada state police discovered Chase's Ford Ranchero lodged in a sand drift near Pyramid Lake. Inside were two rifles, piled clothing and significant blood splatters. The officers tracked down Chase, who was naked and screaming in the sand, soaked from head to toe in blood. When questioned, he claimed that the blood was his own.

The culmination of his personal disintegration resulted in the murder of six individuals including four children between late December 1977 and January 27, 1978. The violence and slaughter involved with each killing was extreme and the press nicknamed him *The Vampire Killer of Sacramento*. Chase had selected his victims randomly and left as much evidence as he could around his home and the crime scene. When later asked by investigators how he selected his victims, Chase indicated that he strolled down neighborhood streets testing doors to find one that was unlocked. That minimal lack of prevention proved invitation enough.

Investigators apprehended Chase within a week of his final murder based on an accurate serial killer profile and a tip from one of his acquaintances. Following his arrest, the carnage inside the apartment surpassed any semblance of decency. Hell had descended upon earth.

His apartment complex and the neighborhood where the murders were committed are located in a declining sector of East Sacramento. A desperate outcast such as Chase would integrate unnoticeably even today. Current residents are completely unaware of the history behind unit #15, the sole door painted white. All other doors in the complex are painted in redwood latex.

On January 2, 1979, Chase's trial began. He was charged with six counts of murder. Given the local notoriety of the case, the trial was moved one hundred twenty miles south to Santa Clara County. The evidence and testimony proved overwhelming. His insanity defense crumbled once psychiatric testimony confirmed that Chase's thought process was not disrupted, he was aware of what he had done and that it was wrong. A jury deliberated five hours before returning a verdict of guilty on six counts of first-degree murder. He was sentenced to die in the gas chamber at San Quentin Penitentiary.

He chose an alternative not offered to his unfortunate victims. On December 26, 1980, a guard doing cell checks found Chase lying awkwardly on his bed, not breathing. An autopsy determined that Chase committed suicide with an overdose of prison doctor-prescribed antidepressants that he had been saving up during the prior few weeks.

A 1992 movie entitled *Rampage* was loosely based on Chase's crimes. Predictably, the film eluded general public interest and was sentenced promptly to DVD rental purgatory.

Richard Trenton Chase's Hellish Apartment

The Boneyards of the Dead Speak: The Speedfreak Killers

The outskirts of the rural town of Linden harbored the remnants of dead souls in at least two major agricultural wells. The monstrous atrocities of Wesley Shermantine and Loren Herzog were temporarily buried into oblivion.

The voices of the silenced perhaps reverberated through the consciousness of the two responsible perpetrators. One hung himself. The other putrefies on San Quentin's death row remorseful and anxious to expose the sins of his peers.

This would be a moralist storyline for two men with a conscience. The truth is grittier. Serial killers as a rule exhibit absolutely no empathy towards their victims. They care little for survivor's grief. They are fractured, damaged and ruined permanently. Rehabilitation is impossible.

They are dehumanized, self-centered narcissists. They cannot conceive the magnitude of their damage. They parrot for public consumption insincere words of attrition, repentance and sorrow. These words cannot actually convey emotions they are incapable of feeling.

Shermantine and Herzog were known in Linden as *Speed Freaks* due to their methamphetamine abuse. They were local boys and childhood friends. In an intimate farming community with few diversions, they were accepted as harmless eccentrics. They were regulars at one of their eventual victims father's bar.

Law enforcement authorities have been unable to accurately tabulate the extent of their homicides. The count may total 8. It may extend past 72. The documented deaths for both included Cyndi Vanderheiden, Henry Howell, Robin Armtrout, Howard King, Paul Cavanaugh, Chevelle Wheeler, Kimberly Ann Billy and Joann Hobson.

They killed the victims between 1994-99 for sport. They killed for sex. They killed because they were high or needed money to get high. They killed violently on impulse. They blamed each other. Shermantine was sentenced to death. Herzog was given a 78-year sentence, later reduced to 14.

An appeals court decision overturned Herzog's conviction citing that his confession was coerced. He was paroled in 2010 to a trailer adjacent to the High Desert Prison in Susanville. In the isolation and silence, the echoes from his ugly past may have compelled him to hang himself on January 16, 2012. This makes a redemptive storyline. That conclusion is probably inaccurate. A bounty hunter, Leonard Padilla made a special visit to Herzog's trailer shortly before to inform him that his partner Shermantine was planning to disclose three burial sites of their victims.

Up until that disclosure, none of their victim's bodies had been discovered. Whether Herzog suffered a crisis of conscience or saw his impending freedom dissipate, we'll never know. The dead rarely reveal their secrets to the living.

It would be encouraging to assume that remorse and perhaps a hope for closure amongst the survivors motivated Shermantine. He wrote several letters to legal authorities and a local newspaper detailing three boneyard gravesite locations. Why suddenly after fifteen years of silence?

The answer becomes clearer. Padilla offered to pay Shermantine $33,000 for the information. The tedium of death row existence perhaps made him envious of the media attention and coverage his case once generated.

He was not disappointed...initially. The first excavated well dredged up more than 1,000 human bone fragments. The second well bore over 300 human bones and personal items. A third well excavation has yet to be detailed. Shermantine has indicated his further interest in revealing other burial locations from fellow death row inmates. Even when you are forgotten and reviled, the extreme need for recognition never disappears.

His revelations and society's revulsion continue.

Former Escalon Road Well Boneyard Site

Waverly Road Well
Boneyard Now Covered

Herbert Mullin: The Blood Sacrifices of Earthquake Preventiveness

The razor thin precipice between reason and insanity manifest itself early in the existence of Herbert Mullin.

His formative stages resembled a toxic theatre between convergent forces of light and darkness, personal penitence and sacrifice for the greater good of the masses. It becomes difficult to distinguish prophetic imagery from the schizophrenic ramblings of madness. From what circumstances do our prophets and serial killers emerge?

Herbert Mullin profited from a reportedly stable and structured upbringing in Santa Cruz. His father was a World War II veteran. His high school classmates voted him *Most Likely to Succeed*. A future of normalcy appeared imminent...but illusionary.

His personality fissures began with the accidental car death of his best friend following graduation. His bedroom became a shrine to his deceased memory. Questions about his sexual orientation tormented him.

And then the voices...

Inaudible to others, their conflicting instructions began to dominate his life. Their volume and frequency were accentuated by his LSD and amphetamine use.

By the age of 21, Mullin was committed by his family to a mental hospital. He would discharge himself and voluntarily re-enter other facilities after short stays. The pattern of his severing attachment to reality was widening.

He started extinguishing cigarettes on his own skin, attempted to enter the priesthood and was evicted from the sole apartment he had lived apart from his family due to disruptive behavior.

It is theorized that by 25, Mullin had formulated his philosophy for existence. His birthday, April 18, was identical to the day of the 1906 San Francisco Earthquake. He foresaw the immediate demands upon him to prevent a subsequent catastrophic California quake he felt inevitable. Blood sacrifice of others on a mass scale was the sole vehicle to temporarily elude the preordained

It is dangerous territory to rationalize or attempt to understand psychosis. The testimony of the afflicted may appear perfectly coherent when articulated through the voice of lunacy or manipulation.

Mullin often confused himself with a contemporary biblical Jonah preserving Nineveh from the ravages of destruction. Madness speaks with the equal conviction of truth but remains idiocy. Within a three-week period during October and November 1972, Mullin bludgeoned a homeless man Lawrence "Whitey" White, 55, with a baseball bat and stabbed a hitchhiker, Mary Guilfoyle, 24, to death. He dissected her body and spread her remains along an inclined roadside.

On a calm November Thursday afternoon, he entered the confessional at St. Mary's Church in Los Gatos to profess his sins. Father Henri Tomei had little idea of the delusional disintegration haunting his parishioner. Mullin kicked, beat and stabbed the priest to death allowing him to expire within the confines of the confessional.

Mullin determined that his killing proficiencies were better suited to an appreciative audience. He decided to join the U.S. Marines and passed the initial physical and psychiatric tests. His documented history of minor arrests and bizarre and disruptive behavior however, ultimately were the causes for his refused entry.

A seeping paranoia of conspiracies tainted his thinking upon his rejection from the armed forces. He decided upon the role of vigilante to clean up the local drug trade, which had plagued the previous years of his life. He had ceased using drugs and cited their abuse as the primary source of his problems.

Between a compressed period of January and February 1973, Mullin was responsible for the deaths of two families who he believed were directly involved with drug trafficking and five completely innocent individuals.

The family victims included Jim Gianera, 25, a former friend and his wife Joan, 21. Kathy Francis, 29, and her sons Daemon, 4, and David, 9, were killed because she had provided him with Gianera's address. Her husband was reputed to be a drug dealer. Her death and those of her sons were Mullin's attempt to remove potential witnesses. At his trial, these actions were cited to eliminate his plea of *not guilty by reason of insanity* since he knew the killings to be morally wrong.

The following month, he encountered four teenage boys camping at Henry Cowell Redwoods State Park. Posing as a park ranger, he ordered them to leave citing their pollution of the forest and warned them he would return. They were armed with their own . 22 rifle and did not take his threat seriously.

He did return, shooting each and abandoning their bodies, which would not be discovered until the week following. The four victims were David Oliker, 18, Robert Spector, 18, Brian Card, 19 and Mark Dreibelbis, 15.

His final murder was on February 13, 1973 when he drove past Fred Perez, 72, weeding his Santa Cruz lawn in full daylight. Mullin passed Perez while driving alone and made a U-turn further down the road. He stopped his station wagon, sighted his victim with a rifle and dispassionately shot Lopez to death. No motive was established. Mullin drove away placidly making no effort to conceal his actions.

Numerous witnesses viewed the killing and furnished police with his vehicle license plate number. Mullin was apprehended within minutes. Santa Cruz, in the throes of three serial killers operating simultaneously (also Edmund Kemper and John Lindley Frazier), could exhale briefly.

Mullin was charged with 10 murders and tried during July 1973. He confessed to each of the crimes. His trial focused principally on the question of his sanity while committing them. The defense argued that he had suffered a lengthy history of mental illness and was an undiagnosed paranoid schizophrenic. The prosecution focused their energies on proving both premeditation and his attempted efforts to conceal his actions.

Mullin was convicted of two counts of first-degree murder due to premeditation and eight counts of second-degree murder due to their impulsivity. Following these verdicts, the killing of Father Tomei was to be tried in Santa Clara County. Before trial, he pled guilty to second-degree murder. As California had abolished the death penalty in 1972, he was sentenced to life imprisonment. He is currently incarcerated at the Mule Creek State Prison in Ione, California.

California has endured several major earthquakes since Mullin's confinement. None have measured close to the apocalyptic dimensions he had prophesized.

St. Mary's Church

Herbert Mullin: The Blood Sacrifices
of Earthquake Preventiveness

David Carpenter: The Devil Behind Bifocals and a Stutter

The remarkable longevity of convicted octogenarian serial killer David Carpenter is testament towards the merits or abuses of the appeal capabilities of convicts. Born in 1930, he is the oldest inmate at San Quentin and one of the oldest in the United States awaiting a death sentence that will doubtlessly be preceded by his own demise by natural causes.

The media labeled *Trailside Killer* was a notably shy, social introvert with a severe stutter. His personality and disability were coupled by a prototype serial killer history of violent crimes and sexual deviancy. His unremarkable, bespectacled and balding appearance separated him from the menacing attributes of assumed maniacal behavior. He spent more than 22 of his first 55 years in custody before his final incarceration.

His only conventional behavior appeared to be his first marriage at 25 that bore three children. His entrenched sexual perversion and disintegrating personality cracks were by then sufficiently evident but usually overlooked due to his nondescript physical features.

The formation behind the notorious predator and deviant were established early by reported animal torturing, physical abuse by his parents and an alcoholic father. At seventeen he was arrested for behavior that later became his defining compulsions. He spent three months at Napa State Hospital for molesting two of his cousins, one only three years old. The seeds towards complete unraveling continued in 1950 as he was arrested for raping a 17-year old girl but the charges were dropped. Throughout his life, he has maintained innocence for his actions. This pattern of denial and disregard has never wavered even into his advanced age.

In 1960, the married Carpenter assaulted and nearly killed a woman he had befriended. She had rebuffed his clumsy seduction advances. Driving her into an isolated sector of San

Francisco's Presidio Woods instead of her workplace, he struck her multiple times with a hammer. He fired upon a responding military patrol officer but missed. The officer wounded Carpenter with return fire and spared an initial murder victim as the woman survived.

He was arrested and sentenced to fourteen years of imprisonment. During his confinement, his wife divorced him. He learned valuable lessons about evading suspicion during his internment. He parroted for evaluating psychologists studied explanations rationalizing his erratic behavior. The ploy was successful as he served only nine years. He had learned to articulate what authorities and potential victims wished to hear, milking his stutter to maximum sympathetic effect. He also discovered that the best way to avoid returning to prison was to eliminate potential witnesses.

Released in 1969, he remarried quickly. Shortly afterwards, he sexually attacked two women in Santa Cruz County, stole a car and drove to the Sierra mountain region. In Calaveras County, he robbed two women, kidnapping one of them. He attempted to rape one woman that same year by striking her car and forcing her out. She resisted and was able to escape despite multiple stab wounds. He was arrested in Modesto in February 1970.

While awaiting trial for his crime spree, Carpenter attempted unsuccessfully to escape the Calaveras County jail. He was sentenced to seven years for kidnapping and robbery plus two for parole violation, He served the full sentence. All sex related offenses were dropped. Freed from the tracking designation of registered sex offender, his worse transgressions were to follow.

Carpenter typified the most dangerous sociopathic form of serial killer. He could superficially pass for a normal, articulate and productive citizen. He made the expected adaptation towards reform following his release from prison. He enrolled in a San Francisco based computer-printing course, graduating with a degree that enabled immediate employment. He became an instructor at an East Bay area agency affiliated with the school. He likewise became an avid hiker with designs on becoming a proficient stalker and camouflaged predator.

His multiple guises proved useful for the killing sequence to follow. Between 1979-1981 months after his release, he raped and murdered ten confirmed victims and two suspected. Based on his pathological cunning and impulses, the fatality totals could be easily understated. During that same period, several remote terrain killers roamed the Marin, Sonoma and Santa Cruz mountain regions.

His tactics were varied, efficient and gruesome. Each victim was alone on isolated stretches of the publicly hiked trails.

All of the victims were surprised from behind or blind vantage points. It is assumed the killer deliberately stalked and patiently awaited his prey. Some were shot, generally to the head or stabbed repeatedly and viciously. One victim was strangled with picture framing wire. Most of the women were attractive, slight and in their 20s. Each was overwhelmed by his superior strength. The victims that he struck were aggressively beaten and often raped. A FBI profiler surmised that an execution-style killing employed on a few of the victims, while on their knees, may have been a forced subservience gesture by Carpenter to assert his perceived male superiority.

A sadist such as Carpenter doubtlessly endured tremendous trauma and ridicule due to his lifelong stutter. His stutter also generated significant empathy, which he manipulated. It was suggested that this sympathy disarmed many of his potential victims before his lethal attacks. Some of his survivors indicated his pronounced stutter was absent during his attacks.

His appearance, which made him invisible as a person, distinguished him as a rapist. A middle-aged balding male wearing glass could be very identifiable in a police line-up. Eliminating his victims became imperative.

The list of confirmed Mt. Tamalpais trail victims included Edda Kane (1979), Barbara Schwartz (1980), Anna Mejivas (1980) and Anne Anderson (1990). Shawna May and Diane O'Connell, strangers to each other, were murdered at the Point Reyes National Seashore Park. They were discovered lain adjacently face down in a shallow ditch. It was speculated that one of victims had appeared inconveniently while Carpenter was violating the other. Both were killed at approximately the same time on November 28, 1980.

On the following day, their bodies and two other buried victims, Cynthia Moreland and Richard Towers, were discovered a half-mile away. Morehead and Towers had been slain the month previously. Investigators surmised that although the locations were different, the killings were committed only days apart from Anne Anderson's.

A concealed eyewitness viewed the stabbing of Barbara Schwartz and provided police with a detailed description of the assailant. Her physical profile proved erroneous and the inaccuracies hindered the police initially. Other hikers fortunately spotted Carpenter following some of the murders ultimately enabling police to compose a more accurate composite profile sketch of the killer.

Like the more renowned Zodiac serial killer, Carpenter only attacked males when they accompanied their female partners. Their appearance may have come as a problematical surprise. Their immediate elimination became paramount to avoid a more equally matched struggle or detection. Stealth and surprise were elemental to his attacking strategy. As with the Zodiac, cowardice towards a male presence threatened his perceived sense of gender dominance.

Expanding his network of killing sites, he killed Ellen Hansen in 1981 at a park near Santa Cruz, but made a crucial error. Her boyfriend, Steve Haertle survived the attack despite being shot four times, twice through his neck. Haertle furnished police with a crucial description of the assailant and his distinctive escape vehicle, a red Fiat.

Carpenter had evaded capture for two years despite widespread public and law enforcement attention. In May of 1981, he kidnapped and killed a co-worker, Heather Scaggs. He had stupidity and in all probability arrogantly killed a victim directly traceable to him.

Scaggs had informed her boyfriend about an impending visit to Carpenter's house because he was going to assist her in purchasing a used car. When investigating officers questioned Carpenter regarding Scagg's visit and subsequent disappearance at his San Francisco residence, they observed his resemblance to the Trailside killer's composite sketch. His red Fiat further linked him to Ellen Hansen's killing. The survivor of the attack, Steve Haertle identified Carpenter in a police line-up.

The focus of examination abruptly honed in on him. His multiple felonies and incarcerations had previously eluded scrutiny due to a variety of bureaucratic errors. Once examined, his profile made him an obvious candidate. The subsequent investigation and apprehension of Carpenter followed swiftly.

Upon the discovery of Heather Scagg's body in Big Basin State Park in the Santa Cruz Mountains, Carpenter was arrested for her homicide. An escalating case of evidence was building against him. A selling party for one of his primary .45 caliber pistols, used in several of the killings, came forward. The gun was never recovered. A second weapon however, used in the final two killings was discovered by investigators and submitted into evidence by the prosecution.

David Carpenter was convicted for the first-degree murders of Hansen and Skaggs in July of 1984 and separately convicted of five Marin murders later in the year. He was sentenced to death on November 16, 1984. He was not charged in some of the

Marin trails cases and two suspected killings. These two included Anna K. Menjivar, a 17-year old high school student killed in 1981 at Castle Rock State Park in the Santa Cruz Mountains. She worked at a bank that Carpenter habitually patronized. In 2009, DNA evidence linked him to the 1979 violent stabbing death of Mary Frances Bennett who had been jogging near the Palace of the Legion of Honor when attacked.

Over three decades have passed in confinement. Carpenter is apparently respected and well regarded by his peers (not surprising) and compliant to prison authority. In a 2013 published interview with convict/journalist Boston Woodard, he maintained his steadfast innocence of all convicted charges and boasted about his good health, despite advanced age. Carpenter indicated that the majority of his time was spent with written correspondence, legal appeal documentation and regular attendance at Catholic worship services. His continued appeals and legal efforts have delayed his ultimate execution.

A profound absence of remorse towards his crimes and murder victims remains entrenched within his crippled and corrupt soul. Instead, his complaints about zealous law enforcement persecution become hollow and as rote as his earlier psychological rationalizations. He is an individual who has learned nothing constructive or introspectively from his life of debauchery.

His life remains conclusive proof that habitual violent criminals are beyond redemption even with an unthreatening demeanor and appearance. Despite certain similarities with the Zodiac killings, he was dismissed long ago as a suspect due to his incarceration at the identical times of the murders.

His legal appeals and requests for new trials have been routinely and systematically denied. Each attempt strains an overloaded legal system and lengthens his condemned life.

Since 1978, the average time served on death row has been 17

1/2 years and 49 is the average age at execution. There are currently approximately 741 prisoners on death row in California, by far the most populous state compared to Texas and Florida, active states for executions. During that same period, over 60 condemned prisoners have died from natural causes, 22 have committed suicide and only 13, predominately white males, have been executed. The last execution was in 2006.

It is unlikely Carpenter will share their fate. The travesty that has defined his delay is an affront society's notion of expedient justice.

What seems difficult to determine is which option is more repulsive, his deeds or his denials.

David Carpenter's San Francisco House

Jim Jones and the People's Temple Massacre: No Way Home

Writer Thomas Wolfe's novel *You Can't Go Home Again* aptly summarized the plight of Peoples Temple members isolated in the jungle of Jonestown, Guyana in 1978. Most of the resident cult's followers had long ago abandoned their own birth families to follow a charismatic orator, the Reverend Jim Jones

For the dispossessed, the marginalized and the forgotten who had abandoned the San Francisco Bay area and relocated to this isolated outpost, a single instruction remained on November 18, 1978. They were commanded to drink a concoction of cyanide-laced, grape-flavored Kool-Aid or face immediate shotgun execution. Each complied.

The resulting mass suicides and killings resulted in 918 deaths including 276 children. Among the victims were US Congressman Leo Ryan whose visit and investigation into the encampment triggered the fatal sequence of events. Jones' security personnel gunned down Ryan and his entourage as they attempted to depart via a nearby airstrip at Port Kaituma. In retrospect, the climatic slaughter should have seemed inevitable given the numerous advance-warning signals.

The Peoples Temple was an organization founded in 1955 by Jim Jones under the guise of a structured religion. By the mid-1970s, the Temple possessed over a dozen locations in California. The headquarters were based in San Francisco. The origins of the movement began in Indianapolis, Indiana inspired by Jones fascination with communism. Jones masqueraded his preaching under as social gospel virtues primarily out of fear of reprisals for his communist leanings.

Borrowing tactics such as clairvoyant revelations, healing tricks and fiery rhetoric from Pentecostal movements, the Peoples Temple expanded. The movement attracted diverse classes of people enabling them to generate income and accomplish Jones' social agenda. Jones and Temple members knowingly faked healings because they discovered as a result, donations increased. These healings involved chicken livers and other animal tissue, claimed by Jones (and confederate Temple members) to be cancerous tissues removed from the body.

Two essential differences separated Jones' operations from comparative cults; the composition of his congregation and his savvy political activism.

The Peoples Temple earned a reputation for aiding the cities' poorest citizens, especially racial minorities, drug addicts, and the homeless. The Temple made strong connections with the California state welfare system. During the 1970s, the Peoples Temple owned and ran at least nine residential care homes for the elderly, six homes for foster children, and a state-licensed 40-acre ranch for developmentally disabled persons. The Temple elite handled members' insurance claims and legal problems, effectively acting as a client-advocacy group.

The Temple further distinguished itself from most religious movements with its overtly political message. It combined Jones' political sympathies with the reality that he could help turn out large numbers of volunteers and votes to gain the support of a number of prominent politicians. Jones' ability to mobilize large numbers of his members within short notice ingratiated him with San Francisco's political elite including Mayor George Moscone, Governor Jerry Brown, Lieutenant Governor Mervyn Dymally, Assemblyman Willie Brown (later Mayor), Harvey Milk, District Attorney Joseph Freitas, State Senator Milton Marks and future Mayor Art Agnos. San Francisco's most visible voice at the San Francisco Chronicle, columnist Herb Caen regularly wrote favorably of Jim Jones in print.

Incredibly, their associations with Jones while he was headquartered in San Francisco barely tarnished their own political legacies despite the Guyana tragedy.

Each evaded close scrutiny, especially Moscone, who staunchly refused investigating the Peoples Temple operations despite repeated requests. Following a narrow election victory in 1975 where Jones' labor resources proved invaluable, Moscone had appointed Jones as Chairman of the San Francisco Housing Authority Commission.

Political obligations to Jones ultimately proved profoundly deeper than any moral concern towards the welfare of his followers. Political debts were owed to Jones and their silence and nonintervention was repayment. Moscone and Milk would be assassinated ten days following the massacre.

In 1974, the Peoples Temple signed a lease to rent land in Guyana. The community created on this property was called the Peoples Temple Agricultural Project, or informally, Jonestown. It had as few as 50 residents in early 1977. Jones saw Jonestown as both a socialist paradise and a sanctuary from media scrutiny.

The Temple's growing political influence and higher local visibility opened the organization up to media inquiry from sources within and outside of San Francisco. An investigative article on their operations was written by Marshall Kilduff and published by *New West Magazine* containing numerous allegations of fraud, assault and potential kidnapping. Subsequent media articles would follow raising a disturbing profile of the Temple's activities and operations.

The exodus to Guyana by Jones' followers required several weeks of preparation and bureaucratic passport formalities. It was reported that Jones himself fled to Guyana the very evening that the contents of Kilduff's *New West* article (yet to be published) was read to him over the phone.

The Temple's pattern of control, beatings and abuse continued upon the their arrival en mass in Jonestown, removed from investigating eyes. Ultimately Congressman Ryan's visit sealed his and the colony's fate. Jones determined that Ryan could not be allowed to return to California with what he had observed and witnessed firsthand.

Today Jim Jones is a conveniently discarded memory. His cult of personality has been forever tarnished. His former political allies have distanced themselves from the man and the movement. The San Francisco Peoples Temple building has become resurrected into a post office station on Geary Street.

The memories of the forgotten and dispossessed Jonestown residents remain so. 412 unclaimed bodies from the Guyana mass suicide are buried at the Evergreen Cemetery in Oakland. Jim Jones name is inscribed on one of the four marble tombstones with no reference to his accountability.

For the forgotten and entombed, few have acknowledging families remaining to mourn their passing.

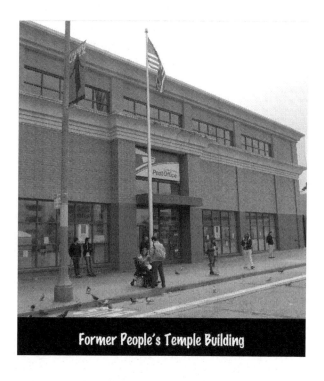

Former People's Temple Building

People's Temple Memorial At Evergreen
Cemetery in Oakland

Lee Johnson · Thomas William Johnson
hnson · Adline "Addie" B. Jones
Ava Phenice Cobb Brown Jones
es · Earnest Jones · Eliza Jones
p Jones · James Warren Jones

Controversial Inclusion of Rev. Jim Jones

The Hillside Strangler Duo: Killing Cousins

The Hillside Strangler tandem of Kenneth Bianchi and Angelo Buono paralyzed Los Angeles and particularly the San Fernando Valley during four months between November 1977 and February 1978. Ten young women were kidnapped, raped, tortured and then killed. Their bodies were randomly dumped in locations ranging from the Forest Lawn Cemetery to residential driveways. The empty hillside dumping terrains earned them their designation.

Bianchi and Buono were cousins bonded in decadence. Initial investigations focused on the responsible party being a single individual. The evidence and patterns of torture revealed the characteristics of a lethal duo.

There were no survivors from their attacks. The confirmed dead included Yolanda Washington, Judith Miller, Lissa Kastin, Dolores Cepeda, Sonja Johnson, Kristina Weckler, Jane King (the oldest victim at 28), Lauren Wagner, Kimberly Martin and Cindy Hudspeth. Others victims likely existed but escaped attribution to the murderers.

One potential victim was reportedly spared. The killers gave a ride to Catharine Lorre, the daughter of actor Peter Lorre with the intent of killing her. Once they determined her identity, they released her without incident. Were they paying homage to his work as a screen killer? More likely they preferred to keep their killings spree under the international publicity radar.

The heat of intensive investigation separated the two cousins. Bianchi fled to Bellingham, Washington where his personal rampage continued with a rape and murder of two women he had lured into a home for a housesitting position. He was arrested soon afterwards.

Buono remained in Glendale where he operated an auto body repair business on a prominent boulevard. His business location was situated centrally to the killings. He was arrested without incident.

Bianchi attempted a poorly executed insanity defense at his trial. A court appointed psychologist conclusively observed that he was faking. Both men were convicted to life sentences since the death penalty had been abolished in California. Buono died of a heart attack in 2002 while incarcerated and Bianchi remains imprisoned at the Washington State Penitentiary in Walla Walla for murders in that state.

Angelo Buono's Former Glendale Body Shop

Rodney Alcala: A Beastly Killing Machine Slaying Beauty

The prolific debauchery of serial killer Rodney Alcala has been estimated to have potentially exceeded one hundred female victims spanning a period between 1968 and 1979. He has been convicted for five killings in California, two in New York and is the prime suspect in two Seattle murders.

Unlike serial killer Ted Bundy, who he is often compared with, Alcala has remained mute on identifying his victims or disclosing any potential dumping locations.

Posing under the guise of a fashion photographer, Alcala would lure his victims with promises of intimate photo shoots. Police discovered his personal collection of more than 1,000 sexually explicit photographs leading to the speculation of an expanded victim count. He was reputed to have studied film under director Roman Polanski at New York University.

Initiated with his army enlistment in 1960, he was professionally diagnosed with an antisocial personality disorder and discharged on medical grounds four years later. He would later be appraised as exhibiting a narcissist personality disorder, borderline personality disorder, psychopathic tendencies and sexual sadism.

None of these professional evaluations spared his later victims, which included Cornelia Crilley, Ellen Hover, Jill Barcomb, Georgia Wixted, Charlotte Lamb, Jill Parenteau and Robin Samsoe. He was accused but not tried for the murder of Pamela Lambson and the prime suspect in two Seattle area murders with Antoinette Wittaker and Joyce Gaunt.

Alcala possessed the sociopathic capacity to flatter and solicit aided by his handsome appearance. He was cruelly calculated in his manner of executions. He often strangled and then revived his victims from consciousness before ultimately killing them. Many of his victims were stabbed and bludgeoned to death.

He was originally labeled *The Dating Game* killer because of a 1978 appearance on the identically named television show. He was selected as the winning bachelor contestant but never actually dated his selector due to her aversion towards his erratic behavior.

This behavior became publicly displayed during his third trial when Alcala elected to act as his own attorney. During one memorable five-hour sequence, he made a mockery of the proceedings by assuming the role of interrogator and witness. He asked himself and then answered questions in varying voice tones. He addressed the jury with rambling monotones and introduced unusual evidence that included footage from his *Dating Game* appearance and a segment from Arlo Guthrie's song *Alice's Restaurant*. DNA matching became the primary source of evidence used against him.

The jury convicted him on five-counts of first-degree murder. The proceedings were heightened by the appearance of his first recorded surviving rape and attempted murder victim, Tali Shapiro during the penalty phase. He was sentenced to death and is currently incarcerated at Corcoran State Prison.

Since his conviction, Alcala has periodically resurfaced for public spectacle as subsequent charges have been leveled against him. His once flowing shoulder length hair grayed hideously before being shorn off in prison. Now past seventy, his former alluring appearance has deteriorated into the degeneration matching the horror of his actions.

Alcala Lived With His Mother In This Monterey Park Residence During Most of His Spree

Visual Artist, Writer and Photographer Marques Vickers is a California native presently living in the San Francisco Bay Area and Seattle, Washington regions.

He was born in 1957 and raised in Vallejo, California. He is a 1979 Business Administration graduate from Azusa Pacific University in the Los Angeles area. Following graduation, he became the Public Relations and ultimately Executive Director of the Burbank Chamber of Commerce between 1979-84. He subsequently became the Vice President of Sales for AsTRA Tours and Travel in Westwood between 1984-86.

Following a one-year residence in Dijon, France where he studied at the University of Bourgogne, he began Marquis Enterprises in 1987. His company operations have included sports apparel exporting, travel and tour operations, wine brokering, publishing, rare book and collectibles reselling. He has established numerous e-commerce, barter exchange and art websites including MarquesV.com, ArtsInAmerica.com, InsiderSeriesBooks.com, DiscountVintages.com and WineScalper.com.

Between 2005-2009, he relocated to the Languedoc region of southern France. He concentrated on his painting and sculptural work while restoring two 19th century stone village residences. His figurative painting, photography and sculptural works have been sold and exhibited internationally since 1986. Between 2008-2011, he was a part-time instructor in the Benicia Unified School district. He re-established his Pacific Coast residence in

2009 and has focused his creative productivity on writing and photography.

His published works span a diverse variety of subjects including true crime, international travel, California wines, architecture, history, Southern France, Pacific Coast attractions, auctions, fine art marketing, poetry, fiction and photojournalism.

He has two daughters, Charline and Caroline who presently reside in Europe.

BOOKS:
Marketing and Buying Fine Art Online, Allworth Press, New York NY (2005)
Making Auction Pay, Marquis Publications, Vallejo CA. (2014)
Unicorns and Dark Chocolate: Eros, Aphrodesia and Existence, Marquis Publications, Vallejo CA (2014)
Amour, Wine and Real Estate, Marquis Publications, Vallejo CA (2014)
Flamenco Jondo: The Paintings of Marques Vickers, Marquis Publications, Vallejo CA (2014)
The Ultimate Guide to Selling Art Online, Marquis Publications, Vallejo CA (2014)
The Lafayette White Cross Protest Memorial, Marquis Publications, Vallejo CA (2014)
2014 Napa Valley Earthquake, Marquis Publications, Vallejo CA (2014)
Fish Head Beach: The Silent and Senseless Murders of Lindsay Cutshall and Jason Allen, Marquis Publications, Vallejo CA (2014)
Muse One: Pantera Linda, Marquis Publications, Vallejo CA (2014)
Nature As Art: One, Marquis Publications, Vallejo CA (2014)
Springtime in New England, Marquis Publications, Vallejo CA (2014)
San Antonio Riverwalk, Marquis Publications, Vallejo CA (2014)
Ruined Castles and Phantom Memories, Marquis Publications, Vallejo CA (2014)

Sand and Water: Desert and Seascapes, Marquis Publications, Vallejo CA (2014)

Napa Rebuilds: Two Months Following Their Devastating Earthquake, Marquis Publications, Vallejo CA (2014)

The 2014 Napa Valley Wine Harvest, Marquis Publications, Vallejo CA (2014)

The Topography of Evil: Notorious Northern California Murder Sites, Marquis Publications, Vallejo CA (2015)

The Disappearing Women, Marquis Publications, Morro Beach CA (2015)

Five Month of Renovation After the 2014 Napa Earthquake, Marquis Publications, Morro Bay CA (2015)

100 Famous Phobias and Obsessions: An Entertaining Portrayal of Anxiety, Fears and Insecurity As Artwork, Marquis Publications, Morro Bay CA (2015)

Visions of Neo-Urbania: The Reinvention of Contemporary Metropolitan Vertical Living and Commerce, Marquis Publications, Tacoma WA (2015)

Nature As Art Two: Photography and Abstract Paintings of Marques Vickers, Marquis Publications, Tacoma WA (2015)

Morro Rock: Veiled Bridge of the Nine Sisters, Marquis Publications, Tacoma WA (2015)

Eternal Spring Street: Los Angeles' Architectural Reincarnation, Marquis Publications, Tacoma WA (2015)

The Reflective Powers of Water As Visual Alchemy, Marquis Publications, Tacoma WA (2015)

Jimi Hendrix, Bruce and Brandon Lee and the Lakeview Cemetery Seattle: Entombing Our Icons, Marquis Publications, Renton WA (2015)

The Artistic Properties of Reflective Glass, Marquis Publications, Renton WA (2015)

The Glass Curtain Architecture of Bellevue, Washington, Marquis Publications, Renton WA (2015)

Murder in California: Notorious California Murder Sites, Marquis Publications, Renton WA (2015)

Coffee Anarchists of the World Unite: The Italian Roasted Elixirs of Tacoma, Washington, Marquis Publications, Renton WA (2015)

The Abandoned Western Cascade Mountain Railroad Tunnels and 1910 Wellington Avalanche, Marquis Publications, Renton WA (2015)
The 2014 Napa Earthquake and Anniversary Aftermath: A Fourteenth Month Retrospective Into Historical Downtown Napa, Marquis Publications, Concord CA (2015)
Murder in Washington: The Topography of Evil, Marquis Publications, Larkspur CA (2016)
The Architectural Elevation of Technology: A Photo Survey of 75 Silicon Valley Headquarters, Marquis Publishing, Edmonds, WA (2016)
Reinventing Broadway Street: Los Angeles Architectural Reincarnation, Marquis Publishing, Edmonds, WA (2016)
So You Think You Know California Wine? (2016) The Grape Divide: Demystifying the Economics of Wine, Marquis Publishing, Edmonds, WA (2016)
Unseen Marin: The Waterways of Marin County, California, Marquis Publications, Edmonds, WA (2016)
Tulip Universe, Marquis Publications, Edmonds, WA (2016)
Unseen Marin: The Waterways of Mill Valley, Marquis Publications, Edmonds, WA (2016)
Unseen Marin: The Waterways of Central Marin County, Marquis Publications, Edmonds, WA (2016)
Unseen Marin: The Waterways of San Rafael and Fairfax, Marquis Publications, Edmonds, WA (2016)
When Letters Still Mattered: An Autobiography Based on Correspondence, Marquis Publications, Edmonds, WA (2016)
Lake Union: The Public Face of Prosperity, The Vertical Seattle Series, Marquis Publications, Edmonds, WA (2016)
101 Surrealistic Phobias and Obsessions, Marquis Publications, Edmonds, WA (2016)
So You Think You Know Washington State Wines? (2016-17) *Demystifying the Economics of Wine*, Marquis Publishing, Edmonds, WA (2016)
Teaching With One Eye Shut, Volume One, Marquis Publications, Edmonds, WA (2016)
Leaving Teaching With Both Eyes Open, Volume Two, Marquis Publications, Edmonds, WA (2016)

Vertical Bellevue: Architecture Above A Boomburb Skyline, Marquis Publications, Edmonds, WA (2016)
Vladimir Putin and Dresden, Germany: The Genesis of Myth Making, Marquis Publications, Frankfurt Am Main, Germany (2016)
The Berlin Wall: Over 25 Years After the Fall, Marquis Publications, Frankfurt Am Main, Germany (2016)
102 Satirical Photographic Ironies: Subtle to Subversive, Marquis Publications, Frankfurt Am Main, Germany (2016)
16-Hour Oregon Coast Road Trip: A Photographic Narrative, Marquis Publications, Larkspur, CA (2016)
Architect John D. Parkinson: Eternally Elevating the Los Angeles Skyline, Marquis Publications, Larkspur, CA (2017)
The Lafayette White Cross Protest Memorial, Marquis Publications, Larkspur, CA (2017)
Death of a Post Office: The Bruised Legacy of Architect William H. Corlett, Marquis Publications, Larkspur, CA (2017)

Made in the USA
Middletown, DE
14 April 2018